# the SOCIAL and EMOTIONAL DEVELOPMENT of GIFTED CHILDREN

## What Do We Know?

# the SOCIAL and EMOTIONAL DEVELOPMENT of GIFTED CHILDREN

## What Do We Know?

edited by
### MAUREEN NEIHART
### SALLY M. REIS
### NANCY M. ROBINSON
### SIDNEY M. MOON

A Service Publication of
**The National Association for Gifted Children**
1707 L Street NW, Suite 550
Washington, DC 20036
(202) 785-4268   http://www.nagc.org

PRUFROCK PRESS, INC.

A Service Publication of
The National Association for Gifted Children

ISBN-13: 978-1-882664-77-1
ISBN 1-882664-77-9

Prufrock Press, Inc.
P.O. Box 8813
Waco, Texas 76714-8813
(800) 998-2208
Fax (800) 240-0333
http://www.prufrock.com

# table of CONTENTS

## SECTION III
### Gifted Children and Youth With Special Needs

# FOREWORD

The field of gifted education is at an important time in its history. While traditional conceptions of giftedness still provide a foundation to much of what we believe about the nature and needs of gifted students, more contemporary notions are also having an effect on our thinking. This period of time may prove to be monumental inasmuch as our historical failure to identify and provide services to the diverse population of American gifted students still plagues us, encouraging us to change our beliefs and approaches. Consequently, interesting and divergent ideas for how the field should proceed have been simultaneously forwarded. Nevertheless, as the various support engines gear up to compete for ownership of postmodern gifted education, our schools must carry on, with students attending classes, reading books, writing papers, conducting experiments and completing college applications.

In an effort to contribute to the resolution of the major questions in the field, leaders of the National Association for Gifted Children have compiled a concise book reporting on the social and emotional lives of gifted students. This collection has value in three important ways. First, it provides logical synopses of differing subsets of the literature base. Second, it provides guidance for researchers to follow as they design their studies. Third, it establishes a watermark of our level of understanding at this time in history, which is quite valuable given the current limitations in the literature base on the psychology of gifted students.

As the population of the United States becomes increasingly diverse, our schools must be able to provide a free and appropriate education for all students. The professionals in gifted education must be able to identify and provide services to gifted students from all backgrounds. This book shares important information that will enable caring professionals the opportunity to act on what they know about the social and emotional lives of gifted students at this time in history and offers researchers a template for expanding our knowledge base in the future—a significant contribution to be sure.

Tracy L. Cross, Ph.D.
Ball State University
November 2001

# INTRODUCTION

by **Nancy M. Robinson, Ph.D.**

There is no more varied group of young people than the diverse group known as gifted children and adolescents. Not only do they come from every walk of life, every ethnic and socioeconomic group, and every nation, but they also exhibit an almost unlimited range of personal characteristics in temperament, risk taking and conservatism, introversion and extroversion, reticence and assertiveness, and degree of effort invested in reaching goals. Furthermore, no standard pattern of talent exists among gifted individuals. Included in this group are both those moderately advanced students who might be overlooked in a regular classroom setting and those whose talents are so far from the usual range that they have an obvious need for dramatic educational adjustments. Despite their diversity, several common threads emerge in the experiences and characteristics of gifted individuals that call for special attention if they are to develop optimally and use their abilities well.

This book summarizes what is known about the social and emotional characteristics of gifted individuals and the issues they encounter. It has been produced by a task force of psychologists and educators associated with the National Association for Gifted Children, some of them members of its counseling and research divisions, and many who work intimately with children of high potential and their families (see page 295 for a list of task force members). Our goal was to produce a book that comprehensively summarizes the best recent research about the social and emotional characteristics of, and issues faced by, gifted children and adolescents. For the most part, the findings are based on research conducted in the last two decades and in the United States, although some findings from older studies and some conducted in other countries are also included.

We have undertaken this effort *not* because these youngsters sustain any inherent vulnerability associated with their giftedness *per se*, but because their needs are so often unrecognized and unmet, with predictable negative consequences. We also believe that this underserved population is worthy of our attention. They cannot be expected to "make it on their own," nor should they.

This book is addressed to a broad audience of adults who are engaged—or may decide to become engaged—with a population of young people who are simultaneously intriguing and challenging, who exhibit the potential for outstanding development and performance in both the immediate and the distant future. The findings summarized here are also relevant to the nurturance of talent development in general, with important implications for the integration of those social and emotional factors necessary for high performance.

To achieve such goals, however, takes support from many understanding adults. Family members and teachers are often on the front line, but so are coaches, counselors, tutors, Scout leaders, and other mentors. Peers also play a very formative role in the lives of these young people, and adults can help to improve the peer climate for high achievement and facilitate access to other young people of similar ability and interests. We hope that describing the issues will encourage adults toward a variety of efforts on behalf of these children so that they can develop their talents to their fullest expression.

# Who Are "Gifted" Students?

As we have mentioned, the students about whom this book is written are a highly diverse group of individuals. They all share ability, in one or more domains, that is sufficiently advanced that it requires adaptation in the ordinary environment that serves the needs of average students their age. *No firm consensus exists among professionals as to precisely who should be considered "gifted," "talented," or both.* This lack of consensus extends to the domains involved (e.g., domains such as leadership and athletic skills are included in some, but not all, definitions) and even the degree of advancement required for designation in this group. In practice, definitions adopted by schools vary greatly and are often more attuned to the programs a school district has decided to offer than to a more general definition of giftedness or talent. Indeed, even the words *gifted* and *talented* are used in conflicting ways by different authors. Rather than becoming too concerned about the precise parameters by which this group may be defined, we offer a widely accepted definition developed by a representative group of experts convened by the Office of Educational Research and Improvement in the U.S. Department of Education (1993):

> Children and youth with outstanding talent perform or show the potential for performing at remarkably high levels of accomplishment when compared with others of their age, experience, or environment.
>
> These children and youth exhibit high performance capability in intellectual, creative, and/or artistic areas, possess an unusual leadership capacity, or excel in specific academic fields. They require services or activities not ordinarily provided by the schools.
>
> Outstanding talents are present in children and youth from all cultural groups, across all economic strata, and in all areas of human endeavor. (p. 26)

While most of the focus in this book is on students with advanced academic abilities, the reader will also find discussion of creatively gifted students, those whose talents lie in areas not represented in the schools, and some who show advancement in areas sometimes described as "emotional intelligence." For the sake of variety and in keeping with the flexible definition above, we have interchangeably used phrases such as "gifted students," "highly capable students," "talented students," and "advanced students," or, on occasion, specific groups such as "math-talented students." Our focus is meant to be broad, rather than narrow, and to encompass students with advanced abilities in almost all socially valued domains, excluding only the athletically gifted, for whom supports and community approbation already exist in abundance.

## What We Have Learned

The research reviewed in the chapters to come indicates that high-ability students are typically at least as well adjusted as any other group of youngsters. Nevertheless, they face a number of situations that, while not unique to them, constitute sources of risk to their social and emotional development. Some of these issues emerge because of the mismatch with educational environments that are not responsive to the pace and level of gifted students' learning and thinking. This situation is exacerbated by a social milieu that is often unsupportive and negative and, indeed, by a larger society that is, in many ways, frankly anti-intellectual. Some issues arise from the creativity, energy, intensity, and high aspirations of these students, as well as the internal unevenness in development that may exist in this group. Still other issues emanate from the difficulty many talented youth experience in finding compatible friends and the pressures they encounter to be and act "like everyone else." Students who are doubly different from the norm by being gifted in addition to being a member of an ethnic or sexual minority group or who have disabilities, such as attention-deficit disorder or a learning disability, have even more complex situations to address.

The conclusions from this comprehensive review are consistent: *There is no research evidence to suggest that gifted and talented children are any less emotionally hardy than their age peers.* There are, however, aspects of their life experiences due to their differences from other children and the fact that most of them demonstrate greater maturity in some domains than others that may put them at risk for specific kinds of social and emotional difficulties if their needs are unmet. Equally important, failure to target explicitly those affective components known to foster optimal talent development may compromise or prevent actualization of their full potential.

The organization of this book follows a three-section outline that we have found useful in conceptualizing the social and emotional issues facing the gifted child and the adults who care for them:

- **Section One:** Issues deriving from students' advancement compared with age peers and from internal unevenness in development
- **Section Two:** Common areas of psychological response
- **Section Three:** Groups of gifted children and youth with special needs
- **Section Four:** Promising practices and interventions

In this chapter, these topics are briefly introduced before proceeding to the research summaries provided in the chapters that follow.

## Issues Deriving From Students' Advancement Compared With Age Peers

First, we describe issues deriving from the maturity of highly capable children in comparison to their age peers, advancement that inevitably puts them "out of sync" with schools, social groups, and other contexts designed for average children of their age. What fits others very well may not fit them at all. Schools provide the primary nonfamily institution to which children are exposed during their growing years. Indeed, children's presence is legally required in classrooms six hours a day for at least 180 days a year, unless parents have elected to school them at home. Unfortunately, our schools have been notably unresponsive to the various ways in which they might provide a better match for the level and pace of development of students with advanced capabilities. Recent research presented in this book clearly indicates that teachers can seldom adequately meet the needs of gifted children in regular classrooms with classmates of their age.

Yet, numerous strategies are available for making the education of gifted students at least as appropriate for them as is the ordinary classroom environment for other students. In fact, many of the techniques developed for gifted students are capable of greatly strengthening educational approaches for *all* children and can benefit gifted students in regular classroom settings, as well as challenge other students. These techniques include "compacting" the curriculum to avoid wasting time teaching what children already know, differentiating and extending what is taught to accommodate varied pacing and levels of development, using high-interest content and hands-on activities to create high engagement and creativity, grouping gifted students together in cluster groups within classrooms or across classrooms to form more homogeneous groups, and so on. Specific for gifted children are various strategies of accelerating instruction, often using regular classes but adjusting the age at which students enter them. Also specific for gifted children are self-contained classes or schools where instruction can be provided appropriately and classmates are sufficiently similar in age, interests, and maturity to provide a true peer context.

Indeed, the social context in which gifted children grow is as significant for their social and emotional health as is the educational context in which they learn. As a group, gifted children demonstrate more mature social competence and occupy more valued positions in their peer networks than do children of average ability, at least during the early school years. On the other hand, gifted children may have a more mature concept of what a friend should be than do their agemates, and they may not feel they have real friends, even though others view them as well accepted or even popular. In the process of developing coping strategies, gifted students may deny their academic needs in order to satisfy their social needs. As early as elementary school, some gifted youngsters try to hide and even deny their talents; by adolescence, the situation becomes much more common. Students who are able to find intellectual peers, either by placement in a special program or by acceleration, generally feel less pressure to conform and more freedom to pursue academic goals. In the absence of peer support, however, the pressures on gifted students may be intense and stressful.

The situation is exacerbated for those students who are extremely intellectually gifted, especially those children with high verbal abilities who demonstrate observable differences nearly every time they speak. Because their exceptional level of ability is rare, it is often difficult for highly gifted students to find compatible friends, especially when they are young and their social sphere is restricted to a particular classroom, school, neighborhood, or small town. Because of this, they are likely to be less socially adept, more introverted, and more inhibited than other gifted children.

Additional issues derive from the fact that almost all gifted children are ahead of the norm in some ways more than in others. Typically, for example, their intellectual development exceeds their development in physical maturity and in fine and gross motor skills. Even within intellectual domains, they are likely to demonstrate more advancement in some abilities than others. They may, for example, be considerably more advanced in verbal than visual-spatial abilities, or vice-versa, to an extent that masks or interferes with expression of their talents and makes them seem "undeserving" of special programming efforts or support. Unevenness in cognitive abilities is correlated with IQ across the spectrum; the higher the IQ, the greater the disparities. By virtue of being ahead in one or more domains, the degree of internal differences gifted children experience is usually greater than those encountered by any average child who does not have a disability.

## Common Areas of Psychological Response

One example of typical unevenness has to do with the fact that affect regulation in gifted children is often (but not always) *more* mature than expected for chronological age, but *less* mature than the child's mental or intellectual age. Affect regulation involves managing emotional experience in a healthy way. Gifted children often have fears like those of older nongifted children (for example, they encounter the dangers of nuclear warfare or the implications of the concept of infinity at an early age), but do not have the emotional control to put these insights aside and go on with their lives. Adults often expect gifted children to behave in all ways like older children and are confused and frustrated when the children prove unexpectedly "immature" by these exaggerated expectations. What many adults do not realize is that a 6-year-old who has the verbal ability of a 12-year-old may still act like a 6-year-old at certain times. These actions are not immature; rather, they are developmentally appropriate.

On the other hand, there is a group of children who have been called "emotionally gifted" who are advanced in understanding their own emotions and are empathic with the feelings and views of others. They may show propensities for expressions of compassion, moral sensitivity, loyalty, resistance to victimization, and forgiveness. Some of them intuitively understand complex emotional issues at very young ages. Some cannot watch the news as they cry over every local or national tragedy. Some carry the burden of family problems on very young shoulders and cannot enjoy or appreciate life as a child because they are so worried about problems in their home or school or the world. Some of their positive traits, such as moral sensitivity, carry risks, however, when their age peers fail to understand their views and subject them to ridicule and the other cruelties of childhood.

Some common areas of psychological vulnerability that are created in part by the intensity of gifted children's experience, their high levels of aspiration, their clarity of insights, and their creativity ("going outside the box"). Some phenomena, like perfectionism, underachievement, and indecision about which of several talents to pursue, can indeed pose particular pitfalls for gifted students. Others, like suicide and delinquency, are often *said* to be problems for gifted persons, although no reliable evidence exists to verify this claim.

Few authors have developed psychological theories specific to gifted persons, and the question is still open as to whether *qualitative* differences exist between gifted and average children or whether the differences are more a matter of maturity. One of the few theories about gifted persons has emerged from the work of the Polish author, Kazimierz Dabrowski (see Chapter 6), who described in gifted individuals what he termed "forms of psychic overexcitability" in psychomotor, sensory, intellectual, imaginational, and emotional experience. He described a developmental progression that involves successive breaking down of inferior cognitive and emotional attributes and reconstructing more mature ones. While this concept emphasizes the positive aspects of experiencing life with greater intensity and sensitivity, some children may be overwhelmed and others may sacrifice sensitivities in order to conform to the expectations of others.

Another area of vulnerability for gifted children occurs for those who have a view of their own ability as a "given entity" or "gift" that should lead to high attainment by itself, without hard work. Opportunities for new learning and true mastery are less important to such children than opportunities to demonstrate their ability—but, they must avoid at all costs situations in which they might not perform well. Such views are often unwittingly encouraged by adults who habitually underchallenge students and overpraise them.

Perfectionism—holding very high standards for one's performance—can be a potent force capable of producing either negative or positive outcomes. Among the causes of negative perfectionism are parents who are themselves perfectionistic or critical; excessive adult adulation; pervasive messages from the media, teachers, and peers that one must be "the best"; and, particularly for the most able students, the fact that they are, in reality, better able than others to meet high standards of performance. Perfectionism that translates into persistence leads to success; perfectionism that results in avoidance, anxiety, and withdrawal guarantees failure.

Underachievement is widely regarded as an epidemic of contemporary society, but is all the more costly for those children whose potential is the highest. Underachievement can arise from multiple sources, including underchallenging schools, peer pressure for conformity, social isolation, family dysfunction, unrecognized disabilities, and so on. The pattern is not easily undone and often persists into adulthood. Students who have succeeded in overcoming underachievement often cite the roles of parents and teachers; changes in their self-image; and stimulating, interest-based classes.

Many gifted students exhibit "multipotentiality," or a variety of talent domains in which they might excel. While, for most students, talent profiles are somewhat uneven, their abilities provide many potential areas for future success. While these are clearly assets in **xix** many ways, some individuals are torn by indecision in the face of this wealth and consequently fail to pursue true expertise in any of them.

With the exception of creatively gifted adolescents who are talented in writing or the visual arts, studies have not confirmed that gifted individuals manifest significantly higher or lower rates or severity of depression than those for the general population. Gifted children's advanced cognitive abilities, social isolation, sensitivity, and uneven development may be etiological factors when they do become depressed. However, their problem-solving abilities, advanced social skills, moral reasoning, out-of-school interests, resilience, and satisfaction in achievement may be protective factors. Similarly, it is not at all clear whether suicide is more or less common in gifted adolescents than other adolescents—the statistics simply are not available—although it is easy to develop rationales why the rates should be higher or lower.

Recent incidents of lethal school violence by bright young people have refueled long-term speculation that gifted youngsters may be at special risk for delinquent, criminal, or violent behavior. Evidence to date suggests the opposite, that gifted students evidence less delinquency than average. The situation is extraordinarily complex, however, and may take decades to sort out.

The concept of risk and resilience constitutes a useful way of understanding the varied responses of gifted students to their circumstances. Gifted young people possess a powerful set of protective assets in their ability to understand situations and to problem solve, and their own achievement in the face of challenge can bring them a valuable sense of inner strength. Yet, they are not immune to stressors such as those associated with dysfunctional families, poverty, disabilities, and racism, in addition to the typical stressors that they share with many other gifted people. Individual circumstances and supports—or their lack—determine in large part the degree to which young people are able to achieve healthy social and emotional adjustment.

## Groups of Gifted Students With Special Needs

In Section Three, we describe the special situations encountered by students who are members of specific groups. Gifted females and gifted males each face unique issues. Other gifted students experience differences, not only in terms of their advanced abilities, but also because they are members of nonmainstream communities or have a psychological disability. These "twice-exceptional" youngsters have their counterparts in the general population, of course, but their needs are sometimes more intense in the context of their high ability.

Talented females' belief in their ability and their feelings of self-confidence tend to be undermined and diminished during childhood and adolescence. This situation derives in large part because of external factors, including stereotypes and barriers to achievement presented by parents, school, and the larger society, and from internal barriers, including personal priorities for social, rather than achievement goals, declines in self-confidence, and competing choices.

While numerous researchers in gifted education have examined issues for gifted females, few have addressed the issues faced by gifted males. A strong belief in self is associated with success in young men. Yet, the criticism and ridicule that may be addressed to sensitive, empathic, intelligent males are unquestionably difficult to deal with, particularly for males who exhibit psychological androgyny (the capacity to experience simultaneously opposing feelings and roles) and reduced gender-stereotyping.

Gifted students who are gay, lesbian, or bisexual also bear the emotional burden of being twice-different. Coming to terms with differences in both ability and sexual orientation may lead to a denial of either aspect of one's identity or, more frequently, to social isolation and loss of self-esteem. No reason exists to suspect that the gifted population includes more (or fewer) such students, but the school climate may be particularly unsafe for these teenagers, who are subjected to a double dose of psychological, if not physical, harassment.

Children from ethnic or racial minority groups are consistently underrepresented in gifted programs, leading to widespread concern. The experience of gifted Black students has been more closely studied than that of other underrepresented minorities. These students encounter more barriers to racial identity development than do White students, particularly when they feel they must choose between academic success and social acceptance. Some gifted Black students sabotage their own school achievement in order to strengthen their sense of belonging in their social group.

Students who are creatively gifted in the arts are often undervalued in traditional educational settings where linear, conventional learning and problem solving are encouraged. Many are gifted in nonacademic areas, such as dance or sculpture, that are not taught in schools. A special risk for bipolar mood disorders exists for those with high creative ability in writing and in the visual arts, although most creative artists and writers are not subject to such diagnosable conditions. Those who become concert musicians may also experience a difficult period as they emerge from the precocity of childhood to the giftedness of the adult. Some emotional volatility and release from conventional thinking may be effective in setting the stage for creative efforts, so again, the situation has both positive and negative components.

Gifted students with learning disabilities are at high risk for having their giftedness or their disabilities pass unnoticed because they appear simply nongifted (because of the disabilities) or "lazy" (because, although known to be gifted, they have trouble producing high-quality work). Even those who are appropriately identified may encounter difficulties in social adjustment because, in settings for gifted students, there is less tolerance for their struggles with self-direction and for the extra time they need to complete high-quality work and because some impairment of social skills may accompany their learning difficulties.

Similarly, gifted children with attention-deficit disorder, with or without hyperactivity (AD/HD), are at risk for difficulties with social and emotional adjustment. Some gifted children who do not have AD/HD but are high-energy youngsters seem disorganized in school settings that fail to capture their attention or satisfy their avid curiosity. For those who do have attention-deficit disorder, however, the issues that increase their risks include misidentification, emotional immaturity, peer rejection, family stress, and school problems, all of which are enhanced by their difficulties with consistent management of attention and organization.

## Promising Practices and Interventions and Recommendations for Future Action

In the fourth section, we describe parenting patterns that are conducive to children's high achievement and creativity, we point to some prevention and intervention approaches that have been found to be useful in supporting the development of gifted young people, and we make some recommendations for future action.

Compared with the general population, gifted children tend to come from families that are more often intact and warmly engaged with one another, that have more financial and educational resources for their use, and have higher aspirations for their children. On average, parents of gifted children invest more time and effort than other parents in engaging the children in learning activities and introducing them to potential talent areas. Some of the findings are, however, counterintuitive, particularly with regard to troubled family contexts that encourage creativity as opposed to attainment of conventional goals.

In recognition of the scarcity of empirical studies of long-term assessment of their efforts, we point to the most promising interventions and supports suggested by the research. As yet, little is known about precisely what kinds of guidance strategies are most effective in nurturing talent and potential and minimizing the effects of the kinds of vulnerable situations we have identified. Nevertheless, the research clearly points to several general practices that facilitate optimal development among our most talented young people. These include practices that support and encourage accelerative learning experiences; time to learn with others of similar abilities, interests, and motivation; engagement in areas of interest with a variety of peers; mentoring and pragmatic coaching to cope with the stress, criticism, and social milieu associated with high levels of performance in any domain; early presentation of career information; and social and emotional curricular approaches to help gifted children support one another.

When children or adolescents do encounter specific difficulties such as isolation and alienation; mood disturbances; perfectionism; or issues of racial, cultural, or sexual identity, a variety of counseling approaches can be made available, including individual counseling, groups, and family interventions.

With respect to the situations of specific subgroups of gifted students, a number of targeted approaches have been suggested. For example, career indecision besets many gifted individuals whose multiple high abilities would make it possible for them to pursue any of a number of paths. Some float aimlessly for years. Others, because of unwise early choices, close doors prematurely to careers that would have brought them satisfaction. Most career counseling for gifted students has stressed academic choices such as college selection, ignoring the multiple complex issues that have to do with the student's personal characteristics, collateral interests, and the contextual demands.

Underachievement among this group of students is a costly and, in many ways, tragic issue, emanating from a variety of sources. Targeted intervention efforts clearly need to be devised to fit student needs and circumstances. Certainly, gifted students with learning disabilities, AD/HD, or both need early identification and intervention. Thus far, a variety of models have been suggested to deal with underachievement, but very few controlled studies have been carried out and almost none have included long-term follow-up. Only a few models or strategies have been proven to work, possibly because of insufficient individualization and certainly because underachievement is difficult to reverse.

Our concluding chapter summarizes and highlights the task force's findings and points the way to agendas for the future. A vigorous research program is called for—a program that will require funding not currently available. Finally, hoped for changes in the national climate of anti-intellectualism and negative stereotyping of gifted and creative individuals are essential. These need to be supported by teacher-training efforts and reform and expansion of educational opportunities for gifted students. Political back is essential.

Finally, it is our hope that this book will inspire activism and commitment to gifted young people and the adults they will become. We cannot afford to sit on the sidelines, nor can the "giftedness" community do this alone. The job is far too important.

## References

U.S. Department of Education, Office of Educational Research and Improvement. (1993). *National excellence: A case for developing America's talent.* Washington, DC: U.S. Department of Education.

# SECTION I

## Issues Deriving From Student Advancement Compared With Age Peers

# EFFECTS OF ACCELERATION ON GIFTED LEARNERS

## by **Karen B. Rogers, Ph.D.**

he drive to excel has long been known to characterize the intellectually or academically gifted individual, although the origins of this drive have been described in a variety of ways. Galton (1869) argued that this "zeal" was an inborn, inherited trait, while Bloom (1985) described it as a product of one's home environment. Dabrowski (Piechowski, 1991), in contrast, argued that this drive evolves as a developmental characteristic. However, when high ability is exercised only in environments that provide little challenge, students tend to abandon hope of real learning and begin to expect themselves to excel at everything they try, avoiding situations at which they might not be instant experts and becoming more involved in demonstrating their ability than in the learning task itself (see Robinson, this volume; Schuler, this volume). To set the stage for high achievement, it is essential that the academically advanced student be afforded an appropriate pace and level of instruction in the domains of talent (Stanley, 1991; Stanley & Benbow, 1982).

The research on social issues among the gifted also supports the gifted individual's need for academic challenge. First, the level of social development of this type of learner is in at least some ways affected by mental age more than by chronological age. In many children, the ability to think abstractly and to reason conceptually leads to advanced development in social, emotional, and moral reasoning domains (Janos & Robinson, 1985; Karnes & Oehler-Stinnett, 1986; Tannenbaum, 1983). Further, gifted individuals tend to be attracted to other gifted youngsters, older children, or adults for their intimate or special interactive relationships (Hollingworth, 1926; O'Shea, 1960; Schunk, 1991). As Foster (1985) and Gross (1989) have both discovered in their studies, when gifted children are not with their intellectual peers, their social self-concept declines and their negative self-criticism increases.

In general, then, in order to address these emotional and social issues, three educational provisions must be in place: (1) placement with others of like ability when the learning is "serious," (2) exposure to progressively more complex tasks in a prestructured continuum of learning experiences based on mastery and readiness, and (3) flexible progression at an appropriately rapid pace. The fortunate gifted student will find a self-contained class of like-talented agemates in a setting that offers academic challenge in the company of peers. Such programs can be of many varieties (special school, school-within-a-school, full-time gifted program, regrouping by talent level for specific subject instruction, within-class grouping, cluster grouping), but the common characteristic is that they furnish not only an academic match, but a peer group.

## When Academic Acceleration Is the Only Choice

In the absence of such grouping options, however, the remaining two educational provisions can still be met through a variety of academic acceleration options, which can be provided either long-term or short-term for the gifted learner. Most of these provisions

**4**

achieve "peer matching" by placing the gifted child with classmates who are older. Five of these options are *grade-based acceleration*—that is, decisions that shorten the number of years a gifted child remains in the K–12 system. These options include:

- grade skipping, double promotion through bypassing one or more years in K–12;
- nongraded classrooms, progression through the curriculum undifferentiated by grade levels;
- grade telescoping, rapid progress through the curriculum at one building level (e.g., three years of middle school in two years);
- early admission to college, enrollment in college without completion of high school diploma; and
- radical acceleration, combination of accelerative forms to shorten student's K–12 progression considerably (e.g., "early-entrance program" whereby student completes both high school and college work in four years).

Seven options comprise *subject-based acceleration*, that is, decisions that bring advanced content and skills to a gifted child earlier than expected for age or grade level. These options include:

- early entrance to school, admission to kindergarten or first grade earlier than the usual age;
- compacted curriculum, streamlining of the regular curriculum so that the student bypasses what was previously mastered but remains in regular classroom settings;
- concurrent enrollment, attending classes at more than one building level (e.g., high school and college classes both taken in the school day);
- subject acceleration, rapid progression within a specific subject curriculum, often accompanied by placement at a higher grade level;
- mentorship, direct experience with an expert for advancing specific subject proficiency and knowledge of career settings;
- credit by examination, testing out of coursework with credit given for course completion; and

- advanced placement program, studying advanced curricula during high school, followed by appropriate college placement and possible college credit.

## Making Good Decisions About Academic Acceleration

On what basis can parents, teachers, and gifted students decide which accelerative option would be best? In terms of academic advancement and high achievement, the evidence is very convincing. There are consistent moderate to high effect sizes for almost every form considered (see Tables 1 and 2). Academic effect sizes can be "translated" generally as the additional grade-equivalent achievement children make when accelerated. An effect size of .30 suggests that children have achieved about three more months of grade-equivalent progress than if they had not participated in the practice. In general, all the grade-based acceleration practices produce moderate achievement gains for children at whatever age the practice is considered. Subject-based acceleration practices produce moderate to high achievement gains, depending upon the practice selected and the magnitude of actual acceleration. Subject acceleration in the lower grades seems to be even more effective than in the older grades.

Socialization effects, which include ratings of social maturity or social cognition, social self-concept ratings, leadership roles and participation in cocurricular activities, and ratings of extroversion, are measured with effect sizes that are not quite as easy to interpret as learning effects, although the statistical analysis is the same. Effect sizes indicate the proportion of the standard deviation unit of the measure by which the accelerated sample that exceeded the gifted sample who did not accelerate. The proportion of higher (more positive) performance, based on the standard deviation unit of the tests or rating scales used to measure self-concept, personality adjustment, and creativity, accounts for the effect sizes reported for psychological effects. As seen in Tables 1 and 2, most forms of acceleration have little or no effect on socialization, that is, on average, accelerated groups resemble nonaccelerated groups. Both grade skipping and radical acceleration appear to have a moderate positive effect, but no research has been conducted on the socialization effects of credit by examination, nongraded classrooms, mentorship, and curriculum compacting.

Psychological effects include ratings of personality characteristics such as mental stability, lack of anxiety and nervousness, happiness, and self-concept (students' views of their own competence in academic, social, global, athletic competence, behavioral, and physical appearance domains). Moderate positive effects have been found for concurrent enrollment and mentorships, while small effects have been found for early entrance, grade skipping, and radical acceleration. Nongraded classrooms and early admission to college have registered no effect, and no research exists on the psychological outcomes of curriculum compacting, grade telescoping, subject acceleration, Advanced Placement, and credit by examination.

How does the parent of a gifted student decide what to do about the issue of acceleration? Even when the research seems to support such practices, it has looked primarily at groups of gifted students, not at individual children. There is another body of "literature" out there that provides the individual anecdotes that the general research does not. Some of these anecdotes relate tales of children who have not been energized by academic advancement, but instead have withdrawn academically, socially, or emotionally.

Acceleration needs groundwork, and children's needs and responses need to be anticipated. Did the practice decided upon create Marsh's (1987) Big-Fish-Little-Pond Effect (BFLPE), eliminating the child's chance to "shine" among classmates? Was the accelerative placement too exaggerated or too abrupt, producing unwanted side effects? Were there skills or content expected of the child that required anticipatory preparation? Did the child experience the unaccustomed degree of challenge as a "failure"? Were the problems that prompted the acceleration actually more complex or serious than a strictly educational approach could take care of? Was social and emotional support so lacking in the accelerative practice that the child was confronted with suspicion and even hostility in the new setting? Or, did the move reduce the child's opportunity to maintain his or her self-concept when the comparison group was removed too suddenly? Considering such possibilities can suggest

Table 1

## Table of Effects for Grade-Based Accelerative Options

| Option | Elementary | | | Secondary | | |
|---|---|---|---|---|---|---|
| | Academic | Social | Self-Concept | Academic | Social | Self-Concept |
| Grades K–2 | .40 | .04 | .05 | — | — | — |
| Grades 3–6 | .42 | .36 | .10 | — | — | — |
| Grades 7–9 | — | — | — | .45 | 0 | 0 |
| Grades 10–12 | — | — | — | .38 | .13 | .13 |
| Grade Skipping | .46 | .31 | .10 | .46 | .31 | .10 |
| Nongraded Classroom | .43 | — | .05 | — | — | — |
| Grade Telescoping | .35 | — | — | .45 | -.05 | — |
| Early Admission to College | — | — | — | .30 | -.05 | .16 |

## Table 2

## Table of Effects for Subject-Based Accelerative Options

| Option | Elementary | | | Secondary | | |
|---|---|---|---|---|---|---|
| | Academic | Social | Self-Concept | Academic | Social | Self-Concept |
| Grades K–2 | .64 | .20 | .16 | — | — | — |
| Grades 3–6 | .59 | .20 | .16 | — | — | — |
| Grades 7–9 | — | — | — | .40 | .07 | .14 |
| Grades 10–12 | — | — | — | .44 | .23 | .37 |
| Early Entrance | .49 | .20 | .16 | .49 | .20 | .16 |
| Compacted Curriculum | .83/.22 | — | — | — | — | — |
| Subject Acceleration | .55 | — | — | .59 | — | -.19 |
| Concurrent Enrollment | — | — | — | .22 | .07 | .47 |
| Mentorship | — | — | — | .47 | .40 | .57 |
| Advanced Placement | — | — | — | .27 | .24 | .07 |
| Credit By Examination | — | — | — | .59 | — | — |

numerous ways that parents and teachers can help to assure a smooth and successful transition.

## Elements of a Predictably Successful Acceleration

Rogers (in press) has identified four prerequisites of successful accelerative placement: (1) cognitive functioning, (2) personal characteristics, (3) learning preferences, and (4) interests. For *cognitive functioning*, the literature suggests that the child must be processing and achieving well above most others at the current grade level in one or more academic subjects. If achievement is not commensurate with ability, then previous underachievement may have led to skill and knowledge gaps that will greatly hinder the child's success in the acceleration option. In terms of *personal characteristics*, the child must generally be motivated by challenge and learning, be independent in thought and action, persist in other-directed and self-directed tasks, be socially mature and comfortable with older children, and have a positive relationship with at least one adult. Without these characteristics, the child will have no robust "self" to fall back on in the face of new challenges. The child's *learning preferences* should include a willingness to work at his or her own pace, but not necessarily always alone. Some consideration of the instructional delivery methods likely to be encountered in the accelerative option would also be helpful. For example, if a gifted high school student were to be concurrently placed in a college history course, it is important to know if he or she usually likes lectures and extensive reading. The *interests* of the child should generally favor academic work, while his or her involvement in a variety of activities and hobbies outside of school might preclude time to supplement school learning in the home. On the other hand, students who have 'over a significant period of time' engaged seriously in an interest area such as music or athletics are often good bets to thrive in the new setting. Although no normative or outcome data are yet available, the Iowa Acceleration Scale (Assouline, 1998), which covers several of these issues, can be of help in the decision-making process.

# Summary

In his book, *Guiding the Social and Emotional Development of Gifted Youth* (1992) Delisle stated:

> It's a daunting task, being an educator, bearing the responsibility for shaping both academics and attitudes . . . No computer-scanned bubble sheet measures how our students feel about learning or their biases toward self and others. These indexes, the true value of learning and education, elude detection and measurement, sometimes for years. . . . So, the brave educators wishing to enhance both students' self-concepts and their achievements must be content with not knowing the immediate or long-term impacts of their actions (p. 50)

Although we may not fully be able to predict the impacts of various educational decisions on an individual gifted student, it is clear that gifted students whose academic needs are not being met face an uncomfortable dilemma. On the one hand, they may choose to stay in the current situation and face inevitable frustration, irritability, anxiety, tedium, and social alienation (Csikszentmihalyi, 1990; Hoekman, McCormick, & Gross, 1999), as well as the dangers of perfectionism and a loss of engagement in the learning enterprise. On the other hand, they may opt to move to a more advanced academic setting, possibly losing age peers and risking the "danger" of not being top of the class, but gaining mental agemates and academic challenge and advancement (Rogers, 1991). Although tedium and repetition may be a fact of life for the highly gifted child at any grade level, acceleration in any of its forms can often diminish its effects, provided that the student's cognitive functioning, personal characteristics, learning preferences, and interests are taken into account.

# References

Assouline, S. (1998). *The Iowa acceleration scale.* Scottsdale. AZ: Gifted Psychology Press.

Bloom, G. S. (1985). *Developing talent in young people.* New York: Ballantine Books.

Csikszentmihalyi, M. (1990). *Flow: The psychology of optimal experience.* New York: Harper & Row.

Delisle, J. R. (1992). *Guiding the social and emotional development of gifted youth: A practical guide for educators and counselors.* New York: Longman.

Foster, W. (1985). Helping a child toward individual excellence. In J. F. Feldhusen (Ed.), *Toward excellence in gifted education* (pp. 135–161). Denver: Love.

Galton, F. (1869). *Hereditary genius.* London: Macmillan.

Gross, M. U. M. (1989). The pursuit of excellence or the search for intimacy? The forced-choice dilemma of gifted youth. *Roeper Review, 11,* 189–194.

Hoekman, K., McCormick, J., & Gross, M. U. M. (1999). The optimal context for gifted students: A preliminary exploration of motivational and affective considerations. *Gifted Child Quarterly, 43,* 170–193.

Hollingworth, L. (1926). *Gifted children: Their nature and nurture.* New York: Macmillan.

Janos, P. M., & Robinson, N. M. (1985). The performance of students in a program of radical acceleration at the university level. *Gifted Child Quarterly, 29,* 175–179.

Karnes, F., & Oehler-Stinnett, J. (1986). Life events as stressors with gifted adolescents. *Psychology in the Schools, 23,* 406–414.

Marsh, H. W. (1987). The big-fish-little-pond effect on academic self-concept. *Journal of Educational Psychology, 79,* 280–295.

O'Shea, H. E. (1960). Friendship and the intellectually gifted child. *Exceptional Children, 26,* 327–335.

Piechowski, M. (1991). Emotional development and emotional giftedness. In N. Colangelo & G. A. Davis (Eds.). *Handbook of gifted education* (pp. 285–306). Needham Heights, MA: Allyn and Bacon.

Rogers, K. B. (1991). *A best evidence synthesis of the research on types of accelerative programs for gifted students.* Unpublished doctoral dissertation, University of Michigan, Ann Arbor.

Rogers, K. B. (in press). *The who, what, when, where, why, and how of educational planning: A handbook for parents.* Scottsdale, AZ: Gifted Psychology Press.

Schunk, D. H. (1991). *Learning theories: An educational perspective.* Upper Saddle River, NJ: Merrill.

Stanley, J. C. (1991). An academic model for educating the mathematically talented. *Gifted Child Quarterly, 35,* 36–42.

Stanley, J. C., & Benbow, C. P. (1982). Educating mathematically precocious youth: Twelve policy recommendations. *Educational Researcher, 11,* 4–9.

Tannenbaum, A. J. (1983). *Gifted children: Psychological and educational perspectives.* New York: Macmillan.

# 2 PEER PRESSURES AND SOCIAL ACCEPTANCE OF GIFTED STUDENTS

by **Sylvia Rimm, Ph.D.**

hether gifted children are socially accepted and respected varies with children's ages, specific school environments, and the extent of their giftedness. No studies show particular biases against gifted elementary school children by their peers. Rather, they are generally well liked and sometimes are even more popular than their peers, although, by age 13, that popularity advantage disappears (Austin & Draper, 1981; Schneider, 1987; Schneider, Clegg, Byrne, Ledingham, & Crombie, 1989; Udvari & Rubin, 1996).

In contrast, gifted adolescents often value being intelligent, yet almost always realize that giftedness exacts a social price. Over 3,500 Minnesota secondary students responded to a newspaper column question asking if they would rather be the best looking, most athletic, or smartest student in their class. Respondents wrote an essay to support their answer (Schroeder-Davis,

1999). Although more students favored "most intelligent" (53.8%), followed by "most athletic" (37.3%), and "best looking" (only 8.9%), content analysis of these student essays showed that the students were aware of the anti-intellectual stigma expressed by peers. Twenty-two percent directly alluded to that stigma, and almost none attributed any immediate social benefits to being smartest.

Gifted adolescents often express feelings of difference (Swiatek & Dorr, 1998; Rimm & Rimm-Kaufman, 2000). Manor-Bullock, Look, and Dixon (1995) have suggested that those feelings result from the gifted label, although women interviewed by Rimm, Rimm-Kaufmann, and Rimm (1999) expressed feelings of difference frequently regardless of whether or not they were in gifted programming. Coleman and Cross (1988) suggested that even when children don't feel different, they sometimes assume that others perceive them as different, thus, they believe that perception will interfere with their social interactions. This study indicates that the stigma of giftedness doesn't have to be proven as real if it is assumed by the students to be real. Their beliefs about the stigma will have an effect on their social relationships.

In contrast to average adolescents and gifted girls, Luftig and Nichols (1990) found that gifted boys ranked as most popular, nongifted boys and nongifted girls as second most popular, and finally, gifted girls as least popular of the four groups. Luftig and Nichols (1989) also found evidence that gifted boys hide or mask their giftedness by being funny.

Many studies that have compared social adjustment of moderately gifted students to students with extremely high IQs have concluded that social acceptance is a much greater problem for students with unusually high intelligence and that extremely gifted students who are not radically accelerated have great difficulty finding true peers, probably because their thinking experiences are so far from the norm (Austin & Draper, 1981; Feldman, 1986; Gallagher, 1958; Hollingworth, 1942). Gross (1993) found that, for students with IQs higher than 160, 80% of them reported that they experienced intense social isolation in a regular classroom and are continuously monitoring their social behavior to conform to the expectations of their peer group. That, in combination with their frequently unchallenging curriculum, caused ongoing emotional stress.

14

A survey conducted by Brown and Steinberg (1990) of 8,000 high school students in California and Wisconsin found that fewer than 10% of the high achievers were willing to be identified as part of the "brain" crowd, and students have been found to withdraw from debate, computer clubs, and honors classes to avoid being labeled a "geek," "dweeb," or "nerd" (Davis & Rimm, 1998). The percentage is even lower for females than for males. A study of over 1,000 successful women (Rimm, Rimm-Kaufman, & Rimm, 1999) found the theme of a social price to pay common among many who were excellent students. Fifteen percent of the successful women in the *See Jane Win* study considered social isolation to be their most negative experience in childhood. Some women commented on intentionally doing poorly on tests or not handing in assignments. However, their backing away from achievement to preserve their social selves was typically temporary, and they, their parents, or a teacher recognized the dysfunction of their brief underachievement.

*None* of the high-achieving African Americans surveyed in the Brown and Steinberg (1990) study was willing to be considered part of the brain crowd. This social pressure was confirmed by Ford (1994/95). In her study of gifted African American girls, peer pressures were found to have a powerfully negative effect on their achievement in school. Over half of the girls in her study indicated that they were teased by their peers for their high achievement, and one-third were accused of "acting White." These negative experiences caused feelings of alienation, rejection, withdrawal, and underachievement.

## What Gifted Students Do About Their Differences

Uncomfortable peer pressures will be reduced for scholarly adolescent boys if they can dissipate their brainy image with excellence in sports and for girls if they have the good fortune to be pretty (Coleman, 1961); but, for most gifted young people, a variety of strategies are used to cope with their interpretations of social stigma. Swiatek and Dorr (1998) developed The Social Coping Questionnaire (SCQ) to identify and measure social-coping strategies typically used by gifted adolescents. Factor analysis of the SCQ

**15**

indicated five social coping factors, including denial of giftedness (saying their ability isn't really that good), emphasis on popularity (the extent to which students acknowledge the importance of popularity), peer acceptance (the perceived impact of giftedness on social interaction), social interaction (the extent to which students get involved in extracurricular activities), and hiding giftedness (not telling people test grades, etc.) They also found that girls were more likely than boys to deny their abilities and report high levels of socialization. The pressure on girls to compete for boys' attention may indeed be an important factor here. Although much has changed for girls, unfair stereotypes continue to place obstacles in their paths to achievement.

There are a number of ways that school and families can help gifted students cope with peer pressures. Maintaining a positive family environment helps gifted children deal with the antigifted peer pressure they may feel during adolescence. Continuous bickering with parents seems to propel adolescents to more acceptance of, and dependence on, peer norms while rejecting parental norms (Hill, 1980). Parents need to be especially careful not to stress popularity and social success.

Parents should value and support their children's talent during this precarious period in their development and not add to the pressures the child already is feeling. Instead, parents may have to counter peer messages of popularity by pointing out that the emphasis on popularity as a competitive form of friendship ends at high school graduation for many people (Rimm, 1988). More importantly, parents should do what they can to arrange for their gifted children to have time to learn with other children who share their passion, drive, and ability. Parents of college-bound students need to support them and point out the rewards ahead, including good scholarships and excellent colleges, and explain that, outside of high school, the stress on popularity will fall away and be viewed as immature.

Assessing adolescents' perceptions of social acceptance seems to fit especially for middle and high schools. Porath (1996) suggested that gifted learners' perceptions of social acceptance should be part of their assessment at the elementary school level because those perceptions affect how they learn in school. The Social Coping Questionnaire, or some similar survey, might be a valuable tool for

**16**

counselors to use in helping gifted students learn how to cope with peer pressure during the teenage years.

The best way to support gifted and talented students, particularly adolescents, is to help assemble a gifted cohort group. That will encourage high achievement and reinforce the full use of students' talents. Youth symphony orchestras, high-level Saturday and summer programs, special classes, debate teams, intellectual and creative teams, and gifted-peer discussion groups help young people to value their talent and build constructive self-concepts and identities.

Perhaps most important, schools need to provide counselors and school psychologists who are trained to understand the peer pressures and isolations that gifted children feel so that social isolation doesn't lead to anger toward themselves or others. If knowledgeable adults are not available to support these gifted students in their schools, they are indeed at risk of using their gifted cognitive abilities and sensitivities to harm themselves and society, instead of making the contributions of which they are capable.

# References

Austin, A. B., & Draper, D. C. (1981). Peer relationships of the academically gifted: A review. *Gifted Child Quarterly, 25*, 129–133.

Brown, B. B., & Steinberg, L. (1990). Academic achievement and social acceptance: Skirting the "brain-nerd" connection. *Education Digest, 55*(7), 55–60.

Coleman, J. S. (1961). *The adolescent society.* New York: The Free Press.

Coleman, L. J., & Cross, T. L. (1988). Is being gifted a social handicap? *Journal for the Education of the Gifted, 11*(4), 41–56.

Davis, G. A., & Rimm, S. B. (1998). *Education of the gifted and talented.* Needham Heights, MA: Allyn and Bacon.

Feldman, D. H. (1986). Giftedness as a developmentalist sees it. In R. J. Sternberg & J. E. Davidson (Eds.), *Conceptions of giftedness* (pp. 285–305). Cambridge, MA: Cambridge University Press.

Ford. D. Y. (1994/95, Winter). Underachievement among gifted and non-gifted Black females: A study of perceptions. *The Journal of Secondary Gifted Education, 6*, 165–175.

Gallagher, J. J. (1958). Peer acceptance of highly gifted children in elementary school. *Elementary School Journal, 58*, 465–470.

Gross, M. U. M. (1993). *Exceptionally gifted children.* London: Routledge.

Hill, J. P. (1980). The family. In M. Johnson (Ed.), *Toward adolescence: The middle school years.* Chicago: National Society for the Study of Education.

**17**

Hollingworth, L. S. (1942). *Children above 180 IQ Stanford-Binet: Origin and development*. New York: World Book.

Luftig, R. L., & Nichols, M. L. (1989). *Assessing the perceived loneliness and self-concept functioning of gifted students in self-contained and integrated settings.* Unpublished manuscript, Department of Educational Psychology, Miami University, Oxford, OH.

Luftig, R. L., & Nichols, M. L. (1990). Assessing the social status of gifted students by their age peers. *Gifted Child Quarterly, 34*, 111–115.

Manor-Bullock, R., Look, C., & Dixon, D. N. (1995). Is giftedness socially stigmatizing? The impact of high achievement on social interactions. *Journal for the Education of the Gifted, 18*, 319–338.

Porath, M. (1996). Affective and motivational considerations in the assessment of gifted learners. *Roeper Review, 19*, 13–17.

Rimm, S. B. (1988 May/June). Popularity ends at grade twelve. *Gifted Child Today, 11*, 42–44.

Rimm, S. B., & Rimm-Kaufman, S. (2000). *How Jane won: Profiles of successful women*. New York: Crown.

Rimm, S. B, Rimm-Kaufman, S., & Rimm, I. (1999). *See Jane win: The Rimm report on how 1,000 girls became successful women*. New York: Crown.

Schneider, B. H. (1987). *The gifted child in peer group perspective*. New York: Springer-Verlag.

Schneider, B. H., Clegg, M. R., Byrne, B. M., Ledingham, J. E., & Crombie, G. (1989). Social relations of gifted children as a function of age and school program. *Journal of Educational Psychology, 81*, 48–56.

Schroeder-Davis, S. J. (1999). Brains, brawn, or beauty: Adolescent attitudes toward three superlatives. *Journal of Secondary Gifted Education, 10*, 134–147.

Swiatek, M. A., & Dorr, R. M. (1998). Revision of the social coping questionnaire: Replication and extension of previous findings. *Journal of Secondary Gifted Education, 10*, 252–59.

Udvari, S. J., & Rubin, K. H. (1996). Gifted and non-selected children's perceptions of academic achievement, academic effort, and athleticism. *Gifted Child Quarterly, 40*, 311–219.

VanTassel-Baska, J. (1986). Acceleration. In C. J. Maker (Ed.), *Critical issues in gifted education* (pp. 179–196). Rockville, MD: Aspen.

# 3 SOCIAL AND EMOTIONAL ISSUES FOR EXCEPTIONALLY INTELLECTUALLY GIFTED STUDENTS

by **Miraca U. M. Gross, Ph.D.**

Most findings reported in reviews (e.g., Robinson & Noble, 1992; Schneider, 1987) of the psychosocial development of intellectually gifted children and adolescents present a positive picture of their adjustment. The majority of the findings, however, originate from studies of moderately gifted children, and the picture may be very different for children who are exceptionally (IQ 160–179) or profoundly (IQ 180+) gifted. Schneider, for example, reported that his own study of peer acceptance of gifted students found significant negative correlations between IQ and peer relationships. Janos and Robinson (1985) warned: "The most highly talented are the most vulnerable, probably because they are exceedingly 'out of sync' with school, friends, and even family. They may become superficially adjusted but sacrifice possibilities for outstanding fulfillment and significant, socially valued contributions" (p. 182).

The paucity of intellectual measures with sufficient "top" for exceptionally and profoundly gifted individuals poses a problem for research about this group. Most such younger children are identified using the admittedly outdated 1972 norms of the Stanford-Binet Intelligence Scale, Form L-M (Silverman & Kearney, 1992), a measure that largely taps abstract verbal reasoning ability. Most exceptionally high-IQ adolescents are identified through their participation as seventh- or eighth-graders in regional talent searches using the SAT (Scholastic Aptitude Test) or the ACT (American College Test), measures of verbal and mathematical reasoning. More recently standardized ability tests such as the the Stanford-Binet Intelligence Scale (4th ed.) and the Wechsler Intelligence Scale for Children (3rd ed.), provide insufficient observation of the most advanced levels of intellectual ability.

## Peer Relationships of Extremely Gifted Children

No review of research on the psychosocial development of extremely gifted children would be complete without reference to the pioneering work of Lewis Terman and Leta Hollingworth. Discussing the social and personality traits of the children in his landmark study, Terman distinguished among children at different levels of intellectual giftedness. He noted that children with IQs higher than 170 tended to have "considerably more difficulty in making social adjustments" than did the moderately gifted children, with two-thirds being reported by their teachers and parents as being definitely solitary or "poor mixers" (Burks, Jensen, & Terman, 1930, p. 175).

It is in the case of extraordinarily high IQ that the social problem is most acute. If the IQ is 180, the intellectual level at 6 is almost on a par with the average 11-year-old, and at 10 or 11 it is not far from that of the average high school graduate. . . . The inevitable result is that the child of IQ 180 has one of the most difficult problems of social adjustment that any human being is ever called upon to meet. (p. 264)

Hollingworth (1926, 1942) was the first psychologist to make a systematic study of peer relationships of children at different levels of intellectual giftedness. She defined the IQ range 125–155 as "socially optimal intelligence" because children in this range typically were well balanced, self-confident, outgoing, and able to win the confidence and friendship of age peers. She observed, however, that above IQ 160, the difference between exceptionally gifted children and their age peers is so great that they are unlikely to find others who share their abilities and interests. Their special problems of development are correlated with social isolation and appear particularly acute between the ages of 4 and 9. She showed that, when exceptionally gifted children who had been rejected by age peers were removed from inappropriate grade placement and permitted to work and play with intellectual peers, the loneliness and social isolation disappeared, and the children were accepted as valued classmates and friends (Hollingworth, 1942).

More recently, Gross's longitudinal study (1993, 1998) of 60 Australian children with IQs higher than 160 has found that children who were retained in an inclusion classroom or permitted a "token" grade advancement of a single year experienced significant and ongoing difficulties with peer relationships. Many reported that they had few friends or no friends at all, despite their deliberate and prolonged academic underachievement in efforts to gain acceptance from age peers.

Dauber and Benbow (1990) compared the popularity and peer acceptance of students who were extremely mathematically or verbally gifted (students in the top 1 in 10,000 among their age peers) with those of students who were moderately gifted in math or language. Moderately gifted students were viewed both by themselves and by their age peers as being more popular, more socially active, and more socially valued than were the extremely gifted. Students with extreme verbal talent rated themselves as having the lowest social standing of the four groups, a finding that Dauber and Benbow attributed to both society's higher valuing of mathematical talent and the fact that, while extreme math ability may be less obvious on social occasions, verbally talented students may be conspicuous due to their sophisticated vocabulary. Moreover, students who wish to mask exceptional mathematical ability for peer acceptance need to moderate their achievements principally in math classes, while students who wish to conceal extreme linguistic precocity have to be much more consistently on guard against "breaking cover."

Swiatek (1995) studied social coping strategies of highly gifted students identified through the Study of Mathematically Precocious Youth. She found that the most highly gifted were most likely to deny their own giftedness. Swiatek suggested this denial could have arisen through a reluctance to believe the validity of their extremely high SAT scores, through a perceived pressure to perform extremely well academically, or through a belief that they might be more socially acceptable if they conformed to the standards of age-peers. As in Dauber and Benbow's study, students who were highly gifted verbally perceived themselves as less socially accepted than did their mathematically gifted counterparts.

## Friendship Studies

Several studies have found that gifted children prefer the companionship of gifted age peers or older children. This finding is congruent with friendship choices in children generally. Most children tend to choose friends on the basis of similarities in mental age, rather than chronological age (Gross, 2001; in press).

Janos, Marwood, and Robinson (1985) queried an exceptionally gifted group (IQ 163+) and a moderately gifted group (IQ 125–140) of elementary school children about their friendships. Exceptionally gifted children were significantly more likely to report that most of their friends were older, that they had too few friends, and that being smart made making friends harder. Parents of the exceptionally gifted children were more likely to report that their child had only one close friend or none at all.

In Britain, Freeman (1979) compared two groups of gifted children: a "target" group with mean IQ of 147 and a comparison group of mean IQ 134. Children in the target group said they felt "different" from other children 17 times more often than did children in the comparison group. Furthermore, 83% of the target group reported having few friends compared to 30% in the comparison group, while 7% said they had no friends at all, compared to only 1% in the control group. The friends that the target group *did* have were described as being older, rather than the same age or younger.

A recent Australian study comparing the conceptions of friendship held by average, moderately gifted, and exceptionally gifted children has found that children's conceptions of friendship form a developmental hierarchy of age-related stages, with expectations of friendship, and beliefs about friendship, becoming more sophisticated and complex with age (Gross, 2001; in press). However, it is mental age, rather than chronological age, that seems to dictate children's progress through the developmental stages.

In this study, a strong relationship was found between children's levels of intellectual ability and their conceptions of friendship. At ages when their age peers of average ability were looking simply for play partners, gifted children were beginning to look for close, stable, and trusting friendships. Children with IQs higher than 160 tend to begin the search for relationships of complete trust and honesty—friendships based on unconditional acceptance—four or five years earlier than their age peers. Indeed, the majority of exceptionally gifted children aged 6 or 7 already displayed conceptions of friendship that did not develop in children of average ability until age 11 or 12. In third and fourth grade, even moderately gifted children had the conceptions of friendship that characterize average-ability children at least two years older.

The differences between the gifted and their age peers were much larger in the earlier years of school than in the later years. This supports Hollingworth's finding that the loneliness and social isolation experienced by many gifted children is most acute before the age of 10. It is at this level of schooling that gifted children are most likely to have difficulty in finding other children who have similar expectations of friendship. Indeed, with increasing age and changes in life circumstances, the field of friendship choices widens. To quote Terman (Burks, Jensen, & Terman, 1930), "Someone has said that genius is necessarily solitary, since the population is so sparse at the highest levels of mental ability. However, adult genius is mobile and can seek out its own kind" (p. 264).

## Motivational Orientation

Rogers (1986) synthesized a range of studies on learning styles and motivational orientations of intellectually gifted children. Her review suggests that gifted students in general are intrinsically, rather than extrinsically, motivated; prefer to study independently, rather than in mixed-ability groups; and dislike being given responsibility for the learning achievements of classmates.

In Australia, Gross (1997), comparing the motivational orientation of academically gifted seventh-grade students with a heterogeneous population of age peers, also found the gifted students to be significantly more task-oriented, focusing on the task and mastery strategies, rather than on the desire for high grades or academic recognition. Similarly in Canada, Kanevsky (1994), comparing differences between the problem-solving strategies used by young children of average ability (mean IQ 104) and those used by highly gifted age peers (mean IQ 153), found ability-related differences in motivational orientation. Highly gifted children were more likely to display intrinsic motivation, enhancing their enjoyment of the problem-solving exercises by monitoring and maintaining the level of challenge available to them, whereas children of average ability appeared more extrinsically motivated by the researcher's interest in their progress.

Case studies of exceptionally and profoundly gifted children often identify, as a dominant affective characteristic, a passionate desire to learn more and improve in the child's talent field. The father of one subject with an IQ above 180 in a study by Morelock (1995) described his son's hunger for intellectual stimulus as "a rage to learn." Several of the extremely gifted children in Gross's longitudinal study gave evidence of this same drive by planning their own programs of radical acceleration through elementary and secondary school over a period of several years, personally negotiating each grade advancement with their teachers and school principals (Gross, 1993, 1998).

**24**

Terman (Burks et al., 1930) found that the majority of his subjects with IQs higher than 170 were reported by their teachers and parents as preferring to work or study alone, rather than with other students. Terman believed strongly that this preference for working independently reflected a natural cognitive and affective orientation. Gross's (1997) study of academically gifted students called this interpretation into question, however, suggesting that the preference for working alone depends on one's situation.

Gross (1997, 1998) found that highly gifted students admitted to a full-time ability-grouped setting designed to telescope six years of secondary schooling into five years swiftly developed a "cohort effect." The group was characterized by peer bonding, affectionate guidance, and mutual encouragement with classmates who were similar in their abilities and interests; were task-oriented, rather than ego-involved; and had been presented with a common, but intellectually challenging, goal (Gross, 1998). Yet many of these children stated that, in the elementary school heterogeneous classroom, they had preferred to work independently and had actively disliked being required to act as tutors for less-able classmates. Collaborative work became a delight, rather than a chore, when the students with whom they were now permitted to work were intellectual peers, rather than simply agemates.

## School Response to Exceptionally and Profoundly Gifted Students

As we have seen, the problems of social isolation, peer rejection, loneliness, and alienation that afflict many extremely gifted children arise *not* out of their exceptional intellectual abilities, but as a result of society's response to them. These problems arise when the school, the education system, or the community refuses to create for the extremely gifted child a peer group based not on the accident of chronological age, but on a commonality of abilities, interests, and values. Ability grouping is an essential interventive response for the highly gifted, and the earlier this occurs, the more effective it is likely to be in preventing social isolation.

Whether or not acceleration occurs within a homogeneous classroom of mental-age peers or for individual children, it is now

**25**

generally recognized (Benbow, 1998; Cronbach, 1996; Hollingworth, 1942) that, for highly gifted children, some form of acceleration is essential if they are to find not only significant numbers of students of their own mental age with whom they can form healthy and productive social relationships, but satisfying intellectual experiences, as well. Since the early 1970s, the findings of the Study of Mathematically Precocious Youth have provided powerful arguments for the intellectual and social benefits of academic acceleration for highly gifted youth (Benbow, Lubinski, & Suchy, 1996). Moreover, the multiplicity of talents displayed by these young people (Rogers & Silverman, 2001) coupled with their social and emotional maturity (Gross, 1993; Hollingworth, 1942; Janos, Robinson, & Lunneborg, 1989) makes them excellent candidates for radical acceleration, a series of grade advancements that results in their entering college three or more years earlier than is customary.

Hollingworth (1942) and Terman and Oden (1947), in their follow-up research on the young adults in Terman's gifted group, argued forcefully that, for extremely gifted children, a single grade skip was not sufficient; they strongly advised several grade skips spaced appropriately through the student's school career. Gross (1992, 1993, 1998) found that, for children with IQs higher than 160, a token grade skip of one year, even when supplemented with in-class enrichment or pull-out, was no more effective, academically or socially, than retention in the heterogeneous classroom.

In Gross's study, the majority of exceptionally gifted children who had not been radically accelerated displayed low levels of motivation and social self-esteem, were more likely to report social rejection by their classmates, and were required to perform in school at levels several years below their tested achievement. Some could recall a time in their lives when deliberate masking of their abilities had not been an automatic survival mechanism, accepted as a painful, but necessary part of living. By contrast, the 17 students who had been radically accelerated developed warm and fulfilling friendships with the older students with whom they learned and socialized through their childhood and adolescence (Gross, 1993, 1994, 1998). Nine of Gross's radical accelerants have already entered university, at ages between 11 and 16. All are experiencing high levels of academic success and have full social lives (Gross, 1998). None regret having taken such an accelerated pathway through school.

## Conclusion

Exceptionally gifted students are those for whom the education system must make exceptions. The social and academic environments that form the core of students' everyday experiences play a critical role in their social and emotional adjustment, as well as their ultimate productivity and life satisfaction. Despite common wisdom and stereotypes to the contrary, exceptionally and profoundly advanced students do not show inherent social deficiencies more frequently than anyone else. It is the mismatch with the environments we afford them that isolates and discourages their efforts to relate to others. This situation is a responsibility we must take seriously.

## References

Benbow, C. P. (1998). Acceleration as a method for meeting the academic needs of intellectually talented children. In J. VanTassel-Baska (Ed.), *Excellence in educating gifted and talented learners* (pp. 279–294). Denver: Love.

Benbow, C. P., Lubinski, D., & Suchy, B. (1996). The impact of SMPY's educational programs from the perspective of the participant. In C. P. Benbow & D. Lubinski (Eds.), *Intellectual talent* (pp. 266–300). Baltimore: Johns Hopkins University Press.

Burks, B. S., Jensen, D. W., & Terman, L. M. (1930). *The promise of youth: Volume 3: Genetic studies of genius.* Stanford, CA: Stanford University Press.

Cronbach, L. J. (1996). Acceleration among the Terman males: Correlates in midlife and after. In C. P. Benbow & D. L. Lubinski (Eds.), *Intellectual talent* (pp. 179–191). Baltimore: Johns Hopkins University Press.

Dauber, S. L., & Benbow, C. P. (1990). Aspects of personality and peer relations of extremely talented adolescents. *Gifted Child Quarterly, 34,* 10–14.

Freeman, J. (1979). *Gifted children.* Lancaster, England: MTP Press.

Gross, M. U. M. (1992). The use of radical acceleration in cases of extreme intellectual precocity. *Gifted Child Quarterly, 36,* 90–98.

Gross, M. U. M. (1993) *Exceptionally gifted children,* London: Routledge.

Gross, M. U. M. (1994). Radical acceleration: Responding to the academic and social needs of extremely gifted adolescents. *Journal of Secondary Gifted Education, 5,* 27–34.

**27**

Gross, M. U. M. (1997). How ability grouping turns big fish into little fish—or does it? Of optical illusions and optimal environments. *Australasian Journal of Gifted Education, 6(2)*, 18–30.

Gross, M. U. M. (1998). "Fishing" for the facts: A response to Marsh and Craven. *Australasian Journal of Gifted Education, 7(1)*, 16–28.

Gross, M. U. M. (2001, Summer). From "play partner" to "sure shelter": What do gifted children seek from friendship? *GERRIC News*, 4–5.

Gross, M. U. M. (in press). From "play partner" to "sure shelter": How do conceptions of friendship differ between average-ability, moderately gifted, and highly gifted children? *Proceedings of the 5th Biennial Henry B. and Jocelyn Wallace National Research Symposium on Talent Development.* Scottsdale, AZ: Gifted Psychology Press.

Hollingworth, L. S. (1926). *Gifted children: Their nature and nurture.* New York: Macmillan.

Hollingworth, L. S. (1942). *Children above IQ 180: Their origin and development.* New York: World Books.

Janos, P. M., Marwood, K. A., & Robinson, N. M. (1985). Friendship patterns in highly intelligent children. *Roeper Review, 8*, 46–49.

Janos, P. M., & Robinson, N. M. (1985). Psychosocial development in intellectually gifted children. In F. D. Horowitz & M. O'Brien (Eds.), *The gifted and talented: Developmental perspectives* (pp. 149–195). Washington, DC: American Psychological Association.

Janos, P. M., Robinson, N. M., & Lunneborg, C. E. (1989). Markedly early entrance to college: A multi-year comparative study of academic performance and psychological adjustment. *Journal of Higher Education, 60*, 496–518.

Kanevsky, L. (1994). A comparative study of children's learning in the zone of proximal development. *European Journal of High Ability, 5*, 163–175.

Morelock, M. J. (1995). *The profoundly gifted child in family context.* Unpublished doctoral dissertation, Tufts University, Boston.

Robinson, N. M., & Noble, K. D. (1992). Social-emotional development and adjustment of gifted children. In M. Wang, M. Reynolds, & H. Walberg (Eds.), *Handbook of special education: Research and practice (Vol. 4,* pp. 57–76). Oxford: Pergamon Press.

Rogers, K. B. (1986). Do the gifted think and learn differently? A review of recent research and its implications for instruction. *Journal for the Education of the Gifted, 10*, 17–39.

Rogers, K. B., & Silverman, L. K. (2001). Personal, social, medical, and psychological factors in children of IQ 160+. *Proceedings of the 4th Biennial Henry B. and Jocelyn Wallace National Research Symposium on Talent Development.* Scottsdale, AZ: Gifted Psychology Press.

Schneider, B. H. (1987). *The gifted child in peer group perspective.* New York: Springer-Verlag.

Silverman, L. K., & Kearney, K. (1992). The case for the Stanford-Binet L-M as a supplemental test. *Roeper Review, 15*, 34–37.

Swiatek, M. A. (1995). An empirical investigation of the social coping strategies used by gifted adolescents. *Gifted Child Quarterly, 39*, 154–161.

Terman, L. M., & Oden, M. H. (1947). *Genetic studies of genius. Volume 4: The gifted child grows up.* Stanford, CA: Stanford University Press.

**29**

# 4 ASYNCHRONOUS DEVELOPMENT

## by **Linda Kreger Silverman, Ph.D.**

*synchrony* means being "out-of-sync." Gifted children are more advanced mentally than others of their chronological age, and most have disparities between their intellectual abilities (as indicated by mental age) and their physical abilities (closely aligned to chronological age). Asynchrony intensifies as IQ increases, as this indicates greater discrepancy between the child's mental and chronological ages. To have the mental maturity of a 14-year-old and the physical maturity of an 8-year-old poses a set of emotional and social challenges analogous to those that face the child with a 14-year-old body and an 8-year-old mind. Hence, asynchrony with chronological peers is an existential dilemma for gifted children, which often creates social and emotional stress (Silverman, 1993). Asynchrony is also amplified by large discrepancies between a child's strengths and weaknesses. With increased asynchrony come greater social and emotional adjustment problems. Thus, exceptionally gifted children (see Gross, this volume) and twice-exceptional children are especially at risk for social and emotional difficulties related to asynchronous development (Moon, this volume; Olenchak & Reis, this volume).

## Asynchronous Development: A Phenomenological Definition of Giftedness

Asynchronous development is a phenomenological, rather than a utilitarian, perspective; it focuses on the conscious experience of the gifted, rather than on their usefulness to society. Roeper (1982) characterized giftedness as "a greater awareness, a greater sensitivity, and a greater ability to understand and to transform perceptions into intellectual and emotional experiences" (p. 21). Similarly, the Columbus Group (1991) defined giftedness as "*asynchronous development* in which advanced cognitive abilities and heightened intensity combine to create inner experiences and awareness that are qualitatively different from the norm."

The definition of giftedness as asynchronous development highlights the complexity of the individual's thought process, the intensity of sensation, emotion, and imagination, and the extraordinary awareness that results from this fusion. Asynchrony also involves uneven development and feeling out of step with societal norms. All of these factors create social and emotional vulnerabilities and require differentiated parenting, teaching, and counseling to promote optimal development in gifted individuals (Columbus Group, 1991).

## Dyssynchrony

Uneven development of gifted children has been noted by numerous clinicians and researchers (Altman, 1983; Delisle, 1990; Gowan, 1974; Hollingworth, 1942; Kerr, 1991; Kline & Meckstroth, 1985; Manaster & Powell, 1983; Munger, 1990; Roedell, 1984; Schetky, 1981; Sebring, 1983; Terrassier, 1985; Webb, Meckstroth, & Tolan, 1982). Terrassier coined the term *dys-*

*synchrony* to refer to the psychological and social ramifications of uneven development in gifted children. Gifted children often suffer from a lack of synchronicity in the rates of development of their intellectual, affective, and motor progress, which has its effect in a number of aspects of their lives, and its results, in turn produce further psychological problems (Terrassier, p. 265).

According to Terrassier (1985), dyssynchrony has two aspects: internal and social. *Internal* dyssynchrony refers to disparate rates of intellectual, psychomotor, and affective development within the individual. For example, children who can read before they can write experience dyssynchrony between their receptive language skills and expressive physical writing skills, which can create great frustration. *Social* dyssynchrony occurs when children feel out of step with their social context, as when gifted children are placed in a school class by chronological, rather than mental, age and so are cognitively out of sync with their classmates.

Hence, dyssynchrony is similar to asynchrony and can be used to refer to similar phenomena. However, the disadvantage of the term *dyssynchrony* is that its prefix *dys* means hard, bad, or difficult. It has pathological overtones. The term *asynchrony* is less value-laden and more useful for conveying the positive cognitive and emotional potentials that exist when high intelligence combines with great sensitivity. In addition, asynchrony incorporates Dabrowski's notion of the intensities (overexcitabilities) that characterize the gifted personality throughout the lifespan (Dabrowski & Piechowski, 1977). There is considerable empirical research substantiating the presence of these intensities in gifted children and adults (e.g., Ackerman, 1997; Gallagher, 1985; Schiever, 1985). For these reasons, asynchrony is a better term to use when discussing the phenomenological experience of giftedness.

## Asynchronous Development as a Conceptual Framework

Asynchrony has deep historical roots. Leta Stetter Hollingworth, the foremother of our field, viewed giftedness as a set of complex psychological issues arising out of the disparities between these children's mental and chronological ages (Grant & Piechowski, 1999).

To have the intelligence of an adult and the emotions of a child combined in a childish body is to encounter certain difficulties. It follows that (after babyhood) the younger the child, the greater the difficulties, and the adjustment becomes easier with every additional year of age. The years between 4 and 9 are probably the most likely to be beset with the problems mentioned (Hollingworth, 1931, p. 13).

Terman (1931) recognized this issue, as well:

> Precocity unavoidably complicates the problem of social adjustment. The child of eight years with a mentality of twelve or fourteen is faced with a situation almost inconceivably difficult. In order to adjust normally such a child has to have an exceptionally well-balanced personality and to be well neigh a social genius. The higher the IQ, the more acute the problem. (p. 579)

These early observations about the social difficulties that asynchrony creates for exceptionally gifted children have been substantiated by more recent research (see Gross, this volume).

Asynchronous development provides a useful conceptual framework to explain many of the existential dilemmas faced by the gifted. It is intensely frustrating when one's awareness outstrips one's emotional control (Hollingworth, 1931; Silverman, 1993, 1997). The construct is particularly germane to those who have been labeled "twice exceptional." When giftedness is equated with high achievement in school, gifted children with learning disabilities fail to be recognized and included. However, through the lens of asynchrony, it becomes apparent that twice-exceptional children are the ones most in need of special provisions. Extreme asynchronous development intensifies their social and emotional issues.

## Research on Asynchronous Development

34

The vast majority of the literature on asynchrony relies on clinical observations. This is fitting, as the concept was born from psychological observations of gifted individuals and intended to describe their phenomenological experience. But, there is some empirical research on this concept. The first to study the emotional and social adjustment of gifted children, Hollingworth (1930a) established that, the farther removed the child is from the average in intelligence, the more pressing his or her adjustment problems become. In Hollingworth's most notable experimental study of social adjustment which employed the Bernreuter Inventory of Personality, she found gifted adolescents to be much less neurotic, much more self-sufficient, and much less submissive than nongifted adolescents (Hollingworth & Rust, 1937). However, as IQ increased, so did difficulties with peer relations (Hollingworth, 1930a, 1930b, 1931).

As noted above, the most asynchronous children are twice exceptional, as they have the largest disparities in their development. For example, many have extraordinary visual-spatial strengths, combined with auditory-sequential weaknesses in reading, writing, spelling, and calculation, which prevent them from being seen as gifted within achievement-based school contexts (Silverman, 2000, 2001). Similarly, gifted children with AD/HD are asynchronous with their chronological peers on two dimensions. Like other gifted children, they are more advanced than their chronological peers cognitively, but, unlike other gifted children, they are less advanced than their age peers in social, emotional, and motivational development (Kaufmann & Castellanos, 2000). Dual asynchronous development in opposite directions creates numerous social and emotional difficulties for gifted children with AD/HD (Moon, Zentall, Grskovic, Hall, & Stormont-Spurgin, 2001).

## Conclusion

In conclusion, while some empirical research exists on the social and emotional impact of the discrepancies in the cognitive profiles of gifted learning-disabled children (Schiff, Kaufman, & Kaufman, 1981) and discrepancies between the cognitive profiles of exceptionally gifted children and their same age peers (Gross, this volume), the complete construct of asynchronous development has not yet been

35

studied systematically. It may be some time before empirical research catches up with the informed observations of psychologists devoted to understanding the emotional lives of gifted children. In the meantime, asynchronous development offers a useful conceptual framework for understanding many of the social and emotional issues faced by these children because of their differences from the norm.

## References

Ackerman, C. M. (1997). Identifying gifted adolescents using personality characteristics: Dabrowski's overexcitabilities. *Roeper Review, 19*, 229–236.

Altman, R. (1983). Social-emotional development of gifted children and adolescents: A research model. *Roeper Review, 6*, 65–68.

Columbus Group. (1991, July). Unpublished transcript of the meeting of the Columbus Group, Columbus, OH.

Dabrowski, K., & Piechowski, M. M. (1977). *Theory of levels of emotional development* (Vols. 1 & 2). Oceanside, NY: Dabor Science.

Delisle, J. R. (1990). The gifted adolescent at risk: Strategies and resources for suicide prevention among gifted youth. *Journal for the Education of the Gifted, 13*, 212–228.

Gallagher, S. A. (1985). A comparison of the concept of overexcitabilities with measures of creativity and school achievement in sixth grade students. *Roeper Review, 8*, 115–119.

Gowan, J. C. (1974). *Development of the psychedelic individual.* Northridge, CA: Gowan.

Grant, B. A., & Piechowski, M. M. (1999). Theories and the good: Toward child-centered gifted education. *Gifted Child Quarterly, 43*, 4–12.

Hollingworth, L. S. (1930a). Personality development of special class children. *University of Pennsylvania Bulletin. Seventeenth Annual Schoolmen's Week Proceedings, 30*, 442–446.

Hollingworth, L. S. (1930b). Playmates for the gifted child. *Child Study, 8*, 103–104.

Hollingworth, L. S. (1931). The child of very superior intelligence as a special problem in social adjustment. *Mental Hygiene, 15*(1), 1–16.

Hollingworth, L. S. (1942). *Children above 180 IQ Stanford–Binet: Origin and development.* Yonkers-on-Hudson, NY: World Book.

Hollingworth, L. S., & Rust, M. M. (1937). Application of the Benreuter Inventory of Personality to highly intelligent adolescents. *Journal of Psychology, 4*, 287–293.

Kaufmann, F., & Castellanos, F. X. (2000). Attention Deficit/Hyperactivity Disorder and gifted students. In K. A. Heller, F. J. Mönks, R. J. Sternberg, & R. F. Subotnik (Eds.), *International handbook of giftedness and talent* (2nd ed., pp. 621–632). Amsterdam: Elsevier.

**36**

Kerr, B. A. (1991). *A handbook for counseling the gifted and talented.* Alexandria, VA: American Association for Counseling and Development.

Kline, B. E., & Meckstroth, E. A. (1985). Understanding and encouraging the exceptionally gifted. *Roeper Review, 8,* 24–30.

Manaster, G. J., & Powell, P. M. (1983). A framework for understanding gifted adolescents' psychological maladjustment. *Roeper Review, 6,* 70–73.

Moon, S. M., Zentall, S., Grskovic, J., Hall, A., & Stormont-Spurgin, M. (2001). Emotional, social, and family characteristics of boys with AD/HD and giftedness: A comparative case study. *Journal for the Education of the Gifted, 24,* 207–247.

Munger, A. (1990). The parent's role in counseling the gifted: The balance between home and school. In J. VanTassel-Baska (Ed.), *A practical guide to counseling the gifted in a school setting* (2nd ed., pp. 57–65). Reston, VA: Council for Exceptional Children.

Roedell, W. C. (1984). Vulnerabilities of highly gifted children. *Roeper Review, 6,* 127–130.

Roeper, A. (1982). How the gifted cope with their emotions. *Roeper Review, 5*(2), 21–24.

Schetky, D. H. (1981). A psychiatrist looks at giftedness: The emotional and social development of the gifted child. *G/C/T, 18,* 2–4.

Schiever, S. W. (1985). Creative personality characteristics and dimensions of mental functioning in gifted adolescents. *Roeper Review, 7,* 223–226.

Schiff, M. M., Kaufman, A. S., & Kaufman, N. L. (1981). Scatter analysis of WISC-R profiles for learning disabled children with superior intelligence. *Journal of Learning Disabilities, 14,* 400–404.

Sebring, A. D. (1983). Parental factors in the social and emotional adjustment of the gifted. *Roeper Review, 6(*2), 97–99.

Silverman, L. K. (1993). Counseling needs and programs for the gifted. In K. A. Heller, F. J. Mönks, & A. H. Passow (Eds.), *International handbook of research and development of giftedness and talent* (pp. 631–647). Oxford, England: Pergamon.

Silverman, L. K. (1997). The construct of asynchronous development. *Peabody Journal of Education, 72*(3–4), 36–58.

Silverman, L. K. (2000). The two-edged sword of compensation: How the gifted cope with learning disabilities. In K. Kay (Ed.). *Uniquely gifted: Identifying and meeting the needs of twice exceptional learners* (pp. 153–159). Gilsum, NH: Avocus.

Silverman, L. K. (2001). *Upside-down brilliance: The visual-spatial learner.* Unpublished manuscript.

Terrassier, J-C. (1985). Dyssynchrony-uneven development. In J. Freeman (Ed.). *The psychology of gifted children* (pp. 265–274). New York: Wiley.

Terman, L. M. (1931). The gifted child. In C. Murchison (Ed.), *A handbook of child psychology* (pp. 568–584). Worcester, MA: Clark University Press.

Webb, J. T., Meckstroth, E. A., & Tolan, S. S. (1982). *Guiding the gifted child: A practical source for parents and teachers.* Columbus: Ohio Psychology Press.

**37**

# Common Areas of Psychological Response

# 5 AFFECT REGULATION AND THE GIFTED

## by Margaret K. Keiley, Ed.D.

In recent years, educators, psychologists, clinicians, and researchers have addressed the educational, social, and emotional needs of intellectually and academically gifted children and adolescents (Colangelo & Davis, 1997; Feldhusen, Van Tassel-Baska, & Seeley, 1989; Horowitz & O'Brien, 1985; Shore, Cornell, Robinson, & Ward, 1991). As in research on other populations (Crick & Dodge, 1994), the focus of research on gifted individuals has been mainly on their cognitive functioning (Sternberg & Davidson, 1986) followed by investigations of their psychosocial functioning (Janos & Robinson, 1985; Robinson & Noble, 1991). Although the affective domain has been heralded as foundational in the development of personal and social talents (Gardner, 1983; Kelly & Moon, 1998; Moon, in press) and an essential component of motivation and social and emotional functioning (Garber & Dodge, 1991;

Martin & Tesser, 1996; Mayer & Salovey, 1997), very little attention has been paid to affect regulation in the gifted. Some research on the emotional development of gifted children has focused on identifying endogenous and exogenous factors related to giftedness that can cause social and emotional difficulties in this population (Moon & Hall, 1997; Moon, Kelly, & Feldhusen, 1997; Neihart, 1999; Robinson & Noble, 1991; Webb, 1993).

## Affect Regulation

Emotions supply information about the impact and relevance of individuals' experiences; what is desired, valued, wanted, or needed (Frijda, 1986; Tomkins, 1963). Emotions are, therefore, crucial in decision-making processes. Affect regulation involves monitoring, tolerating, and coordinating the physiological, behavioral, or experiential aspects of emotional experience (Garber & Dodge, 1991; Keiley, Liu, Moon, & Sprenkle, 2000). Affect that is undercontrolled is a hallmark of externalizing behaviors, such as oppositional defiant disorder, conduct disorder, and violence. Affect that is overcontrolled distinguishes many internalizing disorders, such as anxiety, phobias, and depression (Hinshaw, Lahey, & Hart, 1993). In general, affect is regulated in order to reduce adverse conditions or to increase favorable ones, thus allowing individuals to understand, organize, and act upon that experience (Frijda, 1986; Mayer & Salovey, 1997). Affect management involves both internal relational processes of self-regulation and external relational processes of social regulation (Garber & Dodge). Internally, individuals attempt to modulate affective experience in order to have the time and space in which to decide what external or social regulation processes they want to activate (Magai, 1999). Optimally, individuals are able to tolerate affect with a minimum of controlling strategies aimed at either themselves (internally focused) or at others (externally focused), which enables them to access the information that affect contains about their current experience (Tomkins, 1963), information that is crucial for both effective decision making and the development of talent.

# Affect Regulation in Gifted Children

Until recently, most research on gifted children has focused on academic and social issues, rather than on emotional ones, with the exception of studies of the prevalence of affect-regulation difficulties (Colangelo & Davis, 1997). Reviews of research in this area present conflicting views of the emotional characteristics of intellectually and academically gifted children (Janos & Robinson, 1985; Moon & Hall, 1997; Moon, Kelly, & Feldhusen, 1997; Neihart, 1999; Robinson & Noble, 1991). Some studies suggest that these children are highly motivated, well-adjusted, socially mature, open to new experiences, independent, and possess high self-concepts and a high tolerance for ambiguity. Other studies suggest that gifted children may be vulnerable to social and emotional difficulties related to their giftedness. In addition, certain subpopulations of gifted children (lower socioeconomic status, single parent, African American, gifted children with disabilities, and the highly gifted) have been found to be at risk for poor social adjustment (Ford, 1996; Moon, Zentall, Grskovic, Hall, & Stormont-Spurgin, 2001). Less is known, however, about how these subpopulations of gifted children regulate affect (Ford & Harris, 1995; Frasier, 1993).

Reviews of research on the emotional needs of gifted students (Janos & Robinson, 1985; Robinson, & Noble, 1991; Webb, 1993) suggest that they may be at risk for developing internalizing disorders. They have been found to be vulnerable to isolation and loneliness, which are precursors to depression and anxiety reactions (Kaiser & Berndt, 1986; Jackson, 1998; Kline & Short, 1992). Their intensity, sensitivity, and emotionality can also contribute to anxiety, phobias, and interpersonal problems (Fiedler, 1999; Piechowski, 1997; Silverman, 1993; Webb). Internal, parental, and societal pressures to achieve can result in a fear of failure or in an obsessive-compulsive perfectionism (Weisse, 1990). The negative manifestations of perfectionism that have been identified as pertinent to the gifted are those related to affect regulation (e.g., eating disorders, depression, underachievement, substance abuse, and suicide; Hayes & Sloat, 1992; Hillyer, 1989; Nugent, 2000). If gifted students do experience failure, they may have few strategies to manage their negative affect since they have little experience in dealing with failure. For example, academically gifted junior high students have been found to demonstrate more negative affective, stronger physiological stress reactions, and more irrational beliefs in response to experimentally inducted failure than a comparison group of nongifted peers (Roberts & Lovett, 1994). Gifted students who experience failure may find themselves feeling either anxious or suicidal and depressed (Delisle, 1986; Jackson, 1998; Silverman). Some evidence exists that gifted males may experience more depression than gifted females (Bartell & Reynolds, 1988; Kline & Short). In another study, however, gifted females reported expressions of higher levels of negative affect than the males on a projective story-completion task (Keiley, Moon, Sprenkle, & Liu, 1999).

However, other research suggests that gifted children and adolescents experience either the same or less risk for internalizing difficulties than nongifted children. They have been found to show essentially the same amount of interest and enjoyment in class activities (Gentry, Gable, & Springer, 2000), experience fewer stressful life-changing events (Metha & McWhirter, 1997); demonstrate the same or fewer internalizing symptoms (Galluci, Middleton, & Kline, 1999; Merrell, Gill, McFarland, & McFarland, 1996), and experience similar amounts of depression and suicide ideation (Baker, 1995; Metha & McWhirter; Pearson & Beer, 1991) as their nongifted peers. Similarly, gifted secondary school students have been found to have emotional adjustment scores in the normative range (Garland & Zigler, 1999; Nail & Evans, 1997).

Less evidence exists about the externalizing problems and disorders that the gifted may have. Most studies have shown that, when compared to their nongifted counterparts, gifted children and adolescents showed less physical aggression, restlessness, and lack of respect, all behaviors associated with conduct disorder (Fiedler, 1999; Ludwig & Cullinan, 1985). For example, a study with a large sample second and third graders found no differences in the incidence of any form of behavior problem between gifted and regular education students (Cornell, Delcourt, Bland, Goldberg, & Oram, 1994). Another study (Brody & Benbow, 1987) found similar incidences of discipline problems when comparing gifted and nongifted adolescents.

Research on stressors unique to giftedness is also mixed. An interview study of gifted fifth and sixth graders yielded a number of nega-

**44**

tive affective reactions to perceived stressors related to giftedness, including confusion, embarrassment, annoyance, and guilt (Ford, 1989). However, a study comparing the prevalence of everyday stressors, such as feeling different, boredom, and perfectionism, in groups of gifted and average-ability adolescents found no differences between the groups (Baker, 1996). There is some evidence that gifted students may have buffering traits, such as high self-efficacy (Merrell, Gill, McFarland, & McFarland, 1996), sensitivity (Mendaglio, 1995), and effective coping strategies (Tomchin, Callahan, Sowa, & May, 1996), that can reduce the negative impact of the stressors they experience. This suggests that, although gifted children and adolescents experience stressors related to their giftedness, they may also have advanced ability in managing the negative affect these stressors produce. In other words, their experience of unique stressors related to their giftedness, intensity, and sensitivity may be balanced by their greater resilience, resulting in the development of emotional strength and skill (Bland, Sowa, & Callahan, 1994).

Many intellectually and academically gifted children have families that are child-centered with close, nurturing, and supportive relationships (Friedman, 1994; Moon, Jurich, & Feldhusen, 1998). This suggests that families of the gifted may be doing a good job of facilitating the development of affect-regulation strategies in their children. On the other hand, one of the major difficulties that parents of the gifted experience is a feeling of inadequacy, an inability to help with their children's emotional, social, and cognitive development (Silverman, 1993). At times, the child-centered organization of the gifted child's family can overwhelm their resources, skew relationships, and produce marital conflict (Colangelo, 1997). Disorganization and conflict have been observed among low-income families of gifted children, families of underachieving gifted children, and families of twice-exceptional gifted children.

Sowa and May (1997) described empirically derived, dysfunctional patterns of adjustment in families of the gifted. If a sense of belonging is emphasized to the detriment of a sense of self, gifted children may feel obligated to comply with family rules, rather than explore and express their own ideas and feelings. These compliant gifted children relinquish their sense of agency in order to fit into the environment and are at risk for not developing their potential. If an

**45**

exaggerated sense of individual importance is stressed by families, gifted children may display behavior that is so strange and inappropriate that they do not fit into their environment, are rejected by their peers and teachers, and must rationalize their distress about being rejected. These detached gifted children may relinquish relationships with others in order to fit into their families. The description of these two family types fits into the framework about the differing family environments that are associated with internalizing (compliant, withdrawn) and externalizing (detached, rejected) children currently under investigation by researchers interested in the development of affect regulation and dysregulation (Garber & Dodge, 1991; Katz & Gottman, 1993; Lyons-Ruth, 1996).

Two areas of research on affect regulation in the gifted need attention. First, delineating the *specific* affect-regulation strategies of gifted children who are and are not having difficulties with their social, emotional, or behavioral adjustment would assist in the development of programs and treatments aimed at assisting these children in their adjustment. Second, proposing and researching a model of affective talent development would help in the identification of affectively talented children. Although several scholars have theorized that awareness and management of feelings are crucial in the development of personal and social talents (Dabrowski & Piechowski, 1977; Gardner, 1983; Mayer & Salovey, 1997; Piechowski, 1997), very little research has been conducted on affective talent development processes.

# References

Baker, J. A. (1995). Depression and suicidal ideation among academically gifted adolescents. *Gifted Child Quarterly, 39,* 218–223.

Baker, J. A. (1996). Everyday stressors of academically gifted adolescents. *Journal of Secondary Gifted Education, 7,* 356–368.

Bartell, N. P., & Reynolds, W. M. (1988). Depression and self-esteem in academically gifted and nongifted children: A comparison study. *Journal of School Psychology, 24,* 55–61.

Bland, L. C., Sowa, C. J., & Callahan, C. M. (1994). An overview of resilience in gifted children. *Roeper Review, 17,* 77–80.

Brody, L. E., & Benbow, C. P. (1987). Social and emotional adjustment of adolescents extremely talented in verbal and mathematical reasoning. *Journal of Youth and Adolescence, 15,* 1–18.

Colangelo, N. (1997). Counseling gifted students: Issues and practices. In N. Colangelo & G. A. Davis (Eds.), *Handbook of gifted education* (2nd. ed., pp. 353–365). Boston: Allyn and Bacon.

Colangelo, N., & Davis, G. A. (Eds.). (1997). *Handbook of gifted education* (2nd ed.). Boston: Allyn and Bacon.

Cornell, D. G., Delcourt, M. A. B., Bland, L. C., Goldberg, M. D., & Oram, G. (1994). Low incidence of behavior problems among elementary school students in gifted programs. *Journal for the Education of the Gifted. 18*, 4–19.

Crick, N. R., & Dodge, K. A. (1994). A review and reformulation of social information-processing mechanisms in children's social adjustment. *Psychological Bulletin, 115*(1), 74–101.

Dabrowski, K., & Piechowski, M. M. (1977). *Theory of levels of emotional development.* Oceanside, NY: Dabor.

Delisle, J. R. (1986). Death with honors: Suicide among gifted adolescents. *Journal of Counseling and Development, 64*, 558–560.

Feldhusen, J. F., VanTassel-Baska, J., & Seeley, K. (1989). *Excellence in educating the gifted.* Denver: Love.

Fiedler, E. D. (1999). Gifted children: The promise of potential/the problems of potential. In V. L. Schwean & D. H. Saklofske (Eds.), *Handbook of psychosocial characteristics of exceptional children* (pp. 401–441). New York: Kluwer Academic/Plenum.

Ford, D. Y. (1996). *Reversing underachievement among gifted Black students: Promising practices and programs.* New York: Teachers College Press.

Ford, D. Y., & Harris, J. J., III (1995). Underachievement among gifted African American students: Implications for school counselors. *School Counselor, 42*, 196–203.

Ford, M. (1989). Students' perceptions of affective issues impacting the social emotional development and school performance of gifted/talented youngsters. *Roeper Review 11*, 131–134.

Frasier, M. M. (1993). Issues, problems, and programs in nurturing disadvantaged and culturally different talented. In K. A. Heller, F. J. Mönks, & A. H. Passow (Eds.), *International handbook of research and development of giftedness and talent* (pp. 685–692). Oxford, England: Pergamon Press.

Friedman, R. C. (1994). Upstream helping for low-income families of gifted students: Challenges and opportunities. *Journal of Educational and Psychological Consultation, 5*, 321–338.

Frijda, N. H. (1986). *The emotions.* Cambridge: Cambridge University Press.

Galluci, N. T., Middleton, G., & Kline, A. (1999). Intellectually superior children and behavioral problems and competence. *Roeper Review, 22*, 18–21.

Garber, J., & Dodge, K. A. (Eds.). (1991). *The development of emotion regulation and dysregulation.* New York: Cambridge University Press.

Gardner, H. (1983). *Frames of mind: The theory of multiple intelligences.* New York: Basic Books.

Garland, A. F., & Zigler, E. (1999). Emotional and behavioral problems among highly intellectually gifted youth. *Roeper Review, 22*, 41–44.

**47**

Gentry, M., Gable, R. K., & Springer, P. (2000). Gifted and nongifted middle school students: Are their attitudes toward school different as measured by the new affective instruments, My Class Activities . . . ? *Journal for the Education of the Gifted, 24,* 74–95.

Hayes, M. L., & Sloat, R. S. (1992). Gifted students at risk for suicide. *Roeper Review, 12,* 102–107.

Hillyer, K. (1989). Problems of gifted children. *Journal of the Association for the Study of Perception, 21,* 10–26.

Hinshaw, S. P., Lahey, B. B., & Hart, E. (1993). Issues of taxonomy and comorbidity in the development of conduct disorder. *Development and Psychopathology, 5,* 31–39.

Horowitz, F. D., & O'Brien, M. (Eds.). (1985). *The gifted and talented: Developmental perspectives.* Washington, DC: American Psychological Association.

Jackson, P. S. (1998). Bright star—black sky: A phenomenological study of depression as a window into the psyche of the gifted adolescent. *Roeper Review, 20,* 215–221.

Janos, P. M., & Robinson, N. M. (1985). Psychosocial development in intellectually gifted children. In F. D. Horowitz & M. O'Brien (Eds.), *The gifted and talented: Developmental perspectives* (pp. 149–195). Washington DC: American Psychological Association.

Kaiser, C. F., & Berndt, D. J. (1986). Predictors of loneliness in the gifted adolescent. *Gifted Child Quarterly, 29,* 74–77.

Katz, L. F., & Gottman, J. M. (1993). Patterns of marital conflict predict children's internalizing and externalizing behaviors. *Developmental Psychology, 29,* 940–950.

Kelly, K. R., & Moon, S. M. (1998). Personal and social talents. *Phi Delta Kappan, 79,* 743–746.

Keiley, M. K., Liu, T., Moon, S., & Sprenkle, D. (2000, August). *Affect Regulation Scales for the Gifted: Development and testing.* Paper presented at the annual meeting of the American Psychological Association, Washington, DC.

Keiley, M. K., Moon, S., Sprenkle, D., & Liu, T. (1999, August). *Development of the Affect Regulation Scales for the Gifted.* Paper presented at the annual meeting of the American Psychological Association, Boston.

Kline, B. E., & Short, E. B. (1992). Changes in emotional resilience: Gifted adolescent boys. *Roeper Review, 13,* 184–187.

Ludwig, G., & Cullinan, D. (1985). Behavior problems of gifted and non-gifted elementary school girls and boys. *Gifted Child Quarterly, 28,* 37–39.

Lyons-Ruth, K. (1996). Attachment relationships among children with aggressive behavior problems: The role of disorganized early attachment patterns. *Journal of Consulting and Clinical Psychology, 64,* 64–73.

Magai, C. (1999). Affect, imagery, and attachment: Working models of interpersonal affect and the socialization of emotion. In J. Cassidy & P. R. Shaver (Eds.), *Handbook of attachment: Theory, research, and clinical applications* (pp. 787–802). New York: Guilford Press.

Martin, L. L., & Tesser, A. (Eds.). (1996). *Striving and feeling.* Mahwah, NH: Erlbaum.

Mayer, J. D., & Salovey, P. (1997). What is emotional intelligence? In P. Salovey & D. Sluyter (Eds.), *Emotional development and emotional intelligence: Implications for educators* (pp. 3–34). New York: Basic Books.

Mendaglio, S. (1995). Sensitivity among gifted persons: A multi-faceted perspective. *Roeper Review, 17,* 169–172.

Merrell, K. W., Gill, S. J., McFarland, J., & McFarland, T. (1996). Internalizing symptoms of gifted and non-gifted elementary-age students: A comparative validity study using the Internalizing Symptoms Scale for Children. *Psychology in the Schools, 33,* 185–191.

Metha, A., & McWhirter, E. H. (1997). Suicide ideation, depression, and stressful life events among gifted adolescents. *Journal for the Education of the Gifted, 20,* 284–304.

Moon, S. M. (in press). Personal talent: What is it and how can we study it? In N. Colangelo (Ed.), *Talent development V: Proceedings from the 2000 Henry B. and Jocelyn Wallace National Research Symposium.* Iowa City: University of Iowa Press.

Moon, S. M., & Hall, A. S. (1997). Family therapy with intellectually and creatively gifted children. *Journal of Marital and Family Therapy, 24,* 59–80.

Moon, S. M., Jurich, J. A., & Feldhusen, J. F. (1998). Families of gifted children: Cradles of development. In R. Friedman & K. B. Rogers (Eds.), *Talent in context: Historical and social perspectives* (pp. 81–99). Washington, DC: American Psychological Association.

Moon, S. M., Kelly, K. R., & Feldhusen, J. F. (1997). Specialized counseling services for gifted youth and their families: A needs assessment. *Gifted Child Quarterly, 41,* 16–25.

Moon, S. M., Zentall, S., Grskovic, J., Hall, A., & Stormont-Spurgin, M. (2001) Emotional, social, and family characteristics of boys with AD/HD and giftedness: A comparative case study. *Journal for the Education of the Gifted, 24,* 207–247.

Nail, J. M., & Evans, J. G. (1997). The emotional adjustment of gifted adolescents: A view of global functioning. *Roeper Review, 20,* 18–22.

Neihart, M. (1999). The impact of giftedness on psychological well being: What does the empirical literature say? *Roeper Review, 22,* 10–17.

Nugent, S. A. (2000). Perfectionism: Its manifestations and classroom-based interventions. *Journal of Secondary Gifted Education, 11,* 215–221.

Pearson, M., & Beer, J. (1991). Self-consciousness, self-esteem, and depression of gifted school children. *Psychological Reports, 66,* 960–962.

Piechowski, M. M. (1997). Emotional giftedness: The measure of intrapersonal intelligence. In N. Colangelo & G. A. Davis (Eds.), *Handbook of gifted education* (2nd ed., pp. 366–381). Boston: Allyn and Bacon.

Roberts, S. M., & Lovett, S. B. (1994). Examining the "F" in gifted: Academically gifted adolescents' physiological and affective responses to scholastic failure. *Journal for the Education of the Gifted, 17,* 241–259.

Robinson, N. M., & Noble, K. D. (1991). Social-emotional development and adjustment of gifted children. In M. C. Wang, M. C. Reynolds, & H. J. Walberg (Eds.), *Handbook of special education: Research and practice* (Vol. 4, pp. 57–76). Oxford: Pergamon Press.

Shore, B. M., Cornell, D. G., Robinson, A., & Ward, V. S. (1991). *Recommended practices in gifted education*. New York: Teachers College Press.

Silverman, L. K. (1993). The gifted individual. In L. K. Silverman (Ed.), *Counseling the gifted and talented* (pp. 3–28). Denver: Love.

Sowa, C. J., & May, K. M. (1997). Expanding Lazarus and Folkman's paradigm to the social and emotional adjustment of gifted children and adolescents (SEAM). *Gifted Child Quarterly, 41*, 36–43.

Sternberg, R. J., & Davidson, J. E. (Eds.). (1986). *Conceptions of giftedness*. Cambridge: Cambridge University Press.

Tomchin, E. M., Callahan, C. M., Sowa, C. J., & May, K. M. (1996). Coping and self-concept: Adjustment patterns in gifted adolescents. *Journal of Secondary Gifted Education, 8*, 16–27.

Tomkins, S. (1963). *Affect, imagery, consciousness* (Vol. 1). New York: Springer.

Webb, J. T. (1993). Nurturing social-emotional development of gifted children. In K. A. Heller, F. J. Mönks, & A. H. Passow (Eds.), *International handbook of research and development of giftedness and talent* (pp. 525–538). Oxford: Pergamon Press.

Weisse, D. E. (1990). Gifted adolescents and suicide. *School Counselor, 37*, 351–358.

# 6 THE APPLICATION OF DABROWSKI'S THEORY TO THE GIFTED

## by Kevin J. O'Connor, Ed.M.

any gifted children experience high levels of intensity and sensitivity and may appear at odds with their peers. They may question their "normality" or have it questioned by parents and teachers. Piechowski (1997) has suggested that this line of inquiry may extend into adulthood, as many gifted adults feel the same pressure to be "normal" and continue to question their potential, possibilities, and personality ideal. Dabrowski's (1964) Theory of Positive Disintegration has been discussed as one way of understanding the social and emotional development of gifted children. Relatively little research has addressed the use of Dabrowski's work with gifted students; however, the studies that have been completed indicate that this may be a promising direction for consideration of the unique social and emotional characteristics that some gifted children and adults may exhibit.

51

# Dabrowski's Theory

Dabrowski's theory is based on the belief that emotional development is the most essential dimension of human life (Grant & Piechowski, 1999). The theory defines five levels of personality development, explains the process by which development occurs along these levels, and identifies individual characteristics that equate to developmental potential.

Dabrowski's pentatonic levels represent the mapping of human personality, or emotional development, along a continuum from low (egocentric) to high (altruistic). The levels are in ascending order, with the higher levels representing individuals whose personality is defined by a hierarchy of altruistic values. Piechowski (1997) characterized individuals at each of Dabrowski's levels as follows:

> *Level I: Primary Integration.* Egocentrism prevails. A person at this level lacks the capacity for empathy and self-examination. When things go wrong, someone else is always to blame; self-responsibility is not encountered here. . . .

> *Level II: Unilevel Disintegration.* Individuals are influenced primarily by their social group and by mainstream values . . . They often exhibit ambivalent feelings and indecisive flip-flop behavior because they have no clear-cut set of self-determined internal values. Inner conflicts are horizontal, a contest between equal, competing values. . . .

> *Level III: Spontaneous Multilevel Disintegration.* The person develops a hierarchical sense of values. Inner conflict is vertical, a struggle to bring up one's behavior to higher standards. There is a dissatisfaction with what one is, because of a competing sense of what one could and ought to be (personality ideal). . . .

> *Level IV: Organized Multilevel Disintegration.* Individuals are well on the road to self-actualization. They have found a way to reach their own ideals, and they are effective leaders in society. They show high levels of responsibility,

authenticity, reflective judgment, empathy for others, autonomy of thought and action, self-awareness. . . .

*Level V: Secondary Integration.* The struggle for self-mastery has been won. Inner conflicts regarding the self have been resolved through actualization of the personality ideal. Disintegration has been transcended by the integration of one's values into one's living and being. (p. 374).

Development along Dabrowski's levels comes through a process of lower level cognitive-emotional structures being dismantled and replaced by higher level structures. Dabrowski referred to this process as "positive disintegration" to emphasize the beneficial aspects of breaking down inferior and reconstructing superior personality attributes. The hallmark of Dabrowski's conception of development is inner conflict achieved by a disconnection between "what is" and "what ought to be" in one's self (Dabrowski, in Piechowski, 1975). Dabrowski (1972) believed that many individuals who exhibit neurotic characteristics (i.e., intense inner conflict, feelings of inferiority regarding one's self, dissatisfaction with one's self, feelings of inadequacy, disquietude, anxiety) also possess the greatest potential for development. He further viewed "positive maladjustment" as a prerequisite to the development of authenticity and emphasized its positive effects (Dabrowski; Dabrowski, Kawczak, & Piechowski, 1970; Dabrowski & Piechowski, 1977). In his clinical work, Dabrowski observed that gifted and creative individuals are often in conflict with the demands and expectations of their environment, which are commonly incompatible with their higher value structure (Dabrowski; Dabrowski, Kawczak, & Piechowski).

## The Concept of Developmental Potential

Dabrowski's levels do not represent stages of development; movement to a higher level is not automatic, and most individuals do not advance to the highest levels. In the concept of developmental potential, obtaining higher levels of development is contingent upon one's original endowment of intelligence, special talents and abilities, will to develop, and five forms of experiencing called *overexcitabilities*. Many in the gifted community believe Dabrowski's overexcitabilities, as they contribute to developmental potential, are a measure and indicator of giftedness.

Piechowski (1999) characterized overexcitabilities as enhanced modes of being in the world. The word *over* used in connection with *excitability* connotes responses to stimuli that are beyond normal and often of a different quality. Dabrowski (1937, 1938) identified "psychic overexcitability" in five forms: psychomotor, sensual, intellectual, imaginational, and emotional. Piechowski and Cunningham (1985) explained the expressions of each overexcitability as:

> *Psychomotor overexcitability.* Is an organic excess of energy or heightened excitability of the neuromuscular system. It may manifest itself as a love of movement for its own sake, rapid speech, violent or impulsive activity, restlessness, pressure for action, and drivenness. It may be viewed as a capacity for being active and energetic. . . .

> *Sensual overexcitability.* Is expressed in the heightened experience of sensual pleasure, the seeking of sensual outlets for inner tension. Beyond desires for comfort, luxury, stereotyped or refined beauty, the pleasure in being admired and being in the limelight, sensual overexcitability may be expressed in the simple pleasure derived from touching things . . . or the pleasure of taste and smell. . . . In short, it is a capacity for sensual enjoyment. . . .

> *Intellectual overexcitability.* Is to be distinguished from intelligence. It manifests itself as persistence in asking probing questions, avidity for knowledge and analysis, preoccupation with theoretical problems. Other expressions are: a sharp sense of observation, independence of thought (often expressed in criticism), symbolic thinking, development of new concepts, striving for synthesis of knowledge, and searching for truth. . . .

*Imaginational overexcitability.* Is recognized through rich association of images and impressions, inventiveness, vivid and often animated visualization, use of image and metaphor in verbal expression. . . . Intense living in the world of fantasy, predilection for fairy and magic tales, poetic creations and dramatizing to escape boredom are also observed. . . .

*Emotional overexcitability.* Is recognized in the way emotional relationships are experienced, and in the great intensity of feeling and awareness of its whole range. Characteristic expressions are: inhibition (timidity and shyness) and excitation (enthusiasm), strong affective recall of past experiences or concern with death, fears, anxieties, or depressions. There may be intense loneliness, an intense desire to offer love, a concern for others. There is a high degree of differentiation of interpersonal feeling. (pp. 154–156)

Advanced development, characteristic of a deeper sensitivity and intensity of emotional experiencing, requires a profound knowledge of self and a more meaningful contact with the environment (Dabrowski, 1972). Overexcitabilities assist in meeting these essentials:

One could say that one who manifests a given form of overexcitability, and especially one who manifests several forms of overexcitability, sees reality in a different, stronger, and more multisided manner. Reality for such an individual ceases to be indifferent but affects him deeply and leaves longlasting impressions. Enhanced excitability is thus a means for more frequent interactions and a wider range of experiencing. (Dabrowski, p. 7)

While the concept of developmental potential emphasizes the positive aspects of experiencing life with greater intensity and sensitivity, these same characteristics may also be experienced in negative ways. Individuals with elevated overexcitabilities are more susceptible to being misunderstood and alienated by those who don't share or understand their unique personality traits (Lewis, Kitano, & Lynch, 1992; Lovecky, 1992; Piechowski, 1997; Silverman, 1993). Many individuals with elevated overexcitabilities attempt to hide or learn to control their intensities and sensitivities in order to conform to the expectations of others (Lewis, Kitano, & Lynch). Silverman acknowledges the position of such individuals, explaining that "Feeling everything more deeply than others do is both painful and frightening" (p. 17).

## Research on the Theory

Researchers in the gifted education community have been interested in research and reflection about Dabrowski's theory for its appeal as a means of broadening the conception of giftedness by taking into account the personality attributes related to high ability (Piechowski, 1986). While adult biographical and case study analyses have provided evidence in support of Dabrowski's levels (Brennan, 1987; Brennan & Piechowski, 1991; Grant, 1990; Piechowski, 1975, 1978, 1990), studies with gifted students have focused strictly on the concept of developmental potential. This reflects what Piechowski (1986) described as a research direction aimed at measuring the presence and strength of the overexcitabilities as they contribute to the definition and identification of the gifted.

Measuring overexcitability is made possible through the use of the Overexcitability Questionnaire—Two (Falk, Lind, Miller, Piechowski, & Silverman, 1999), a 50-item, Likert-type scale instrument that is designed to measure the presence and degree of the five overexcitabilities. The studies discussed in this review used an earlier version of the questionnaire with 21-item free responses (Lysy & Piechowski, 1983). Piechowski and Colangelo (1984) compared gifted students with gifted adults and nongifted adults. Their results showed that elevated emotional, intellectual, and imaginational overexcitability scores clearly distinguished the gifted participants, both students and adults, from the nongifted. Gallagher (1986) found this overexcitability pattern could distinguish a group of gifted sixth-grade students from their nonidentified peers, and Schiever (1985) used the same profile to differentiate between high-creative and low-creative seventh- and eighth-grade students. Breard (1994) found that gifted upper elementary students obtained higher overexcitability scores than nongifted students across all five forms of overexcitability. Ackerman (1997) found similar results with a comparison of gifted and nongifted high school students with psychomotor, intellectual, and emotional overexcitabilities acting as the major discriminates between the groups. In a study that compared the overexcitability profiles of intellectually gifted and creatively gifted middle school students, no significant differences were found (Ely, 1995).

Research using adult gifted and nongifted samples illustrates how the distinguishing characteristic of overexcitability may exist throughout the life span (Falk, Manzanero, & Miller, 1997; Miller, Silverman, & Falk, 1994; Piechowski & Cunningham, 1985; Piechowski, Silverman, & Falk, 1985; Silverman & Ellsworth, 1981). Overexcitabilities have also been exhibited in young (preschool) gifted children (Howard, 1994; Kitano, 1990; Silverman, 1983; Tucker & Hafenstein, 1997).

## Discussion

The ideas that neurotic symptoms may be a sign of emotional development, that individuals can be "positively maladjusted," and that "overexcitability" can be considered a positive attribute make Dabrowski's theory more controversial in mainstream psychological theory and practice. However, parents of gifted children and gifted individuals themselves may find that Dabrowski's ideas provide a useful "framework for understanding and explaining the developmental patterns and challenges that occur for those of high ability" (Nelson, 1989, p. 11).

Those providing counseling services to the gifted should consider adding Dabrowski's concepts to their knowledge of developmental and psychological theory. As maladjustment and inner conflict may be necessary for some to gain a deeper and more emotional development, counselors and therapists can provide an empathic environment. This sentiment is echoed by Silverman (1993), who wrote, "One of the greatest gifts a counselor can give

**57**

gifted young people is an appreciation of their sensitivities, intensities, and passions" (p. 17).

For educators interested in alternate means of identifying students for gifted programs, Dabrowski's concept of developmental potential through enhanced overexcitabilities may provide a viable option. By moving beyond IQ measures and defining giftedness in terms of an elevated overexcitability profile, a wider range of students may be identified for gifted programs (Ackerman, 1997; Breard, 1994; Nelson 1989; Piechowski, 1979, 1986). Currently, overexcitability instruments are not conducive for schoolwide identification procedures; the Overexcitability Questionnaire—Two is designed solely for research with group data and not intended to provide individual diagnostic information (Falk, Lind, Miller, Piechowski, & Silverman, 1999), and the original Overexcitability Questionnaire is limited by its length of administration time, required level of writing skills and expressive language, and cost of scoring or training raters (Ackerman, 1997). Future research can help to develop an overexcitability instrument that can be used as part of an identification procedure in schools.

Since Dabrowski's (1964) first discussion of his theory, some research has been sporadically conducted in support of the theory's relevance to and implications for the gifted and talented. While this contemplation and discussion of the viability of Dabrowski's work continues, supporters of the theory should consider enhancing their argument by providing further empirical data that strengthen the link between the theory and the life experiences of gifted individuals.

# References

Ackerman, C. M. (1997). Identifying gifted adolescents using personality characteristics: Dabrowski's overexcitabilities. *Roeper Review, 19*, 229–236.

Breard, N. S. (1994). *Exploring a different way to identify gifted African-American students.* Unpublished doctoral dissertation, University of Georgia, Athens.

Brennan, T. P. (1987). *Case studies of multilevel development.* Unpublished doctoral dissertation, Northwestern University, Evanston, IL.

Brennan, T. P., & Piechowski, M. M. (1991). A developmental framework for self-actualization: Evidence from case studies. *Journal of Humanistic Psychology, 31*(3), 43–64.

Dabrowski, K. (1937). Psychological basis of self-mutilation. *Genetic Psychology Monographs, 19*, 1–104.

Dabrowski, K. (1938). Typy wzmozonej pobudliwosci psychicznej. *Biul. Inst. Higieny Psychicznej, 1*(3, 4), 3–26.

Dabrowski, K. (1964). *Positive disintegration.* Boston: Little, Brown.

Dabrowski, K. (1972). *Psychoneurosis is not an illness.* London: Gryf.

Dabrowski, K., Kawczak, A., & Piechowski, M. M. (1970). *Mental growth through positive disintegration.* London: Gryf.

Dabrowski, K., & Piechowski, M. M. (1977). *Theory of levels of emotional development: Volume I—Multilevelness and positive disintegration.* Oceanside, NY: Dabor Science.

Ely, E. I. (1995). *The overexcitability questionnaire: An alternative method for identifying creative giftedness in seventh grade junior high school students.* Unpublished doctoral dissertation, Kent State University, Kent, OH.

Falk, R. F., Lind, S., Miller, N. B., Piechowski, M. M., & Silverman, L. K. (1999). *The overexcitability questionnaire —II: Manual, scoring system, and questionnaire.* Unpublished manuscript.

Falk, R. F., Manzanero, J. B., & Miller, N. B. (1997). Developmental potential in Venezuelan and American artists: A cross-cultural validity study. *Creativity Research Journal, 10*, 201–206.

Gallagher, S. A. (1986). A comparison of the concept of overexcitabilities with measures of creativity and school achievement in sixth-grade students. *Roeper Review, 8*, 115–119.

Grant, B. A. (1990). Moral development: Theories and lives. *Advanced Development, 2*, 85–91.

Grant, B. A., & Piechowski, M. M. (1999). Theories and the good: Toward child-centered gifted education. *Gifted Child Quarterly, 41*, 4–12.

Howard, D. D. (1994). *A naturalistic study of the psychosocial development of highly gifted girls.* Unpublished doctoral dissertation, University of Denver.

Kitano, M. K. (1990). Intellectual abilities and psychological intensities in young children: Implications for the gifted. *Roeper Review, 13*, 5–10.

Lewis, R. B., Kitano, M. K., & Lynch, E. W. (1992). Psychological intensities in gifted adults. *Roeper Review, 15*, 25–31.

Lovecky, D. V. (1992). Exploring social and emotional aspects of giftedness in children. *Roeper Review, 15*, 18–25.

Lysy, K. Z., & Piechowski, M. M. (1983). Personal growth: An empirical study using Jungian and Dabrowskian measures. *Genetic Psychology Monographs, 108*, 267–320.

Miller, N. B., Silverman, L. K., & Falk, R. F. (1994). Emotional development, intellectual ability, and gender. *Journal for the Education of the Gifted, 18*, 20–38.

Nelson, K. C. (1989). Dabrowski's theory of positive disintegration. *Advanced Development, 1*, 1–14.

Piechowski, M. M. (1975). A theoretical and empirical approach to the study of development. *Genetic Psychology Monographs, 92*, 231–297.

Piechowski, M. M. (1978). Self-actualization as a developmental structure: A profile of Antoine de Saint-Exupery. *Genetic Psychology Monographs, 97,* 181–242.

Piechowski, M. M. (1979). Developmental potential. In N. Colangelo & R. T. Zaffrann (Eds.), *New voices in counseling the gifted* (pp. 25–57). Dubuque, IA: Kendall/Hunt.

Piechowski, M. M. (1986). The concept of developmental potential. *Roeper Review, 8,* 190–197.

Piechowski, M. M. (1990). Inner growth and transformation in the life of Eleanor Roosevelt. *Advanced Development, 2,* 35–53.

Piechowski, M. M. (1997). Emotional giftedness: The measure of intrapersonal intelligence. In N. Colangelo & G. A. Davis (Eds.). *Handbook of gifted education* (2nd ed., pp. 366–381). Boston: Allyn and Bacon.

Piechowski, M. M. (1999). Overexcitabilities. In M. A. Runco, & S. R. Pritzker (Eds.), *Encyclopedia of creativity (Vol. 2,* pp. 325–334). San Diego: Academic Press.

Piechowski, M. M., & Colangelo, N. (1984). Developmental potential of the gifted. *Gifted Child Quarterly, 28,* 80–88.

Piechowski, M. M., & Cunningham, K. (1985). Patterns of overexcitability in a group of artists. *Journal of Creative Behavior, 19,* 153–174.

Piechowski, M. M., Silverman, L. K., & Falk, R. F. (1985). Comparison of intellectually and artistically gifted on five dimensions of mental functioning. *Perceptual and Motor Skill, 60,* 539–549.

Schiever, S. W. (1985). Creative personality characteristics and dimensions of mental functioning in gifted adolescents. *Roeper Review, 7,* 223–226.

Silverman, L. K. (1983). Personality development: The pursuit of excellence. *Journal for the Education of the Gifted, 6,* 5–19.

Silverman, L. K. (1993). The gifted individual. In L. K. Silverman (Ed.), *Counseling the gifted and talented* (pp. 3–28). Denver: Love.

Silverman, L. K., & Ellsworth, B. (1981). *The theory of positive disintegration and its implications for giftedness: Proceedings of the third international conference.* Miami, FL.: University of Miami School of Medicine.

Tucker, B., & Hafenstein, N. L. (1997). Psychological intensities in young gifted children. *Gifted Child Quarterly, 41,* 66–75.

# 7 INDIVIDUAL DIFFERENCES IN GIFTED STUDENTS' ATTRIBUTIONS FOR ACADEMIC PERFORMANCES

by **Nancy M. Robinson, Ph.D.**

otivation and its origins constitute an area in which research is especially complex and contradictory, particularly with regard to gifted children (Dai, Moon, & Feldhusen, 1998). The translation of high intellectual ability to high achievement requires sustained investment in thinking and learning, as well as the production of actual contributions of worth. The foundation for high achievement lies in areas such as academic self-concept, self-confidence, achievement orientation, appropriate goal setting, and the healthy ability to weather setbacks.

Most (but not all) research comparing high-ability students to others has found gifted students to have more positive self-concepts, particularly with regard to academic abilities (Chamrad, Robinson, Treder, & Janos, 1995; Hoge & Renzulli, 1993; Kelly & Colangelo, 1984; but not Csikszentmihalyi, Rathunde, & Whalen, 1993); to be more accurate in predicting their performance (Pajares, 1996); to be more strongly motivated by intrinsic than extrinsic motivation (i.e., by the pleasures of the activity rather than prizes; Gottfried & Gottfried, 1996; Rogers, 1986); and to be more invested in learning and challenge (Gottfried, Gottfried, Bathurst, & Guerin, 1994).

The research is, however, problematic in that few investigators have focused on individual differences in these constructs among gifted students (Dweck, 2000, being one important exception), rather than comparing gifted groups with nongifted groups. Furthermore, most have focused on gifted students enrolled in specialized programs designed to promote this very constellation of healthy motivational characteristics. In addition, most students in such programs have a prior record of achievement appropriate to their ability; have opted, with parental encouragement, for enrollment in the more challenging school environment; and, in some studies, have volunteered for summer programs constituting extra challenge in a domain in which they expect to succeed (e.g., Dai & Feldhusen, 1996). We need to be extremely cautious in generalizing from these positive findings about selected gifted students to others who have not been so identified and served (Kammer, 1986), and we need additional rubrics to understand individual differences in motivation and challenge seeking among high-ability students.

## Self-Concept

*Self-concept* is a general term encompassing more specific constructs such as *self-confidence, self-perceptions*, and *self-efficacy* (Dai, Moon, & Feldhusen, 1998). Contemporary research tends to discriminate self-views and their consequences in specific domains (e.g., specific courses [Marsh & Yeung, 1997] or academic as distinct from social self-views [Harter, 1982]), in specific social-comparison contexts (e.g., regular classes vs. special classes [Kammer, 1986; Marsh, 1987, 1990; Marsh, Chessor, Crowen, & Roche, 1995]), and after specific experiences (e.g., success or failure [Bogie & Buckhalt, 1987]). This chapter deals specifically with academic self-concept and its effects.

Generally speaking, gifted children tend to exhibit relatively more positive self-concepts than do nongifted peers, especially in

62

intellectual and school status as compared with self-perceptions of social skills and self-satisfaction. Of the age groups, however, high school students attain the lowest scores on self-concept scales. The drop is most significant for gifted high school girls (Colangelo & Assouline, 2000).

Early research tended to assume that the higher the self-concept, the healthier the person, but recent research tends to recognize more realistic or accurate self-perceptions as healthier (e.g., the ability to predict accurately one's own performance or to remain confident in the company of other high achievers; Phillips, 1984). The limited research that exists on gifted children suggests that, as a group, they tend to be more accurate in their appraisals of task difficulty and of the likelihood that they will succeed in a given situation (Pajares, 1996). Those who are steadfast in developing their talents tend to show high commitment and a willingness to persevere, to be less prone than other students to question their own worth, and to be willing to display their accomplishments (Csikszentmihalyi, Rathunde, & Whalen, 1993). There may be some variation in self-concept by domain of talent; For example, Csikszentmihalyi et al. found that adolescent male scientists showed a more positive self-image than males who were musicians, artists, or mathematicians.

## Attributions

At least as important as one's academic self-appraisal is one's set of attributions for the source of one's ability and reasons for one's successful or unsuccessful academic performance. Rotter's (1990) concept of *locus of control,* distinguishes between attributions of internal influences (e.g., ability, effort) and external influences (e.g., luck). One's explanation for success or failure at a task might likewise rest on task difficulty, degree of preparation, boredom versus interest, and so on. Some attributions are immediate and situation-linked, and others are more enduring (Dai et al., 1998). *Giftedness* is experienced by many students as a mixed blessing (e.g., positive with regard to personal growth and recognition of academic achievement, but negative in social relationships; Kerr, Colangelo,

**63**

& Gaeth, 1988). Many gifted students are concerned that others' attitudes toward them may be directed to the label, rather than their personal qualities. Such perceptions tend to have a reverse effect on performance, as students may deliberately underachieve academically in an effort to gain social acceptance (Gross, 1993).

## Implicit Theories of Intelligence

Among attribution categories, implicit theories of intelligence are a powerful example that we will use as a prototype of the extensive research in the field highlighting the complex interplay of attributions, goals, and achievement motivation applicable to individual differences among gifted students. In a body of careful work dating back to the 1970s, Dweck (1975, 2000; Dweck & Elliot, 1983) delineated the effects of two competing beliefs about the nature of intelligence. Surprisingly, about 85% of people ascribe distinctively to one belief or the other, although both beliefs have validity. The first, termed by Dweck an *entity theory*, maintains that intelligence is a fixed trait of which we each have an allotted share and that there is little we can do to change it. The other belief, an *incremental theory*, is that, even though we differ in ability, intelligence is malleable and can be cultivated and increased through effort. Younger children tend to hold to an incremental theory, but the situation shifts as they grow older (Stipek & Mac Iver, 1989). Because gifted children tend to be more "mature," they may make the shift earlier.

For people who hold an entity theory of intelligence, it becomes important to appear "smart" at all times and to pull this off with as little effort as possible. Entity theorists generally believe that their ability is stable and that there is little they can do to change their own "gift." Such entity believers need to excel over others and generally seek safe, low-effort successes in order to achieve *performance goals* such as good grades or praise for attainment. They are willing to try something new only if they are assured of being, or appearing to be, an instant expert. Paradoxically, although they often thereby enter new situations with a history of successes that one would ordinarily expect to produce a strong and positive academic self-concept, their brittle views of themselves make them highly vulnerable to minor setbacks and ineffective defensive maneuvers. In the face of criticism, their response may be one of helplessness, rather than resolve, and they may leave the field and pass up valuable learning opportunities, rather than give them another try.

In contrast, for those who hold an incremental theory of intelligence, the focus is on challenge, engagement with learning even at the cost of sometimes appearing less smart, and sticking with difficult tasks to a level of mastery. They establish *learning goals* and achieve a robust feeling of confidence by engaging energetically and persistently with next steps, rather than already mastered ones; seeing their own progress sustained; and focusing on using, rather than demonstrating, their new knowledge.

Dweck (2000) and her colleagues reported a high frequency of entity theorists among gifted students, particularly among those who have been underchallenged in school. In the ordinary course of events, gifted children encounter many traps that put them at greater risk for seeing their abilities as fixed. First, they typically do not encounter many school tasks they cannot master the first time, handily and quickly. Because the work is easy, they know that they are "smart." They build the expectation that they should be able to handle new situations and remain at the top of the class with minimal effort. Second, the well-meaning praise from adults as to how bright and talented they are solidifies their hold on an entity theory. Rather than expecting, and praising children for, hard work, trying new challenges, persistent efforts, and hardiness in the face of difficulties, adults simply confirm their feeling of being "special" because of their natural abilities.

Dweck's (2000) research clearly shows that praise for intelligence, rather than effort, creates vulnerability in high-ability students that does not show up until they experience setbacks and failure. Hence, when students eventually do encounter an appropriately challenging academic situation, as is especially likely to happen if they transfer into a special class or are academically accelerated at the middle or senior high school level, they are likely to be in trouble. To maintain the reputation of being "smart," they cannot invest enough effort to master the challenges. At this point, the minor transgressions formerly forgiven because of obvious competence (e.g., projects and papers sloppily completed or not turned in) are taken more seriously, students are trapped by their shattered self-evaluations and habits of avoidance (and now conclude that they must not be smart after all), and too often fall prey to helplessness and full-blown underachievement (Moon, Swift, & Shallenberger, in press).

Dweck's research suggests that the situation may be even more exacerbated for girls. She has found gifted girls to be more likely than gifted boys to hold an entity view, to opt for low-risk tasks, and to exhibit helplessness in the face of challenge (Dweck, 2000; Licht & Dweck, 1984).

When gifted students are given appropriate intellectual challenges, when they have families who support and expect the best of them (see Olszewski-Kubilius, this volume), their attributions about the origins of their abilities may be quite different. There is, for example, evidence that students who choose challenges such as academically advanced summer programs are predominantly incremental theorists (Dai & Feldhusen, 1996). Moreover, there is also evidence that children who see their ability as stable, but who emphasize its stability in the face of external forces (such as a move to a new school), as opposed to the more common entity view of ability as resistant to internal forces (our own efforts to change it), tend to act more like incremental theorists in their responses to success and failure (Pomerantz & Saxon, 2001).

## Implications for Intervention

Those gifted children who escape this cycle are the continuing high achievers who ascribe only moderately high importance to ability as the source of their attainment (Shell, Colvin, & Bruning, 1995) and who attribute failure to internal, controllable causes such as lack of effort (Chan, 1996). Dweck (2000) has advocated "success training" that encourages an incremental view and emphasizes effort and strategizing, rather than ability. Students might, for example, receive "attribution retraining" in which they learn to attribute lack of success to a need to try harder. In a recent study (Kamins & Dweck, in press), young children praised on a learning task for being "really good at this," or being a "good boy/girl" were

66

the most helpless in the face of subsequent failure; those given praise for effort and strategy were much more mastery-oriented in subsequent encounters and rated themselves more positively in ability and happiness.

## Conclusion

It is clear that, in general, gifted students—especially those who are challenged and who have developed healthy habits of self-appraisal and application—tend to excel over other students in their views of their academic ability, their eagerness for challenge, and their willingness to invest what it takes to succeed. Yet, there are others who are distinctly at risk for underachievement and unhappiness because they have not achieved such self-views, motivational patterns, or goals of learning. Future research should be directed at understanding the sources of these individual differences and intervening at an early age so that gifted students are enabled to become the high-achieving, energetic, optimistic people they have every right to be.

## References

Bogie, C. E., & Buckhalt, J. A. (1987). Reactions to failure and success among gifted, average, and EMR students. *Gifted Child Quarterly, 31*, 70–74.

Chamrad, D. L., Robinson, N. M., Treder, R., & Janos, P. M. (1995). Consequences of having a gifted sibling: Myths and realities. *Gifted Child Quarterly, 39*, 135–145.

Chan, L. K. S. (1996). Motivational orientations and metacognitive abilities of intellectually gifted students. *Gifted Child Quarterly, 40*, 184–193.

Colangelo, N., & Assouline, S. G. (2000). Counseling gifted students. In K. A. Heller, F. J. Mönks, R. J. Sternberg, & R. F. Subotnik (Eds.). *International handbook of giftedness and talent,* (2nd ed., pp. 595–607). Oxford, England: Elsevier.

Csikszentmihalyi, M., Rathunde, K., & Whalen, S. (1993). *Talented teenagers: The roots of success and failure.* New York: Cambridge University Press.

Dai, D. Y., & Feldhusen, J. F. (1996). Goal orientations of gifted students. *Gifted and Talented International, 11*, 84–88.

Dai, D. Y., Moon, S. M., & Feldhusen, J. F. (1998). Achievement motivation and gifted students: A social cognitive perspective. *Educational Psychologist, 33*, 45–63.

Dweck, C. S. (1975) The role of expectations and attributions in the alleviation of learned helplessness. *Journal of Personality and Social Psychology, 31,* 674–685.

Dweck, C. S. (2000) *Self-theories: Their role in motivation, personality, and development.* Philadelphia: Taylor and Francis.

Dweck, C. S., & Elliot, E. S. (1983) Achievement motivation. In P. Mussen & E. M. Hetherington (Eds.), *Handbook of child psychology* (pp. 643–692). New York: Wiley.

Gottfried, A. E., & Gottfried, A. W. (1996). A longitudinal study of academic intrinsic motivation in intellectually gifted children: Childhood through early adolescence. *Gifted Child Quarterly, 40,* 179–183.

Gottfried, A. W., Gottfried, A. E., Bathurst, K., & Guerin, D. W. (1994). *Gifted IQ: Early developmental aspects. The Fullerton longitudinal study.* New York: Plenum.

Gross, M. U. M. (1993). *Exceptionally gifted children.* London: Routledge.

Harter, S. (1982). The Perceived Competence Scale for Children. *Child Development, 53,* 87–97.

Hoge, R. D., & Renzulli, J. S. (1993). Exploring the link between giftedness and self-concept. *Review of Educational Research, 63,* 449–465.

Kammer, P. P. (1986). Attribution for academic successes and failures of students participating and not participating in programs for the gifted. *Journal for the Education of the Gifted, 9,* 123–131.

Kamins, M., & Dweck, C. S. (in press). Person vs. process praise and criticism: Implications for contingent self-worth and coping. *Developmental Psychology.*

Kelly, K. R., & Colangelo, N. (1984). Academic and social self-concepts of gifted, general, and special students. *Exceptional Children, 50,* 551–554.

Kerr, B., Colangelo, N., & Gaeth, J. (1988). Gifted adolescents' attitudes toward their giftedness. *Gifted Child Quarterly, 32,* 245–247.

Licht, B. G., & Dweck, C. S. (1984) Determinants of academic achievement: The interaction of children's achievement orientations with skill area. *Developmental Psychology, 20,* 628–636.

Marsh, H. W. (1987). The big-fish-little-pond effect on academic self-concept. *Journal of Educational Psychology, 79,* 280–295.

Marsh, H. W. (1990). Influences of internal and external frames of reference on the formation of math and English self-concepts: A multiwave, longitudinal panel analysis. *Journal of Educational Psychology, 82,* 107–116.

Marsh, H. W., Chessor, D., Craven, R., & Roche, L. (1995). The effects of gifted and talented programs on academic self–concept: The big fish strikes again. *American Educational Research Journal, 32,* 285–319.

Marsh, H. W., & Yeung, A. S. (1997). Coursework selection: Relations to academic self-concept and achievement. *American Educational Research Journal, 34,* 691–720.

Moon, S. M., Swift, M., & Shallenberger, A. (in press). Perceptions of a self-contained class for fourth- and fifth-grade students with high to extreme levels of intellectual giftedness. *Gifted Child Quarterly.*

Pajares, F. (1996). Self-efficacy beliefs and mathematical problem solving of gifted students. *Contemporary Educational Psychology, 86,* 543–578.

**68**

Phillips, D. (1984). The illusion of incompetence among academically competent children. *Child Development, 55,* 2000–2016.

Pomerantz, E. M., & Saxon, J. L. (2001). Children's conceptions of ability as stable and self-evaluative processes: A longitudinal examination. *Child Development, 72,* 152–173.

Rogers, K. B. (1986). Do the gifted think and learn differently? A review of recent research and its implications for instruction. *Journal for the Education of the Gifted, 10,* 17–39.

Rotter, J. B. (1990). Internal versus external control of reinforcements: A case history of a variable. *American Psychologist, 45,* 489–493.

Shell, D. F., Colvin, C., & Bruning, R. H. (1995). Self-efficacy, attribution, and outcome expectancy mechanisms in reading and writing achievement: Grade-level and achievement-level differences. *Journal of Educational Psychology, 87,* 386–398.

Stipek, D., & Mac Iver, D. (1989). Developmental change in children's assessment of intellectual competence. *Child Development, 60,* 521–538.

# 8 PERFECTIONISM IN GIFTED CHILDREN AND ADOLESCENTS

by **Patricia Schuler, Ph.D.**

ost professionals, as well as the general public, regard perfectionism as psychologically unhealthy. Perfectionism covers a variety of issues and has repeatedly been cited as a major counseling focus for gifted children and adolescents (Adderholdt-Elliott, 1991; Kerr, 1991; Silverman, 1990b; Webb, Meckstroth, & Tolan, 1982), especially when addressing underachievement and emotional turmoil (Pyryt, 1994). In actuality, however, perfectionism must be seen as a potent force capable of bringing either intense frustration and paralysis or intense satisfaction and creative contribution, depending on how it is channeled.

Perfectionism is a combination of thoughts and behaviors generally associated with high standards or expectations for one's own performance (Burns, 1980; Hamachek, 1978). Research and clinical studies of gifted children and adolescents draw three conclusions about perfectionism: (1) as a group, gifted students are perfectionistic; (2) they seem to be more perfectionistic than average-ability peers; and (3) their perfectionism can be a positive force for high achievement. (Adderholdt, 1984; Ford, 1989; Hollingworth, 1926; Karnes & Oeher-Stinnett, 1986; Lovecky, 1994; Oden, 1968; Roeper, 1982; Silverman, 1990a; Whitmore, 1980). This chapter briefly describes the construct of perfectionism and its measurement and summarizes what is known about perfectionism among gifted children and adolescents. It concludes with several recommendations for intervention and support.

## The Construct of Perfectionism

A review of the literature highlights the lack of agreement as to perfectionism's inherent nature. While several personality theorists view perfectionism as a healthy and salient part of human development (Adler, 1973; Dabrowski, 1972; Lazarfeld, 1991; Maslow, 1970), others view it as negative and destructive (Burns, 1980; Pacht, 1984).

Several researchers have proposed that perfectionism be viewed from a multidimensional perspective. Hamacheck (1978) viewed perfectionism both as a manger of behaving and as a manger of thinking about the behavior and described two types of perfectionism, normal and neurotic, that form a continuum of perfectionistic behaviors. Healthy perfectionists are those who "derive a very real sense of pleasure from the labors of a painstaking effort and who feel free to be less precise as the situation permits" (p. 27). Neurotic perfectionists, on the other hand, "are unable to feel satisfaction because in their own eyes they never seem to do things good enough to warrant that feeling" (p. 27).

Bransky, Jenkins-Friedman, and Murphy (1987) also discussed two types of perfectionism, distinguishing between enabling perfectionism, which empowers, and disabling perfectionism, which cripples. Like Bransky et al., Hamachek identified six specific, overlapping behaviors associated with perfectionism that describe both normal and neurotic perfectionists with the difference lying in the duration and intensity of these behaviors. They include: (1)

**72**

depression, (2) a nagging "I should" feeling, (3) shame and guilt feelings, (4) face-saving behavior, (5) shyness and procrastination, and (6) self-deprecation.

Pacht (1984) disagreed with these multidimensional theories and viewed perfectionism as inherently destructive. Pacht agreed with Burns' (1980) definition of perfectionism as a compulsive and unrelenting strain toward impossible goals. According to Pacht and Burns, perfectionists are those who measure their self-worth in terms of accomplishment and productivity; the drive to excel is self-defeating. Perfectionistic tendencies are distortions in one's thinking that can be related to a variety of psychological maladjustments. Reviewing the literature, Pacht found perfectionism to be associated with depression, eating disorders, writer's block, migraines, sexual dysfunction, obsessive-compulsive personality disorders, dysmorphophobia, suicide, and Type-A coronary-prone behavior. Furthermore, perfectionism has also been associated with underachievement (Lind, 1992), academic procrastination (Ferrari, 1992), and career obstacles and failure (Connolly, 1994).

However, one cannot conclude from the research literature that perfectionism causes these conditions or that it is necessarily destructive. Hamachek (1978) viewed these types of linkages as consequences only of neurotic perfectionism, while normal perfectionism is linked to healthy consequences. Likewise, Whitmore (1980) believed that perfectionism could either be a positive force for achievement or a negative force for underachievement.

Many hypotheses exist about the causes of perfectionism. Dabrowski (1972), Kerr (1991), and Silverman (1990a) have maintained that perfectionism is inborn in some individuals and that the pressure of high standards comes from within the child. Others believe that perfectionistic children have perfectionistic parents (Rowell, 1986), have parents who are more interested in their performance than in their learning (Ablard & Parker, 1997), are first-born or only children (Leman, 1985), or have dysfunctional families (Brophy, 1986; Crespi, 1990). Additional reasons given for unhealthy perfectionism include "hothousing" or giving babies intensive, early academic training (Elkind, 1981), pervasive messages from the media to be perfect, and pressure from teachers and peers to be the best (Barrow & Moore, 1983).

**73**

## Measurement of Perfectionism

Just as elusive as a consensus on the definitions and dimensions of perfectionism is its measurement. Throughout the 1980s, the Burns Perfectionism Scale (Burns, 1980) was widely used; its unidimensional focus is on personal standards and concern over mistakes. Hewitt and Flett (1989) developed the Multidimensional Perfectionism Scale, which emphasizes the interpersonal aspects of perfectionism: self-oriented, other-oriented, and socially prescribed perfectionism.

Frost, Marten, Lahart, and Rosenblate (1990) developed a perfectionism questionnaire, also called the Multidimensional Perfectionism Scale, which examines the intrapersonal nature of perfectionism based on Hamachek's (1978) construct of perfectionism. The major dimensions of this measure include concern over making mistakes, high personal standards, the perception of high parental criticism, the doubting of the quality of one's actions, the perception of high parental expectations, and a high preference for order and organization (Frost et al., p. 449). The results of two studies (Parker & Stumpf, 1995; Schuler & Siegle, 2000) support the use of the Multidimensional Perfectionism Scale to measure perfectionism in academically talented children and adolescents.

## Perfectionism and Gifted Adolescents

Case studies and anecdotal records have been the main source of data on perfectionism in children and adolescents, while empirical studies have focused primarily on adults and college students (Adderholdt, 1984; Adkins, 1994; Brown, 1993; Frost et al., 1990; Hewitt & Flett, 1993; Mosher, 1995). Few empirical studies, however, have been done with gifted children and adolescents who are perfectionistic (Bellamy, 1993; Bransky, 1989; Orange, 1997; Parker, 1997, 2000; Parker & Mills, 1996; Parker & Stumpf, 1995; Schuler, 1997; Schuler & Siegle, 2000).

Bransky (1989) reported that perfectionistic junior high students see themselves as the principle agents of their academic outcomes and take more responsibility for them. Baker (1996) and Roberts and Lovett (1994) also found statistically significant higher levels of perfectionism among gifted adolescents in grades 7–9 than academic achievers and nongifted students. Schuler and Siegle (2000) reported perfectionistic tendencies in all socioeconomic and racial/ethnic statuses for gifted students in grades 6, 7, and 8. Schuler (2000) noted that gifted adolescents perceive perfectionism as both a helpful and harmful influence in their relationships, schoolwork, and view of their future. Baker, as part of her study on stressors of the academically gifted, stated that exceptional girls in ninth grade report statistically significantly higher levels of perfectionism than average-ability girls. Girls in general may show more perfectionistic tendencies than boys (Kramer, 1988), and, indeed, the level of perfectionism in gifted girls increases as they go from elementary to high school (Kline & Short, 1991).

There are probably a number of reasons underlying this association between giftedness and perfectionism (Silverman, 1999). Among them:

- The lofty goals for which gifted students reach are often abstract concepts that require the kind of facility with conceptual thinking that are the hallmark of gifted students.
- Gifted children set standards appropriate to their mental age although the asynchronous nature of their abilities (e.g., lagging fine motor skills) may frustrate their efforts.
- Gifted children often have older friends and set their goals accordingly.
- From their earliest years, gifted children have tended to be successful in almost everything they have tried because they have been underchallenged and, paradoxically, become failure-avoidant as a consequence (Dweck, 2000).
- When students find the work they are expected to do to be unchallenging, they may strive for perfect performance instead of mastery. Artificial rewards, such as grades, become the only satisfaction possible.
- Even when challenges are appropriate, as in specialized programs, perfectionistic teachers and competitive peers may exacerbate the situation (Adderholdt-Elliott, 1991).

**75**

- Finally, introverts, who represent half the gifted population (Gallagher, 1990), tend to be strong perfectionists (Dauber & Benbow, 1990).

## Recommendations

Only with high goals will there be high accomplishment. Whether perfectionism is perceived as an innate drive, a learned behavior, or a combination of both, there are many ways to address its negative manifestations (Adderholdt & Goldberg, 1999; Cohen & Frydenberg, 1996; Nugent, 2000; Schuler, 1999; Silverman, 1999). Parents and teachers should be cautious about viewing perfectionism as unhealthy. Gifted children and adolescents need assistance from parents, teachers, and counselors to understand that wanting to achieve at a high level, having a drive to excel, and enjoying order and organization can be positive assets, while learning to set priorities, taking time to reflect on the value of mistakes and relaxation, and pursuing one's passion will reduce the stress that results from unhealthy perfectionism.

Perfectionism that translates into trying again and again leads to success; perfectionism that results in paralysis, avoidance, anxiety attacks, and withdrawal guarantees failure. By helping gifted students to take pleasure in their accomplishments and to see their setbacks as learning opportunities, by praising them for their efforts and determination, rather than being "smart" or "talented"; and by encouraging them to channel their efforts into what they care about most, rather than trying to do everything equally well, adults can help them toward passion, progress, creative achievement, and celebration of their attainment.

## References

Ablard, K. E., & Parker, W. D. (1997). Parents' achievement goals and perfectionism in their academically talented children. *Journal of Youth and Adolescence, 26*, 65–667.

Adderholdt, M. R. (1984). *The effects of perfectionism upon the self-concepts of undergraduate women at The University of Georgia.* Unpublished doctoral dissertation, University of Georgia, Athens.

Adderholdt, M. R., & Goldberg, J. (1999). *Perfectionism: What's bad about being too good?* Minneapolis, MN: Free Spirit

Adderholdt-Elliott, M. R. (1991). Perfectionism and the gifted adolescent. In M. Bireley & J. Genshaft (Eds.), *Understanding the gifted adolescent: Educational, developmental, and multicultural issues* (pp. 65–75). New York: Teachers College Press.

Adkins, K. K. (1994). *Relationship between perfectionism and suicidal ideation for students in a college honors program and students in a regular college program.* Unpublished doctoral dissertation, University of Alabama, Birmingham.

Adler, A. (1973). *Superiority and the social interest: A collection of later writings.* New York: Viking Press.

Baker, J. A. (1996). Everyday stressors of academically gifted adolescents. *Journal of Secondary Gifted Education, 7,* 356–368.

Barrow, J. C., & Moore, C. A. (1983). Group interventions with perfectionist thinking. *Personnel and Guidance Journal, 61,* 612–615.

Bellamy, J. (1993). *Perfectionism in adolescents: A comparison of private and public school students.* Unpublished master's thesis, University of Manitoba, Canada.

Bransky, P. S. (1989). *Academic perfectionism in intellectually gifted adolescents: The roles of attribution, response to failure, and irrational beliefs.* Unpublished doctoral dissertation, University of Kansas, Lawrence.

Bransky, T., Jenkins-Friedman, R., & Murphy, D. (1987). *Identifying gifted students at risk for disabling perfectionism: The role of the school psychologist.* Paper presented at the annual meeting of the American Psychological Association, New York.

Brophy, B. (1986, April 7). Workaholics beware: Long hours may not pay. *U.S. News and World Report,* 60.

Brown, S. R. (1993). *Perfectionistic thinking and self-efficacy as predictors of college student's psychological development.* Unpublished doctoral dissertation, University of Georgia, Athens.

Burns, D. D. (1980, November). The perfectionist's script for self-defeat. *Psychology Today,* 70–76.

Cohen, L. M., & Frydenberg, E. (1996). *Coping for capable kids: Strategies for parents, teachers, and students.* Waco, TX: Prufrock Press.

Connolly, M. (1994). Are you drowning in details? *Supervisory Management, 39*(1), 1–2.

Crespi, T. D. (1990). *Becoming an adult child of an alcoholic.* Springfield, IL: Thomas.

Dabrowski, K. (1972). *Psychoneurosis is not an illness.* London: Little, Brown & Co.

Dauber, S. L., & Benbow, C. P. (1990). Aspects of personality and peer relations of extremely talented adolescents. *Gifted Child Quarterly, 34,* 10–15.

Dweck, C. S. (2000). *Self-theories: Their role in motivation, personality, and development.* Philadelphia: Taylor & Francis.

Elkind, D. (1981). *The hurried child: Growing up too fast too soon.* Reading, MA: Addison-Wesley.

Ferrari, J. R. (1992). Procrastinators and perfect behavior: An exploratory factor analysis of self-presentation, self-awareness, and self-handicapping components. *Journal of Research In Personality, 26*, 75–84.

Ford, M. A. (1989). Students' perceptions of affective issues impacting the social and emotional development and school performance of gifted/talented youngsters. *Roeper Review, 11*, 131–134.

Frost, R. O., Marten, P., Lahart, C., & Rosenblate, R. (1990). The dimensions of perfectionism. *Cognitive Therapy and Research,14*, 449–468.

Gallagher, S. A. (1990). Personality patterns of the gifted. *Understanding Our Gifted, 3*(2), 11–13.

Hamachek, D. E. (1978). Psychodynamics of normal and neurotic perfectionism. *Psychology, 15*, 27–33.

Hewitt, P. L., & Flett, G. L. (1989). The Multidimensional Perfectionism Scale: Development and validation. *Canadian Psychology, 30*, 339.

Hewitt, P. L., & Flett, G. L. (1993). Dimensions of perfectionism, daily stress, and depression: A test of the specific vulnerability hypothesis. *Journal of Abnormal Psychology, 102*, 58–65.

Hollingworth, L. S. (1926). *Gifted children: Their nature and nurture.* New York: Macmillan.

Karnes, F., & Oehler-Stinnett, J. (1986). Life events as stressors with gifted adolescents. *Psychology in the Schools, 23*, 406–414.

Kerr, B. A. (1991). *A handbook for counseling the gifted and talented.* Alexandria, VA: American Association for Counseling and Development.

Kline, B. E., & Short, E. B. (1991). Changes in emotional resilience: Gifted adolescent girls. *Roeper Review*, 13, 184–187.

Kramer, H. J. (1988). Anxiety, perfectionism, and attributions for failure in gifted and nongifted junior high school students. *Dissertation Abstracts International*, 48, 3077A (University Microfilms No. 88–03–891)

Lazarfeld, S. (1991). The courage for imperfection. *Individual Psychology, 47*(1), 93–96.

Leman, K. (1985). *The birth order book: Why you are the way you are.* New York: Dell.

Lind, S. (1992). Perfectionism and the gifted underachiever. *AEGUS Newsletter, 3*(2), 1–2.

Lovecky, D. V. (1994). Exceptionally gifted children: Different minds. *Roeper Review, 17*, 116–120.

Maslow, A. (1970). *Motivation and personality* (Rev. ed.). New York: Harper & Row.

Mosher, S. W. (1995). *Perfectionism and personal project appraisals in psychological strain and depression.* Unpublished master's thesis, York University, Canada.

Nugent, S. (2000). Perfectionism: Its manifestations and classroom-based interventions. *Journal of Secondary Gifted Education, 12*, 215–221.

Oden, M. H. (1968). The fulfillment of promise: 40-year follow-up of the Terman gifted group. *Genetic Psychology Monographs, 77*, 3–93.

Orange, C. (1997). Gifted students and perfectionism. *Roeper Review, 20*, 39–41.

Pacht, A. R. (1984). Reflections on perfectionism. *American Psychologist, 39,* 386–390.

Parker, W. D. (2000). Healthy perfectionism in the gifted. *Journal of Secondary Gifted Education, 12,* 173–182.

Parker, W. D. (1997). An empirical typology of perfectionism in academically talented children. *American Educational Research Journal, 34,* 545–562.

Parker, W. D., & Mills, C. (1996). The incidence of perfectionism in gifted students. *Gifted Child Quarterly, 40,* 194–199.

Parker, W. D., & Stumpf, H. (1995). An examination of the Multidimensional Perfectionism Scale with a sample of academically talented students. *Journal of Psychoeducational Assessment, 13,* 372–383.

Pyryt, M. C. (1994, September). *Perfectionism and giftedness: Examining the connection.* Paper presented at the annual meeting of the Society for the Advancement of Gifted Education, Calgary, Canada.

Roberts, S. M., & Lovett, S. B. (1994). Examining the "F" in gifted: Academically gifted adolescents' physiological and affective responses to scholastic failure. *Journal for the Education of the Gifted, 17,* 241–259.

Roeper, A. (1982). How the gifted cope with their emotions. *Roeper Review, 5*(2), 21–26.

Rowell, J. (1986, Spring). Who says perfect is best? *Growing Up Magazine,* 8–9.

Schuler, P. (1997). *Characteristics and perceptions of perfectionism in gifted adolescents in a rural school environment.* Unpublished doctoral dissertation, The University of Connecticut, Storrs.

Schuler, P. (1999). *Voices of perfectionism: Perfectionistic gifted adolescents in a rural middle school.* Storrs: National Research Center on the Gifted and Talented, The University of Connecticut.

Schuler, P. (2000). Perfectionism and gifted adolescents. *The Journal of Secondary Gifted Education, 11,* 183–196.

Schuler, P., & Siegle, D. (2000). Perfectionism differences in gifted middle school students. *Roeper Review, 23,* 39–44.

Silverman, L. K. (1990a). The crucible of perfectionism. In B. Holyst (Ed.), *Mental health in a changing world* (pp. 39–49). Warsaw: The Polish Society for Mental Health.

Silverman, L. K. (1990b). Issues in affective development of the gifted. In J. VanTassel-Baska (Ed.), *A practical guide to counseling the gifted in a school setting* (pp. 15–30). Reston, VA: Council for Exceptional Children.

Silverman, L. K. (1999). Perfectionism. *Gifted Education International, 13,* 216–255.

Webb, T. J., Meckstroth, E. A., & Tolan, S. S. (1982). *Guiding the gifted child: A practical source for parents and teachers.* Columbus: Ohio Psychology Press.

Whitmore, J. R. (1980). *Giftedness, conflict, and underachievement.* Boston: Allyn and Bacon.

# 9 UNDERACHIEVEMENT IN GIFTED STUDENTS

by **Sally M. Reis, Ph.D.** and **D. Betsy McCoach, M.A.**

The underachievement of gifted students is a perplexing phenomenon. Too often, for no apparent reason, students who show great academic promise fail to perform at a level commensurate with their abilities, frustrating both parents and teachers (Whitmore, 1986). Many gifted students continue to do well on achievement or reasoning tests, but, in their failure to turn in assignments or to attend or participate in class, demonstrate their disengagement from the educational process. Issues concerned with defining underachievement, identifying underachieving gifted students, and explaining the reasons for this underachievement continue to stir controversy among practitioners, researchers, and clinicians. Legitimate problems exist in determining whether or not these students are at greater risk for social or emotional problems than other students, and, to date, most interventions to reverse underachievement have met with limited success.

# Defining Underachievement in Gifted Students

Any discussion of issues relating to underachievement in gifted students must carefully define both the constructs of giftedness and underachievement. The most common component of the various definitions of underachievement in gifted students involves identifying a discrepancy between ability and achievement (Baum, Renzulli, & Hébert, 1995a, 1995b; Butler-Por, 1987; Dowdall & Colangelo, 1982; Emerick, 1992; Rimm, 1997a, 1997b; Supplee, 1990; Whitmore, 1980; Wolfle, 1991).

## Identifying Underachievers

Criteria for identifying gifted underachievers should include a method for determining observable discrepancies between ability and achievement over a substantial period of time (Mandel & Marcus, 1995). Although students may experience short-term lags that may not indicate a long-term problem, whenever a student's performance drops substantially over a short time period, it merits the attention of a teacher or a counselor.

Some professionals may try to gauge an age/performance discrepancy when identifying underachievers (Mandel & Marcus, 1995). In other words, they may not identify a student as an underachiever unless performance in at least one major subject area is at least one year below grade level. Although this may be a suitable method for the general school population, such an age/performance discrepancy may only identify the most severely underachieving gifted students. Rimm, Cornale, Manos, and Behrend (1989) suggested using longitudinal test data to screen for possible underachievement. IQ test scores, achievement percentile scores, or grades that have declined for three years in a row are strong indicators of an underachievement problem. However, using such a formula may not only underestimate the number of students who are falling into patterns of underachievement (Rimm et al.), but do so too late for effective intervention.

## Causes of Underachievement

Underachievement constitutes a symptom that may be indicative of any—often a combination—of a number of causes. Some of these originate in the environment, some in the child, some in a mismatch of the two (Baker, Bridger, & Evans, 1998; Reis & McCoach, 2000). The following are examples of an almost infinite number of possibilities:

### Environmental causes

- chronically underchallenging, slow-moving classroom experiences (Whitmore, 1986), or moving from a regular classroom to an appropriately challenging one (Krissman, 1989);
- peer pressure to conform to "regular" norms, to "be like everyone else," which may be particularly intense for students from underrepresented minorities (Diaz, 1998; Ford, 1992, 1996);
- loneliness, isolation from classmates and the educational enterprise (Mandel & Marcus, 1988, 1995); and
- family dynamics (family conflict drains energies; parents' centering on the underachieving child masks other conflicts; (Green, Fine, & Tollefson, 1988); family has too-low, too-variable, or too-rigid expectations (Rimm, 1995; Rimm & Lowe, 1988).

### Factors within the individual (may be generalized traits or responses to the above)

- internalizing issues: depression, anxiety, perfectionism, failure-avoidance, low self-esteem (Bruns, 1992; Mandel & Marcus, 1988; Supplee, 1990);
- externalizing issues: rebelliousness, irritability, nonconformity, anger (Bricklin & Bricklin, 1967; Bruns, 1992; Rimm, 1995);
- unrecognized learning deficits that interfere with learning/performance (Vail, 1987);

**83**

- nontraditional gifts (e.g., spatial reasoning) that do not fit teachers' expectations (Gohm, Humphreys, & Yao, 1998);
- deficits in self-regulation: disorganization, impulsivity, attention deficit (Baum, Olenchak, & Owen, 1998; Borkowski & Thorpe, 1994; Krouse & Krouse, 1981; Schunk, 1998);
- maladaptive strategies, such as failure to set realistic goals (Van Boxtel & Mönks, 1992), short-term rather than long-term coping strategies (Gallagher, 1991); and
- social immaturity (Whitmore, 1980) or overemphasis on social, as opposed to academic, pursuits (Mandel & Marcus, 1988; Van Boxtel & Mönks, 1992).

## Interventions

Although conducting case studies and qualitative research on underachieving gifted students has become quite popular, very few researchers have attempted to utilize true quasi-experimental designs to study the efficacy of various interventions. Most of the interventions reported in the literature (Supplee, 1990; Whitmore, 1980) were designed to effect immediate results with a group of acutely underachieving gifted students. The documented effectiveness of most interventions designed to reverse underachievement in gifted students has been inconsistent and inconclusive (Emerick, 1988), with limited long-term success (Dowdall & Colangelo, 1982; Emerick, 1992). Interventions aimed at reversing gifted underachievement fall into two general categories: counseling and instructional interventions (Butler-Por, 1993; Dowdall & Colangelo, 1982).

Counseling interventions concentrate on changing the personal, family, or ambition of both dynamics that contribute to a student's underachievement. Counseling interventions may include individual, group, or family, or some combination of all three (Jeon, 1990). Many early attempts to improve underachievers' academic achievement through counseling treatments were unsuccessful (Baymur & Patterson, 1965; Broedel, Ohlsen, Proff, & Southard, 1965). In most counseling situations, the counselor's goal is not to force the underachiever to become a more successful student, but rather to help the student decide whether success is a desirable goal and, if so, to help reverse counterproductive habits and cognitions.

Certain treatments aimed at combating underachievement combine counseling and school-centered interventions. For example, Rimm's (1995; Rimm et al., 1989) trifocal model is an approach that involves parents and school personnel in an effort to reverse student underachievement. This plan involves assessing students' underachievement; changing student, parent, and teacher expectations for these underachievers; and providing differentiated modifications for these students both at home and at school.

The best-known school-based educational interventions for gifted students have established either part-time or full-time special classrooms for gifted underachievers (e.g., Butler-Por, 1987; Fehrenbach, 1993; Supplee, 1990; Whitmore, 1980). Usually, a smaller student-to-teacher ratio exists, teachers create less conventional types of teaching and learning activities, teachers give students some choice and freedom in exercising control, and students are encouraged to utilize different learning strategies. Whitmore, for example, designed and implemented a full-time elementary program for gifted underachievers. Supplee instituted a part-time program for gifted elementary underachievers. Both programs stressed the importance of addressing affective education, as well as the necessity of creating student-centered classroom environments.

The literature is lacking a group of studies that utilize a control or comparison group or a truly longitudinal design, and investigators have yet to track on a long-term basis the progress of students once they leave a program. Although some underachieving students appear to progress during academic interventions, the long-term effects of such programs are less clear. What happens when the student re-enters the regular class and is once again faced with nonstimulating schoolwork? How can the underachievement of older students be reversed? These and many other questions remain unanswered.

Emerick (1992) investigated the reasons that some students are able to reverse their academic underachievement without the assistance of formal interventions. Her qualitative research study examined the patterns of underachievement and subsequent achievement of 10 young adults. Several common factors appeared to play a part in the students' reversal of underachievement. Participants in

Emerick's study perceived that out-of-school interests and activities, parents, development of goals associated with grades, teachers, and changes in "selves" had a positive impact on achievement. In addition, participants were most likely to develop achievement-oriented behaviors when they were stimulated in class and given the opportunity to pursue topics of interest to them.

This study indicates that one type of effective intervention may be based on students' strengths and interests (Renzulli, 1977; Renzulli & Reis, 1985, 1997). In a recent study (Baum, Renzulli, & Hébert, 1995a, 1995b), researchers used self-selected Type III enrichment projects as a systematic intervention for underachieving gifted students. This approach (Renzulli) specifically targets student strengths and interests in order to help reverse academic underachievement.

Because the factors influencing the development and manifestation of underachievement vary, no one type of intervention will be effective for the full range of underachieving gifted students. Rather, a continuum of strategies and services may be necessary if we are to address this problem systematically. Therefore, future researchers in this field will not only need to posit coherent, complete models of gifted underachievement and design interventions in accordance with their proposed models, but take into account individual student needs.

## Areas for Future Research

We do not know how many talented students underachieve, but we know that this issue is foremost in the minds of practitioners (Renzulli, Reid, & Gubbins, 1992). Future research must attempt to unravel the complex causes of academic underachievement and provide interventions that help reverse underachievement behavior. Several lines of research remain inadequately explored.

We need to move beyond correlational studies of common characteristics of underachieving students and begin to explore linkages and flow of causality among these different characteristics and student achievement. For example, according to several authors (e.g., Belcastro, 1985; Bricklin & Bricklin, 1967; Bruns, 1992; Diaz, 1998; Dowdall & Colangelo, 1982; Fine & Pitts, 1980; Fink,

1965; Ford, 1996; Kanoy, Johnson, & Kanoy, 1980; Schunk, 1998; Supplee, 1990; Van Boxtel & Mönks, 1992; Whitmore, 1980), positive self-concept appears to correlate with student achievement, raising an interesting but unanswered question: Does low self-concept cause underachievement, or does underachievement result in a deterioration of self-concept, or does a third exogenous variable influence both self-concept and scholastic achievement? If low self-concept causes underachievement, interventions such as counseling approaches designed to raise self-concept should enhance student achievement. However, counseling treatments have met with limited success. Research on the flow of causality between student achievement and self-efficacy, self-regulation, student attitudes, peer attitudes, and other factors believed to influence underachievement will help researchers to develop more effective intervention strategies to combat underachievement in gifted students.

Another area for research involves studying whether or not gifted underachievers differ significantly from other underachievers and, if so, how McCall, Evahn, and Kratzer (1992) observed that most of the comparison-group research within this area compares gifted underachievers to their achieving mental-ability cohorts, often finding qualitative differences between the groups. However, an interesting, though less studied, line of research involves comparing gifted underachievers to other students at the same achievement level according to GPA, achievement test scores, and similar measures regardless of their measured mental ability. Do gifted underachievers have more in common with gifted students who do achieve or low-achieving students who are not gifted? Dowdall and Colangelo (1982) observed that gifted underachievers seem to share more characteristics with other underachievers than they do with gifted achievers. Whether gifted students require interventions that are qualitatively different from nongifted underachievers has yet to be determined.

Finally, researchers must translate insights about causes and correlates of underachievement into models and strategies that educators can use to develop more effective prevention and intervention programs. If unchallenging scholastic environments produce underachieving gifted students, then providing intellectual challenge and stimulation at all grade levels should decrease underachievement. Do schools that differentiate instruction, provide gifted programming, or both for high-ability students have lower incidences of underachievement? Is providing intellectual challenge especially critical during a particular age range? Bright, underachieving students might benefit from curriculum differentiation techniques (Reis, Burns, & Renzulli, 1992; Renzulli & Smith, 1978), such as curriculum compacting, interesting Type III enrichment opportunities, and acceleration. The literature also presents a variety of other classroom designs, such as self-contained classrooms and home and school partnerships. Because causes and correlates of underachievement differ, no single intervention reverses underachievement patterns in the full spectrum of gifted underachievers. Further research in this area must focus on developing multiple approaches to both preventing and reversing underachievement. Such approaches would differentiate among different types of underachievement, incorporating both proactive and preventative counseling and innovative instructional interventions. In addition, researchers should incorporate the knowledge gained from social cognitive theory to combat underachievement (Dai, Moon, & Feldhusen, 1998; Schunk, 1998; Zimmerman, 1989). Interventions that enhance self-efficacy or develop self-regulation may complement other intervention strategies and increase their effectiveness. Different types of underachievers may require different proportions of counseling, self-regulation training, and instructional or curricular modifications.

## Conclusion

The concept of underachievement, though often discussed, is still vaguely defined in the professional literature. The absence of any clear, precise definition of gifted underachievement restricts research-based comparisons and hinders the quest for suitable interventions. Precise operational definitions of gifted underachievement may prevent the identification of certain types of potential gifted underachievers, while more flexible, inclusive definitions of gifted underachievement may not adequately distinguish between gifted students who achieve and those who underachieve. The psychological characteristics ascribed to gifted underachievers vary and sometimes contradict each other. Further, more adequate research is needed in this area in order to unravel the mystery of why gifted students underachieve and how we can help them to succeed.

# References

Baker, J. A., Bridger, R., & Evans, K. (1998). Models of underachievement among gifted preadolescents: The role of personal, family, and school factors. *Gifted Child Quarterly, 42*, 5–14.

Baum, S. M., Olenchak, F. R., & Owen, S. V. (1998). Gifted students with attention deficits: Fact and/or fiction? Or, can we see the forest for the trees? *Gifted Child Quarterly, 42*, 96–104.

Baum, S. M., Renzulli, J. S., & Hébert, T. P. (1995a). *The prism metaphor: A new paradigm for reversing underachievement* (CRS95310). Storrs: National Research Center on the Gifted and Talented, The University of Connecticut.

Baum, S. M., Renzulli, J. S., & Hébert, T. P. (1995b). Reversing underachievement: Creative productivity as a systematic intervention. *Gifted Child Quarterly, 39*, 224–235.

Baymur, F., & Patterson, C. H. (1965). Three methods of assisting underachieving high school students. In M. Kornrich (Ed.), *Underachievement* (pp. 501–513). Springfield, IL: Thomas.

Belcastro, F. P. (1985). Use of behavior modification strategies: A review of the research. *Roeper Review, 7*, 184– 189.

Borkowski, J. G., & Thorpe, P. K. (1994). Self-regulation and motivation: A lifespan perspective on underachievement. In D. H. Schunk & B. J. Zimmerman (Eds.), *Self-regulation of learning and practice* (pp. 45–74). Hillsdale, NJ: Erlbaum.

Bricklin B., & Bricklin, P. M. (1967). *Bright child, poor grades: The psychology of underachievement.* New York: Delacorte.

Broedel, J., Ohlsen, M., Proff, F., & Southard, C. (1965). The effects of group counseling on  gifted underachieving adolescents. In M. Kornrich (Ed.), *Underachievement* (pp. 514–528). Springfield, IL: Thomas.

Bruns, J. H. (1992). *They can but they don't.* New York: Viking Penguin.

Butler-Por, N. (1987). *Underachievers in school: Issues and intervention.* Chichester, England: John Wiley and Sons.

Butler-Por, N. (1993). Underachieving gifted students. In K. A. Heller, F. J. Mönks, & A. H. Passow (Eds.), *International handbook of research and development of giftedness and talent* (pp. 649–668). Oxford: Pergamon.

Dai, D. Y., Moon, S. M., & Feldhusen, J. F. (1998). Achievement motivation and gifted students: A social cognitive perspective. *Educational Psychologist, 33*(2/3), 45–63.

Diaz, E. I. (1998). Perceived factors influencing the academic underachievement of talented students of Puerto Rican descent. *Gifted Child Quarterly, 42*, 105–122.

Dowdall, C. B., & Colangelo, N. (1982). Underachieving gifted students: Review and implications. *Gifted Child Quarterly, 26*, 179–184.

Emerick, L. J. (1988). *Academic underachievement among the gifted: Students' perceptions of factors that reverse the pattern.* Unpublished doctoral dissertation, University of Connecticut, Storrs.

Emerick, L. J. (1992). Academic underachievement among the gifted: Students' perceptions of factors that reverse the pattern. *Gifted Child Quarterly, 36*, 140–146.

Fehrenbach, C. R. (1993). Underachieving students: Intervention programs that work. *Roeper Review, 16*, 88–90.

Fine, M. J., & Pitts, R. (1980). Intervention with underachieving gifted children: Rationale and strategies. *Gifted Child Quarterly, 24*, 51–55.

Fink, M. B. (1965). Objectification of data used in underachievement self-concept study. In M. Kornrich (Ed.), *Underachievement* (pp. 79–86). Springfield, IL: Thomas.

Ford, D. Y. (1992). Determinants of underachievement as perceived by gifted, above-average, and average Black students. *Roeper Review, 14*, 130–136.

Ford, D. Y. (1996). *Reversing underachievement among gifted Black students.* New York: Teacher's College Press.

Gallagher, J. J. (1991). Personal patterns of underachievement. *Journal for the Education of the Gifted, 14*, 221–233.

Gohm, C. L., Humphreys, L. G., & Yao, G. (1998). Underachievement among spatially gifted students. *American Educational Research Journal, 35*, 515–531.

Green, K., Fine, M. J., & Tollefson, N. (1988). Family systems characteristics and underachieving gifted males. *Gifted Child Quarterly, 32*, 267–272.

Jeon, K. (1990, August). *Counseling and guidance for gifted underachievers.* Paper presented at the First Southeast Asian Regional Conference on Giftedness, Manila, Philippines. (ERIC Document Delivery Service ED328051)

Kanoy, R. C., Johnson, B. W., & Kanoy, K. W. (1980). Locus of control and self-concept in achieving and underachieving bright elementary students. *Psychology in the Schools, 17*, 395–399.

Krissman, A. L. (1989). The "Trillium" child: A new type of gifted underachiever. *Roeper Review, 11,* 160–162.

Krouse, J. H., & Krouse, H. J. (1981). Toward a multimodal theory of underachievement. *Educational Psychologist, 16*, 151–164.

Mandel, H. P., & Marcus, S. I. (1988). *The psychology of underachievement.* New York: Wiley & Sons.

Mandel, H. P., & Marcus, S. I. (1995). *Could do better.* New York: Wiley & Sons.

McCall, R. B., Evahn, C., & Kratzer, L. (1992). *High school underachievers: What do they achieve as adults?* Newbury Park: SAGE.

Reis, S. M., Burns, D. E., & Renzulli, J. S. (1992). *Curriculum compacting: A guide for teachers.* Mansfield Center, CT: Creative Learning Press.

Reis, S. M., & McCoach, D. B. (2000). The underachievement of gifted students: What do we know and where do we go? *Gifted Child Quarterly, 44*, 152–170.

Renzulli, J. S., Reid, B. D., & Gubbins, E. J. (1992). *Setting an agenda: Research priorities for the gifted and talented through the year 2000.* Storrs: National Research Center on the Gifted and Talented, The University of Connecticut.

Renzulli, J. S. (1977). *The Enrichment Triad Model: A guide for developing defensible programs for the gifted and talented.* Mansfield Center, CT: Creative Learning Press.

Renzulli, J. S., & Reis, S. R. (1985). *The schoolwide enrichment model: A comprehensive plan for educational excellence.* Mansfield Center, CT: Creative Learning Press.

Renzulli, J. S., & Reis, S. R. (1997). *The schoolwide enrichment model: A how-to guide for educational excellence.* Mansfield Center, CT: Creative Learning Press.

Renzulli, J. S., & Smith, L. H. (1978). *The learning styles inventory: A measure of student preference for instructional techniques.* Mansfield Center, CT: Creative Learning Press.

Rimm, S. (1995). *Why bright kids get poor grades and what you can do about it.* New York: Crown Trade Paperbacks.

Rimm, S. (1997a). An underachievement epidemic. *Educational Leadership, 54*(7), 18–22.

Rimm, S. (1997b). Underachievement syndrome: A national epidemic. In N. Colangelo & G. A. Davis (Eds.), *Handbook of gifted education* (2nd ed., pp. 416–435). Boston: Allyn and Bacon.

Rimm, S., Cornale, M., Manos, R., & Behrend, J. (1989). *Guidebook for implementing the trifocal underachievement program in schools.* Watertown, WI: Apple.

Rimm, S., & Lowe, B. (1988). Family environments of underachieving gifted students. *Gifted Child Quarterly, 32,* 353–358.

Schunk, D. H. (1998, November). *Motivation and self-regulation among gifted learners.* Paper presented at the annual meeting of the National Association of Gifted Children, Louisville, KY.

Supplee, P. L. (1990). *Reaching the gifted underachiever.* New York: Teacher College Press.

Vail, P. L. (1987). *Smart kids with school problems: Things to know and ways to help.* New York: Dutton.

Van Boxtel, H. W., & Mönks, F. J. (1992). General, social, and academic self-concepts of gifted adolescents. *Journal of Youth and Adolescence, 21,* 169–186.

Whitmore, J. R. (1980). *Giftedness, conflict, and underachievement.* Boston: Allen and Bacon.

Whitmore, J. R. (1986). Understanding a lack of motivation to excel. *Gifted Child Quarterly, 30,* 66–69.

Wolfle, J. A. (1991). Underachieving gifted males: Are we missing the boat? *Roeper Review, 13,* 181–184.

Zimmerman, B. J. (1989). A social cognitive view of self-regulated academic learning. *Journal of Educational Psychology, 81,* 329–339.

**91**

# 10 GIFTED CHILDREN AND DEPRESSION

by **Maureen Neihart, Psy.D.**

Although it is a popular notion that gifted children are at risk for higher rates of depression and suicide than their average peers, no empirical data supports this belief, except for students who are creatively gifted in the visual arts and writing (see Neihart & Olenchak, this volume). Nor, however is there good evidence that rates of depression and suicide are significantly lower among populations of gifted children.

Epidemiological studies indicate that rates of depression among children and adolescents are at an all-time high and climbing. Prevalence estimates for clinical depression are as high as 9% for young adolescents, and the age of onset continues to drop (Garrison, Addy, & Jackson, 1992; Lewinshohn, Rohde, Seeley, & Fischer, 1993). Girls are twice as likely as boys to develop depression (Birhmaher, Ryan, Williamson, Brent, & Kaufman, 1996). Many depressed children think about suicide, and the rate of suicide among adolescents has sky-rocketed in the last three decades, up as much as 300% for older adolescent males (Kerr & Milliones, 1995). As many as 10% of adolescents make at least one suicide attempt or gesture, and suicide is the second leading cause of death in this age group. In their thorough review of the literature, Gust-Brey and Cross (1999) concluded that there is no empirical evidence that rates of depression or suicide among gifted youth are higher or lower than the rates observed in epidemiological studies.

## Risk Factors for Depression

Several writers have proposed that some of the identified characteristics of high-ability children may be risk factors for depression (Altman, 1983; Delisle, 1982; Dixon & Scheckel, 1996; Hayes & Sloat, 1990; Jackson, 1998; Lajoie & Shore, 1981; Leroux, 1986; Webb, Meckstroth, & Tolan, 1993). Specifically, gifted children's high cognitive functioning, asynchronous development, and tendency toward perfectionism, sensitivity, and social isolation are viewed by some writers as risk factors for psychopathology in general and depression and suicide in particular (see Silverman, Gross, & Schuler, this volume). On one level, this syllogistic reasoning seems to make good sense. Advanced cognitive functioning might be stressful if and when it leads to imposing critical judgments and high standards on oneself and others. Unrealistic expectations can cause chronic stress, which may, in turn, lead to poor self-esteem, anxiety, and depression (Blatt, 1995; Hamachek, 1978; Seligman, Peterson, Kaslow, Tannenbaum, Alloy, & Abramson, 1984). Advanced intellectual abilities also incline gifted youth to affiliate with older individuals than themselves, resulting in greater exposure to adult conflicts and problems (Gross, 1993; Janos, Marwood, & Robinson, 1985). This exposure may be an additional source of stress that average-ability children do not experience. It may also leave gifted children with a greater sense of frustration or powerlessness if they perceive themselves as helpless to change situations that they view as grossly unjust.

## Asynchronous Development

Asynchronous development (defined as the early onset of some developmental stages) has been identified as an etiological factor in psychopathology during adolescence (Peterson & Craighead, 1986; see also Silverman, this volume) and has been proposed as a risk factor for depression among gifted children. The high-ability child's development may differ so much from the norm that he or she experiences additional stress and social isolation. Gifted children may experience less predictability about their development and may not receive the emotional or social support of a peer group that experiences similar kinds of changes.

## Perfectionism

Perfectionism is a multidimensional construct often described as a combination of thoughts and behaviors associated with high expectations for self and others. In its negative or neurotic form, perfectionism is associated in the clinical literature on general populations with a wide range of medical and emotional problems, including depression and suicide (Adkins & Parker, 1996; Blatt, 1995; Callahan, 1993; Hewitt, Flett, & Ediger, 1996; Parker, 2000). This association has led some to conclude that perfectionism is a risk factor that contributes to depression. Perceived parental and societal pressures to perform combined with feelings of inadequacy may contribute to an exaggerated fear of failure and negative self-evaluations. However, recent studies on perfectionism in gifted students conclude that, while many gifted students are perfectionists, they tend to have the adaptive form of perfectionism that stimulates high achievement, rather than the maladaptive form associated with depression and suicide (Parker; Parker & Mills, 1996; Schuler, 2000).

## Social Isolation

Since social isolation is often associated with depressed mood in children and adolescents, it has been speculated that the social isolation some gifted children experience may increase their risk for depression and suicide (Jackson, 1998; Webb, Meckstroth, & Tolan, 1993). Social isolation may be a common experience among highly gifted children who are not radically accelerated and among many moderately gifted students who do not receive appropriate educational services (Freeman, 1979; Gross, 1993; Janos, Marwood, & Robinson, 1985; Kaiser & Berndt, 1985). It seems to be more of a problem for gifted children under the age of 10 who have less mobility to access intellectual peers.

However, developmental studies of depression in children have not found social isolation *per se* to be a risk factor for depression in the general child or adolescent population. Also, the fact that social isolation is often associated with depressed mood does not mean it causes or contributes to the depression. It may be the reverse: Depression may lead children to withdraw, creating greater social isolation (National Institute for Mental Health, 2000). Further, the evidence indicates that various groups of gifted children interpret their social isolation differently, with some not perceiving it as negatively as others (Cross & Coleman, 1988; Cross, Coleman, & Stewart, 1995; Gross, 1993). It is also important to distinguish between loneliness and solitude because only loneliness correlates with depression (Kaiser & Berndt, 1985), while solitude can be adaptive in reducing stress and encouraging independent, creative work. Hence, the role of social isolation in the development of depression among gifted children is simply not clear at this time.

## Sensitivity

It is easy to imagine how people who are sensitive may suffer more from social injustices, personal losses, slights, and perceived rejections. Gifted children may experience high levels of frustration or concern when they are intellectually capable of understanding the nature and severity of personal and global injustices, yet feel powerless to act toward them (Gross, 1993). Although it is reasonable to conclude that this sensitivity might be a contributing factor in a gifted child's depression, no studies have confirmed this to be the case.

## Group Differences

Many studies have explored differences in depression among samples of average and gifted students by comparing subscale and composite scores on standardized inventories or checklists (Baker, 1995; Bartell & Reynolds, 1986; Demoss, Milich, & DeMers, 1993; Kaiser, Berndt, & Stanley, 1987; Metha & McWhirter, 1997). Scores on these measures consistently suggest that gifted students do not manifest higher levels of depression than their peers, and that when significant differences do arise between scores of high- and average-ability students, differences are in the positive direction for the high-ability group.

However, this research does have serious limitations in regard to sample selection. It tends to focus primarily on White gifted students who are already formally identified and participating in special programs. It is quite possible that many gifted students, particularly those with serious behavior problems or emotional concerns, are not referred for identification for such programs or that they may choose not to participate. The samples used in most of the available studies may be biased against gifted students with the most serious mental health concerns.

Some writers have concluded that there are qualitative differences in the depression of gifted and average children (Berndt, Kaiser, & Van Aalst, 1982; Jackson, 1998; Webb, Meckstroth, & Tolan, 1993). One frequent observation is that gifted adolescents are more likely to experience a premature existential depression (struggling with questions about the meaning of life) than are their average peers as a result of mature cognitive abilities, advanced moral reasoning, and heightened sensitivity, although this idea has not been tested empirically.

## Protective Factors

The role of protective factors is usually overlooked in discussions about the emotional adjustment of gifted children, but it is an important consideration that may help explain the differences observed in subgroups of gifted children. Some characteristics common among gifted students have been cited as protective factors in studies that examine variables associated with the achievement of social competence and emotional health in children and adolescents. For instance, high intelligence, problem-solving abilities, advanced social skills, androgyny, advanced moral reasoning, and outside interests have been identified in risk and resilience research as factors that mediate the potential negative effects of adversity in children, contributing to lower rates of depression (Earls, Beardslee, & Garrison, 1987; Garmezy, 1984; Rolf, Masten, Cicchetti, Nuechterlein, & Weintraub, 1990; Rutter, 1987). Findings like these suggest that, even when some gifted children are exposed to higher levels of stress, their personal characteristics may ameliorate the negative impact that leads to negative outcomes in other children.

## Summary

With the exception of creatively gifted adolescents who are pursuing high achievement in the visual arts and writing (see Neihart & Olenchak, this volume), studies have not confirmed that gifted children and adolescents manifest significantly higher or lower rates or severity of depression than is observed in the general population. Gifted children's advanced intellectual functioning, social isolation, sensitivity, and asynchronous development may be etiological factors when they become depressed, but this link has not yet been systematically investigated. What are needed are controlled studies that compare depressed gifted children with gifted children who are not depressed and studies that compare quantitative and qualitative differences in the course and outcome of depression between gifted and nongifted youth. There is also a need for careful studies of subpopulations of gifted students, such as those with learning disabilities, those who are primarily gifted in nonacademic areas, and gifted children from various cultural groups, all of whom are often underrepresented in studies of gifted children's adjustment.

Those interested in the emotional well-being of gifted children should not neglect the important role of protective factors in ameliorating risk for depression and suicide. Evidence from research on risk

98

and resilience in children and adolescents suggest that, just as there are characteristics of gifted children that may heighten risk, there are also characteristics that may buffer them from the negative effects of unique stressors. Future studies will need to consider the broader picture. It is possible that it will be among some of the most able young people that we will discover the clues to lifelong optimal health.

## References

Adkins, K. K., & Parker, W. D. (1996). Perfectionism and suicidal preoccupation. *Journal of Personality, 64*, 529–543.

Altman, R. (1983). Social-emotional development of gifted children and adolescents: A research model. *Roeper Review, 6*, 65–67.

Baker, J. A. (1995). Depression and suicidal ideation among academically talented adolescents. *Gifted Child Quarterly, 39*, 218–223.

Bartell, N. P., & Reynolds, W. M. (1986). Depression and self-esteem in academically gifted and nongifted children. *Journal of School Psychology, 24*, 55–61.

Berndt, D. J., Kaiser, C. F., & Van Aalst, F. (1982). Depression and self-actualization in gifted adolescents. *Journal of Clinical Psychology, 38*, 142–150.

Birhmaher, B., Ryan, N. D., Williamson, D., Brent, D. A., & Kaufman, J. (1996). Childhood and adolescent depression: A review of the past ten years. Part I. *Journal of the American Academy of Child and Adolescent Psychiatry, 35*, 1575–1583.

Blatt, S. J. (1995). The destructiveness of perfectionism: Implications for the treatment of depression. *American Psychologist, 50*, 1103–1020.

Callahan, J. (1993). Blueprint for an adolescent suicidal crisis. *Psychiatric Annals, 23*, 263–270.

Cross, T. L., & Coleman, L. J. (1988). Is being gifted a social handicap? *Journal for the Education of the Gifted, 11*, 41–56.

Cross, T. L., Coleman, L. J., & Stewart, R. A. (1995). Psychosocial diversity among gifted adolescents: An exploratory study of two groups. *Roeper Review, 17*, 181–185.

Delisle, J. R. (1982). Striking out: Suicide and the gifted adolescent. *Gifted/Creative/Talented, 24*, 16–19.

Demoss, K., Milich, R., & DeMers, S. (1993). Gender, creativity, depression, and attributional style in adolescents with high academic ability. *Journal of Abnormal Child Psychology, 21*, 455–467.

Dixon, D. N., & Scheckel, J. R. (1996). Gifted adolescent suicide: The empirical base. *The Journal of Secondary Gifted Education, 7*, 386–392.

Earls, F., Beardslee, W., & Garrison, W. (1987). Correlates and predictors of competence in young children. In A. Cohler & B. J. Cohler (Eds.), *The invulnerable child* (pp. 70–83). New York: Guilford Press.

Freeman, J. (1979). *Gifted children*. Lancaster, England: MTP Press.

Garmezy, N. (1984). Stress-resistant children: The search for protective factors. In J. E. Stevenson (Ed.), *Aspects of current child psychiatry research* (pp. 213–233). Oxford: Pergamon Press.

Garrison, C., Addy, C., & Jackson, K. (1992). Major depressive disorder and dysthymia in young adolescents. *American Journal of Epidemiology, 135,* 792–802.

Gross, M. (1993). *Exceptionally gifted children.* London: Routledge.

Gust-Brey, K., & Cross, T. L. (1999). An examination of the literature base on the suicidal behaviors of gifted children. *Roeper Review, 22,* 28–35.

Hamacheck, D. E. (1978). Psychodynamics of normal and neurotic perfectionism. *Psychology, 15,* 27–33.

Hayes, M., & Sloat, R. (1990). Suicide and the gifted adolescent. *Journal for the Education of the Gifted, 13,* 229–244.

Hewitt, P. L., Flett, G. L., & Ediger, E. (1996). Perfectionism and depression: Longitudinal assessment of a specific vulnerability hypothesis. *Journal of Abnormal Psychology, 105,* 276–280.

Jackson, S. (1998). Bright star—black sky: A phenomenological study of depression as a window into the psyche of the gifted adolescent. *Roeper Review, 20,* 215–221.

Janos, P. M., Marwood, K. A., & Robinson, N. M. (1985). Friendship patterns in highly intelligent children. *Roeper Review, 8,* 46–49.

Kaiser, C. F., & Berndt, D. J. (1985). Predictors of loneliness in the gifted adolescent. *Gifted Child Quarterly, 29,* 74–77.

Kaiser, C. F., Berndt, D. J., & Stanley, G. (1987). *Moral judgment and depression in gifted adolescents.* Paper presented at the Seventh World Conference on Gifted and Talented Children, Salt Lake City, UT.

Kerr, M. M., & Milliones, J. (1995). Suicide and suicidal behavior. In V. B. Van Hasselt & M. Hersen, (Eds.), *Handbook of adolescent psychopathology: A guide to diagnosis and treatment.* (pp. 653–664). New York: Lexington Books.

Lajoie, S. P., & Shore, B. M. (1981). Three myths? The over-representations of the gifted among dropouts, delinquents, and suicides. *Gifted Child Quarterly, 25,* 183–243.

Leroux, J. A. (1986). Suicidal behavior and gifted adolescents. *Roeper Review, 9,* 77–79.

Lewinshohn, P., Rohde, P., Seeley, J., & Fischer, S. (1993). Age-cohort changes in the lifetime occurrence of depression and other mental disorders, *Journal of Abnormal Psychology, 102,* 110–120.

Metha, A., & McWhirter, E. H. (1997). Suicide ideation, depression, and stressful life events among gifted adolescents. *Journal for the Education of the Gifted, 20,* 284–304.

National Institute for Mental Health (NIMH). (2000). *Depression in children and adolescents: A fact sheet for physicians.* Maryland: Author

Parker, W. D. (2000). Healthy perfectionism in the gifted. *Journal of Secondary Gifted Education, 11,* 173–182.

Parker, W. D., & Mills, C. J. (1996). The incidence of perfectionism in gifted students. *Gifted Child Quarterly, 40,* 194–199.

Peterson, A. C., & Craighead, W. E. (1986). Emotional and personality development in normal adolescents and young adults. In G. L. Klerman (Ed.), *Suicide and depression among adolescents and young adults* (pp. 17–52). Washington, DC: American Psychiatric Press.

Rolf, J., Masten, A., Cicchetti, D., Nuechterlein, K., & Weintraub, S. (Eds.). (1990). *Risk and protective factors in the development of psychopathology.* New York: Cambridge University Press.

Rutter, M. (1987). Psychosocial resilience and protective mechanisms. *American Journal of Orthopsychiatry, 57,* 316–331.

Seligman, M. E. P., Peterson, C., Kaslow, N. J., Tannenbaum, R. L., Alloy, L. B., & Abramson, L. Y. (1984). Attributional style and depressive symptoms among children. *Journal of Abnormal Psychology, 93,* 235–238.

Schuler, P. (2000). Perfectionism and gifted adolescents. *Journal of Secondary Gifted Education, 11,* 183–196.

Webb, J., Meckstroth, E., & Tolan, S. (1993). *Guiding the gifted child.* Columbus: Ohio Psychology Press.

**101**

Depression

# 11

# DELINQUENCY AND GIFTED CHILDREN

## by **Maureen Neihart, Psy.D.**

ational media attention given to academically capable kids who commit heinous acts of violence in the last decade has again raised the question of gifted children's vulnerability to antisocial behavior, or delinquency. Is there any evidence to suggest that gifted youth are more likely than their average peers to engage in antisocial acts or violence? Like other concerns about the adjustment of gifted children, thoughts about the potential relationship between giftedness and delinquency are roughly categorized into two camps: the vulnerability thesis and the protection thesis (Seeley, 1984).

One line of thinking says that gifted youth are more vulnerable to delinquency because they are more sensitive to environmental factors as a result of their heightened awareness and arousal. Also, a gifted child's differences may contribute to experiences with social alienation and rejection, thereby contributing to identification and alliances with out-groups and involvement in antisocial behavior as a way to exert control or power (Jackson, 1998; Mahoney, 1980; Seeley & Mahoney, 1981).

The other perspective sees giftedness as a protection against delinquency, primarily as a result of strong problem-solving skills, good insight into the behaviors of self and others, and the ability to foresee long-range consequences of behaviors. The gifted child, it is reasoned, is better able to understand and cope with environmental adversity than children with less intellectual ability. Much of the empirical data supports this view (Bartell & Reynolds, 1986; Cornell, Delcourt, Bland, Goldberg, & Oram, 1994; Gallucci, Middleton, & Kline, 1999a, 1999b; Garland & Ziegler, 1999; Janos & Robinson, 1985).

## Prevalence of Delinquency Among Gifted Children and Adolescents

Numerous epidemiological and longitudinal studies of delinquent youths and adult criminals consistently observe lower levels of intelligence and school achievement than what is represented in the general population, although the mean intelligence of delinquents is well within the average range. In longitudinal studies, *lower* IQ has been identified as a predictor of aggressive behavior patterns and school failure that, in turn, contribute to delinquent tendencies in adolescence and low school achievement (Farrington, 1991; Patterson, DeBaryshe, & Ramsey, 1989). Lower IQ is associated with delinquency even after controlling for social background and low scholastic attainment (Gath & Tennent, 1972; Rutter, Giller, & Hagell, 1998; Tremblay, Masse, Perron, Leblanc, Schwartzman, & Ledingham, 1992).

The association of lower IQ with crime has proved very robust. The association applies particularly to *persistent* antisocial behavior. Intelligence scores of adolescents engaged in *transient* antisocial behavior do not differ appreciably from the scores in the general population (Moffit, 1993).

**104**

# Prevalence of Giftedness
## Among Delinquent Youth

However, these findings may not accurately reflect the intellectual and achievement potential of juvenile and adult offenders for several reasons. First, antisocial individuals often have a history of not applying themselves in school and, therefore, do poorly on traditional tests of vocabulary, general information, and arithmetic. Also, scores on nonverbal tests of potential are usually strongly influenced by an individual's motivation and persistence. The fact that an offender achieves little academically or professionally sometimes has nothing to do with ability or potential and everything to do with antisocial thinking patterns. He or she doesn't make an effort because he or she thinks there is no reason to (Samenow, 1998a; Young, 1999).

Second, there is some evidence that delinquents may possess nontraditional types of intelligence. For example, Samenow (1998a) observed that some offenders who score poorly on standardized measures are "extremely resourceful and effective in pursuing their day-to-day objectives. They were street-smart, savvy men and women who could assess other people for their own purposes and carry out elaborate schemes" (p. 67). In other words, these youth had high practical intelligence (Sternberg, 1985), which is the ability to adapt, shape, and select everyday environments to achieve certain goals. It is an "untaught" intelligence developed through everyday interactions in specific contexts. Similarly, in a two-year study of 1,000 youths who came in contact with the juvenile court system in one county in Colorado, Seeley (1984) found a "substantial number" of gifted youth in the delinquent population. However, the intelligence profile of these gifted delinquents was nontraditional: They had high creative and fluid intelligence combined with relatively lower verbal and crystallized intelligence, lower scores on achievement tests, and poor school performance. Seeley concluded that the intelligence of these bright delinquents was developed through incidental learning, rather than through school learning, and was characterized by the type of "nonverbal quick perceptiveness" that is found in individuals with practical intelligence. Hence, it may be that we would find larger numbers of gifted youth among delinquents if we looked for superior levels of creative and practical intelligence, rather than verbal or analytic intelligence.

## Possible Reasons for the Under-representation of Gifted Youth Among Delinquents

Some people wonder if gifted youth are underrepresented among delinquent populations simply because they are too clever to be apprehended and convicted. Are less intelligent delinquents more likely to get caught? Moffitt's (1993) research strongly suggests that this is not the case and that the association observed between lower IQ and delinquency is with the antisocial behavior specifically. More likely—though it has not been demonstrated yet—is that intelligence covaries with some behavioral mediators associated with delinquency. It may be that risk lies not so much in cognitive deficits, but in these behavioral mediators.

In addition to the direct evidence, there is also indirect evidence to suggest that gifted children may be less at risk for delinquent behavior than their average peers. For example, since poor social problem solving and low levels of moral reasoning are commonly associated with antisocial acts in both juveniles and adults, one might speculate that the lower levels of delinquency observed among the gifted are related to their advanced capacities in these two areas. First, they tend to reach higher levels of moral reasoning at younger ages (Boehm, 1962; Janos, Robinson, & Lunneborg, 1989; Kohlberg, 1984). Delinquents, on the other hand, tend to be characterized by low levels of moral reasoning that don't advance much with age. It may be that the gifted child's early, advanced moral reasoning serves as a protective factor against the development of delinquent or antisocial behavior.

Further, several common characteristics of gifted children are protective factors that have been demonstrated to mitigate the negative effects of adversity in a child's life and are believed to enhance a child's capacity for resilience (Garmezy, Masters, & Tellegen, 1984; Luthar & Zigler, 1991; Young, 1999). These factors include high intelligence, problem-solving abilities, a sense of humor, moral regard, androgyny, and involvement with a talent or hobby. Even social isolation, often considered a risk factor in the minds of parents and teachers (see Neihart on depression, this volume), has been noted as a protective factor against delinquency in one study (Farrington, Gallagher, Morley, St. Ledger, & West, 1988).

## Other Comparisons

Few studies have compared high-ability delinquents with average-ability delinquents, and most of those that have are old and methodologically flawed (Caplan & Powell, 1964; Gath, Tennent, Pidduck, 1971; Mahoney, 1980). The existing studies have found only a few differences between the two groups (i.e., high-ability delinquents seem to be emotionally disturbed more often, their parents have more education, and they are not as far behind scholastically as delinquents of average intelligence).

Some older studies have also compared bright delinquents with bright nondelinquents, concluding that the former are more often truant, hold aspirations far below their capacity, and have major school problems. Bright delinquents are more likely to be referred to the courts by their parents for being "out of control" and are less likely to be runaways (Caplan & Powell, 1964; Seeley, 1984). They are also more likely to be living with both parents and score higher on tests of verbal creativity (Kuo, 1967).

## Criminal Logic

Delinquent youth view life differently than responsible people. To understand how some young people can repeatedly violate the rules, exploit other people, and feel little or no remorse, it is necessary to grasp the antisocial thinking that characterizes criminality. Antisocial individuals are motivated by five needs: the need for power, for control, to look good, to feel good, and to be right. It is this "criminal logic" that enables them to persist in violating the rules and expected norms of behavior (Goldstein, Glick, & Gibbs, 1998; Samenow, 1998a, 1998b). They make decisions from a low level of moral reasoning, choosing to avoid pain and pursue pleasure (Little

& Robinson, 1988; Yochelson & Samenow, 1976). When asked to make an effort to figure out a complex sequence of patterns, the anti-social student may make a poor effort because he or she doesn't care.

## What Causes Some Gifted Youth to Be Violent?

Recent media attention on high-ability youth who commit lethal acts of violence prompts the question, "What causes some talented adolescents to snap?" Juvenile homicide is difficult to research because it is an extremely rare event. There are only a few studies of the dynamics of juvenile homicide, and none of violent, talented teens (Benedek & Cornell, 1989; Cornell, Benedek, & Benedek; 1987; Ewing, 1990). For now, we can conclude that gifted children are neither more prone to violence than other children, nor are they exempt from perpetrating the most heinous of offenses.

While most violent, gifted youth have histories of previous psychiatric or behavioral problems, there are some who have no history of problems and a few who have rather sterling records of comportment and achievement in their schools and communities (Ewing, 1990). How do we explain the latter? Although there is no direct empirical evidence to support the idea that there are conditions or characteristics of gifted children that increase their risk for violence, there is a proposed dynamic that may be worth consideration.

"Episodic dyscontrol" is an alleged syndrome in which a person with severe ego deficits suffers an extreme loss of impulse control (Ewing, 1990; King, 1975). It may explain how good kids with no history of behavior problems might commit horrifying acts of violence. Individuals with episodic dyscontrol are believed to be in a state of "diminished capacity" at the time of their violence. Such children go into a rage and lack the internal resources to stop themselves from harming themselves or others. Among gifted children, this dyscontrol may arise because they have not adequately developed their capacities to modulate impulses and emotions. It is hypothesized that a few intellectually precocious children may establish the habit of thinking away impulses, rather than expressing them and resolving them experientially.

Clinical experience (Neihart, 1999) has suggested that gifted youth who appear to be doing very well on the surface and then one day break down and commit lethal acts of violence are strongly defended and poorly integrated. They rely too much on their cognitive abilities to explain away, avoid, or distract themselves from their intense negative emotions, and they fail to integrate a capacity to modulate strong feelings. These children eventually reach a point where they can no longer keep up these strong defenses. Their psychological resources become depleted, and emotions and impulses then overwhelm them, erupting in full force. Sometimes, this results in a loss of impulse control, sometimes there is a loss of reality testing (i.e., the person becomes psychotic), and sometimes there is an emotional breakdown.

## Conclusion

Intense media coverage of several incidents of lethal violence by high-ability youth has led to some speculation that gifted students may be at risk for delinquent, criminal, or violent behavior. Although research evidence to date suggests that gifted students evidence less delinquency than average, the impression that behavior problems are more common among high-ability youth persists among some teachers, parents, and clinicians. The discrepancy between research findings and these impressions may be due to attributional and selection factors. Some professionals may attribute normal differences in gifted children's behavior to psychopathology. Alternatively, there might be selection bias in the research samples because the studies are conducted with students who are already identified as gifted and participating in gifted programs. It could be that gifted children with the most serious behavior problems are either not identified for such programs or they choose not to participate when identified.

Delinquent youth are not a homogenous group. Any attempt to understand the developmental trajectories of antisocial behavior in children, adolescents, and adults must consider the interaction of multiple risk and protective factors. Research to date suggests overall that high-ability children and adolescents are underrepresented among delinquent youth. Contrary to representations in popular film and news media, it is not usually the gifted teen who commits crimes or acts of violence. Research tells us that the most effective prevention and intervention efforts are those that are tailored to children's developmental levels and address social thinking processes. There remains much research to be done to elucidate the multiple pathways to delinquent and violent behavior.

## References

Bartell, N. P., & Reynolds, W. M. (1986). Depression and self-esteem in academically gifted and nongifted children. *Journal of School Psychology, 24,* 55–61.

Benedek, E. P., & Cornell, D. G. (Eds.). (1989). *Juvenile homicide.* Washington, DC: American Psychiatric Association.

Boehm, L. (1962). The development of conscience: A comparison of American children of different mental and socioeconomic levels. *Child Development, 33,* 575–590.

Caplan, N. S., & Powell, M. (1964). A cross comparison of average and superior IQ delinquents. *The Journal of Psychology, 57,* 307–318.

Cornell, D., Benedek, E., & Benedek, D. (1987). Characteristics of adolescents charged with homicide: Review of 72 cases. *Behavioral Science and the Law, 5,* 11–23.

Cornell, D. G., Delcourt, M. A. B., Bland, L. C., Goldberg, M. D., & Oram, G. (1994). Low incidence of behavior problems among elementary school students in gifted programs. *Journal for the Education of the Gifted, 18,* 4–19.

Ewing, C. (1990). *When children kill: The dynamics of juvenile homicide.* Lexington, MA: Lexington Books.

Farrington, D. P. (1991). Childhood aggression and adult violence: Early precursors and later life outcomes. In D. J. Pepler & K. H. Rubin (Eds.), *The development and treatment of childhood aggression* (pp. 5–29). Hillsdale, NJ: Erlbaum.

Farrington, D. P., Gallagher, B., Morely, L., St. Ledger, R. J., & West, D. J. (1988). Are there any successful men from criminogenic backgrounds? *Psychiatry, 51,* 116–130.

Gallucci, N. T., Middleton, G., & Kline, A. (1999a). Intellectually superior children and behavioral problems and competence. *Roeper Review, 22,* 18–21.

Gallucci, N. T., Middleton, G., & Kline, A. (1999b). The independence of creative potential and behavior disorders in gifted children. *Gifted Child Quarterly, 43,* 194–203.

Garland, A. F., & Ziegler, E. (1999). Emotional and behavioral problems among highly intellectually gifted youth. *Roeper Review, 22,* 41–44.

Garmezy, N., Masters, A., & Tellegen, A. (1984). The study of stress and competence in children: A building block for developmental psychopathology. *Child Development, 55,* 97–111.

Gath, D., & Tennent, G. (1972). High intelligence and delinquency: A review. *The British Journal of Criminology, 12,* 174–181.

Gath, D., Tennet, G., & Pidduck, R. (1971). Criminological characteristics of bright delinquents. *British Journal of Criminology, 11,* 275–279.

Goldstein, A. P., Glick, B., & Gibbs, J. C. (1998). *Aggression replacement training: A comprehensive intervention for aggressive youth.* Champaign, IL: Research Press.

Jackson, P. S. (1998). Bright star—black sky: A phenomenological study of depression as a window into the psyche of the gifted adolescent. *Roeper Review, 20,* 215–221.

Janos, P. M., & Robinson, N. M. (1985). Psychosocial development in intellectually gifted children. In F. D. Horowitz & M. O'Brien (Eds.), *The gifted and talented: Developmental perspectives* (pp. 149–196). Washington DC: American Psychological Association.

Janos, P. M., Robinson, N. M., & Lunneborg, C. E. (1989). Markedly early entrance to college: A multi-year comparative study of academic performance and psychological adjustment. *Journal of Higher Education, 60,* 496–518.

King, C. H. (1975). The ego and the integration of homicidal youth. *American Journal of Orthopsychiatry, 45,* 134–145.

Kohlberg, L. (1984). *The psychology of moral development.* New York: Harper & Row.

Kuo, Y. Y. (1967). Creative thinking: Delinquent vs. nondelinquent boys. *Journal of Creative Behavior, 1,* 411–417.

Little, G. L., & Robinson, K. D. (1988). Moral reconation therapy: A systematic step-by-step treatment system for treatment resistant clients. *Psychological Reports, 62,* 135–151.

Luthar, S. S., & Zigler, E. (1991). Vulnerability and competence: A review of research on resilience in childhood. *American Journal of Orthopsychiatry, 61,* 6–22.

Mahoney, A. R. (1980). Gifted delinquents: What do we know about them? *Children and Youth Services Review, 2,* 315–330.

Moffit, T. E. (1993). The neuropsychology of conduct disorder. *Development and Psychopathology, 5,* 135–152.

Neihart, M. (1999). The treatment of juvenile homicide offenders. *Psychotherapy, 36,* 36–46.

Patterson, G. R., DeBaryshe, B. D., & Ramsey, E. (1989). A developmental perspective on antisocial behavior. *American Psychologist, 44,* 329–335.

Rutter, M., Giller, H., & Hagell, A. (1998) *Antisocial behavior by young people.* Cambridge: Cambridge University Press.

Samenow, S. (1998a). *Straight talk about criminals.* Northvale, NJ: Aronson.

Samenow, S. (1998b). *Before it's too late: Why some kids get into trouble—and what parents can do about it.* New York: Random House.

Seeley, K. R. (1984). Giftedness and juvenile delinquency in perspective. *Journal for the Education of the Gifted, 8,* 59–72.

Seeley, K. R., & Mahoney, A. R. (1981). Giftedness and delinquency: A small beginning toward some answers. In R. E. Clasen et al. (Eds.), *Programming for the gifted, talented, and creative: Models and methods* (2nd. ed., pp. 247–258). Madison: University of Wisconsin Extension.

Sternberg, R. J. (1985). *Beyond IQ: A triarchic theory of human intelligence.* New York: Cambridge University Press.

Tremblay, R. E., Masse, B., Perron, D., Leblanc, M., Schwartzman, A. E., & Ledingham, J. E. (1992). Early disruptive behavior, poor school achievement, delinquent behavior, and delinquent personality: Longitudinal analyses. *Journal of Consulting and Clinical Psychology, 60,* 64–72.

Yochelson, S., & Samenow, S. (1976). *The criminal personality. Volume One: A profile for change.* Northvale, NJ: Aronson.

Young, D. W. (1999). *Wayward kids: Understanding and treating antisocial youth.* Northvale, NJ: Aronson.

# 12 RISK AND RESILIENCE IN GIFTED CHILDREN: A CONCEPTUAL FRAMEWORK

by **Maureen Neihart, Psy.D.**

Although there has been considerable discussion over the years about meeting the social and emotional needs of gifted students, there has been little mention of the conceptual foundations underlying recommendations, models, or strategies. Without a conceptual foundation for the work, efforts to provide affective supports for gifted students might proceed willy-nilly, resulting in a crazy quilt of services that may or may not cover the need. Building from the vast literature on risk and resilience and from the handful of studies that have explored resilience in gifted children, this chapter describes how the concepts of risk and resilience might serve as a theoretical framework for addressing the social and emotional needs of gifted children.

# Risk and Resilience Research

Risk and resilience are concepts that have been explored in the developmental sciences for about 50 years (Cohen & Willis, 1985; Glueck & Glueck, 1950; Luthar & Ziglar, 1991; Murphy & Moriarty, 1976; Rutter, 1987; Werner, 1984). Resilience can be defined as the ability to achieve emotional health and social competence in spite of a history of adversity or stress (Anthony, & Cohler, 1987; Garmezy, 1985; Werner & Smith, 1982). A resilient child beats the odds for negative outcomes.

The first two generations of research focused on the *risk and protective factors* associated with different outcomes for children and outlined the developmental trajectories for specific outcomes like mental illness or delinquency. Risk and protective factors are individual and contextual variables that shift developmental pathways toward positive or negative outcomes. Risk factors heighten vulnerability, and protective factors buffer children from the harmful impact of certain circumstances. Doll and Lyon (1998) have pointed out that risk and protective factors are best conceptualized as constellations of hazards and benefits. The contribution of each factor is not clear, but there is wide consensus that the impact of multiple factors is probably geometric, rather than additive.

We learned from these initial studies that certain types of life experiences are indeed correlated with increased risk for negative results for children and that individual differences exist in how people respond to stress. For instance, we learned that poverty heightens vulnerability in children and predicts criminality and that childhood abuse predicts later physical and mental health difficulties (Cicchetti, 1990; Garmezy & Tellegen, 1984; Glueck & Glueck, 1950; Gordon & Song, 1994; Rutter, 1983). Noteworthy from these and subsequent studies is the consistent finding that the single most powerful predictor of positive outcomes for vulnerable children is a relationship with a caring adult.

The third generation of risk studies asks the question, "What goes right?" for the 25% of children who achieve emotional health and social competence in spite of a history of adversity or stress. This generation of research is seeing a shift from static research on isolated factors to a more organic consideration of negotiating risk situations (Consortium on the School-Based Promotion of Social Competence, 1994; Cowen, 1991, 1994; Doll & Lyon, 1998; Haggerty, Sherrod, Garmezy, & Rutter, 1994; Luthar & Zigler, 1991). The focus of studies is now on the transactional processes among risk and protective factors within the child, family, school, and community.

## Resilience and Giftedness

Studies of resilient children indicate that they share traits in common with gifted children: intelligent curiosity (Anthony & Cohler, 1987; Garmezy & Rutter, 1983), self-efficacy (Garmezy & Rutter; Masten & Garmezy, 1990; McMillan & Reed, 1994), a high moral regard (Coles, 1986), a positive explanatory style (Dai & Feldhusen, 1996; Pajares, 1996), a keen sense of humor (Hébert & Beardsley, 2001; Rutter, 1987), and problem-solving ability (Masten & Garmezy). In addition, numerous people writing about resilient children and gifted children underscore the overriding influence a relationship with a caring adult can make in the life and achievement of children who live or learn in disconfirming environments (Allen, 1996; Cohen & Willis, 1985; Elder, Caspi, & van Nguyen, 1986; Emerick, 1992; Hébert & Beardsley; Masten & Garmezy; McMillan & Reed; Rhodes, 1994; Werner & Smith, 1982). The similarities between resilient and gifted children suggest that common characteristics of gifted children may serve as developmental assets.

A few investigators have examined resilience in gifted children specifically (Bland, Sowa, & Callahan, 1994; Ford, 1994; Ford & Harris, 1990; Hébert & Beardsley, 2001; Kline & Short, 1991a, 1991b; Reis, Hébert, Diaz, Maxfield, & Ratley, 1995). A common observation is that disadvantaged gifted children who succeed tend to manifest a number of personal qualities associated with resilience. For example, Reis et al. observed that characteristics of resilience distinguished talented students who achieved at an urban high school from those who did not achieve. Ford (1994) and Ford and Harris (1990) noted characteristics of resilience in gifted Black youth and also identified several barriers to resilience in this group, including peer pressures, racial identity, relationships with teachers and counselors, and discrimination experiences. These studies and the vast literature on resilience in general suggest that an effective approach to supporting the psychosocial needs of gifted children is to reduce known risk factors in their lives, enhance protective factors, and strengthen personal qualities known to promote emotional health and social competence.

Applying these foundational ideas to the guidance of the gifted provides a practical framework for the identification and development of differentiated affective supports necessary to facilitate positive outcomes for gifted students. Counseling and guidance for gifted children should focus on reducing the risks of maladjustment while strengthening the factors that enhance positive outcomes. This goal should also be the underlying focus of program planning and program evaluation: Attenuate the negative impact of some events while building resources that enable the child to cope effectively. When we use these concepts as the scaffolding on which to build affective supports for the gifted, we are led to ask, "What are the risk factors for gifted children? What are the protective factors? What are the mediating mechanisms that help keep a gifted child on the developmental trajectory for positive outcomes?"

## Risk and Protective Factors for Gifted Children

Does the empirical research on social and emotional adjustment point to specific risk and protective factors for gifted children? Yes, it does. We've seen in the previous chapters that a lack of appropriate educational programming can be a risk factor for underachievement and for some problems with emotional or social adjustment. Low ceiling in the curriculum content and lack of access to intellectual peers are also factors that can increase negative outcomes. Disabling perfectionism can heighten risk for gifted children (see Schuler, this volume). Gifted children's intensity, or overexcitability, and their internal asynchronies may also be risk factors, though this association is mainly supported by clinical and educational observations, rather than controlled studies. It may be that a gifted child's intensity serves as a trigger for one of a number of transactional processes in the

**116**

child's environment that in turn are the causal mechanism largely responsible for positive or negative developmental outcomes.

Gifted children's problem-solving abilities, intellectual curiosity, concern about moral issues, sense of humor, and self-efficacy contribute to their resilience. These common qualities may serve as protective factors, enabling some students to succeed in spite of having to live or learn in indifferent or rejecting environments. Most importantly, we've seen that strong connections to social networks that are accepting and supporting can make the difference between achievement and underachievement, effort and apathy, engagement and withdrawal, or delight and despair.

## Mediating Mechanisms of Positive and Negative Outcomes for Gifted Children

Investigators have only recently begun to address the transactional and ecological nature of the adjustment of gifted children (Moon, Jurich, & Feldhusen, 1998; Noble, Subotnik, & Arnold, 1999; Pufal-Struzik, 1999). The predominant trend is still to study discrete factors (Garland & Zigler, 1999; Schuler, 2000), and practitioners in the field have not done much to apply findings on transactional processes to intervention and programming. Little attention is given to the mechanisms that seem to mediate positive and negative outcomes for gifted children. For example, the finding from Cross, Coleman, and Stewart's (1995) study that the extent to which a gifted adolescent feels different from others is a mechanism that mediates social self-esteem and, perhaps, social competence merits further investigation. In this study, the more different gifted high school students felt from their peers, the more negative was their perception of their social competence. This finding is especially noteworthy given that we already know that the meaning or interpretation a person attaches to an event is a significant mediating process that can alter the eventual outcome of the event for the individual (Burns & Seligman, 1989; Herman, 1992; Seligman, 1995).

It is the mechanisms by which people successfully negotiate adversity or stress that are most important in understanding risk and resilience. Bland, Sowa, and Callahan (1994) have suggested that Lazarus and Folkman's (1984) cognitive appraisal paradigm may help explain the resilience observed in many gifted children. It may be that the early cognitive maturity of gifted children mitigates against the negative effects of underchallenging environments and unsympathetic adults.

The subjectivity of individual experiences needs to be explored further. It should be the initial focus in counseling and guidance with gifted children and their families. What meaning does the student and his or her family attach to the label and experience of gifted? What is their perception of how others respond to their abilities? In the future, qualitative studies that compare the phenomenological worlds of successful gifted individuals will be invaluable in advancing our understanding of the processes involved. Doll and Lyon (1998) have suggested that structural equation modeling (Connell, 1987) and pattern analysis (Magnusson & Bergmum, 1990) will help elucidate the transactional processes involved in risk and resilience outcomes.

Risk and resilience are systemic phenomena that cannot be understood fully outside the systems in which they develop (Doll & Lyon, 1998). The crucial importance of school environments in developmental outcomes has been demonstrated (Doll & Lyon), and we know that the school environment has protective potential. However, evidence indicates that, while elementary schools tend to incorporate affective supports into the daily curriculum, secondary schools do not (Doll & Lyon; Forman & Kalafat, 1998). For example, Sytsma (2000) found that only 13% of the high schools represented offered any affective components in addition to the academic components for gifted students. The failure at the secondary level to infuse affective supports into the daily classroom experience reflects a lack of support for known protective factors, and needs to be corrected.

## Conclusion

The conceptual foundations of risk and resilience offer a theoretical framework for understanding the adjustment of gifted children and further research. It is possible to begin to identify risk factors, protective factors, and mediating mechanisms. This schema can be used by caring adults to assess individually a gifted child's guidance needs simply by asking, "What are the risk factors operating in this child's life? What are the protective factors? What can be done to reduce the risk factors and enhance or increase protective factors? Are there any mediating mechanisms that should be addressed (e.g. parental responses to the child's giftedness or the child's perceptions of his or her abilities)?" Like the early risk research, studies in the psychology of the gifted have clearly identified a few risk factors specific to gifted children: lack of challenge or low ceiling in the curriculum; internal asynchronies; and insufficient learning time with children with similar interests, abilities, and drive. Based on the conceptual foundations of risk and resilience, efforts to insert affective supports for gifted students should focus on reducing or eliminating risk factors, enhancing protective factors, and developing the mediating mechanisms known to facilitate positive outcomes (Doll & Lyon, 1998; Pianta & Walsh, 1998). Resilience research demonstrates that emotional health and social competence are attained not so much as a result of individual characteristics, but from a transaction among children, their families, and the community.

## References

Allen, J. G. (1996). *Coping with trauma*. Washington, DC: American Psychiatric Press.

Anthony, E. J., & Cohler, B. J. (Eds.). (1987). *The invulnerable child*. New York: Guilford Press.

Bland, L. C., Sowa, C. J., & Callahan, C. M. (1994). An overview of resilience in gifted children. *Roeper Review, 17,* 77–80.

Burns, M., & Seligman, M. (1989). Explanatory style across the lifespan: Evidence for stability over 52 years. *Journal of Personality and Social Psychology, 56,* 118–124.

Cicchetti, D. (1990). A historical perspective on the discipline of developmental psychopathology . In J. Rolf, A. Masten, D. Cicchettie, K. Nuechterlein, & S. Weinteraub (Eds.), *Risk and protective factors in the development of psychopathology* (pp. 2–28). New York: Cambridge University Press.

Cohen, S., & Willis, T. A. (1985). Stress, social support, and the buffering hypothesis. *Psychological Bulletin, 98,* 310–357.

Coles, R. (1986). *The moral life of children*. New York: The Atlantic Monthly Press.

Connell, J. P. (1987). Structural equation modeling and the study of child development: A question of goodness of fit. *Child Development, 58*, 167–175.

Consortium on the School-Based Promotion of Social Competence. (1994). The school-based promotion of social competence: Theory, research, practice, and policy. In R. J. Haggerty, L. R. Sherrod, N. Garmezy, &. M. Rutter (Eds.), *Stress, risk, and resilience in children and adolescents: Process, mechanisms, and interventions* (pp. 268–316). Cambridge, England: Cambridge University Press.

Cowen, E. L. (1991). In pursuit of wellness. *American Psychologist, 46*, 404–408.

Cowen, E. L. (1994). The enhancement of psychological wellness: Challenges and opportunities. *American Journal of Community Psychology, 22*, 401–415.

Cross, T. L., Coleman, L. J., & Stewart, R. A. (1995). Psychosocial diversity among gifted adolescents: An exploratory study of two groups. *Roeper Review, 17*, 181–185.

Dai, D. Y., & Feldhusen, J. F. (1996). Goal orientations of gifted students. *Gifted and Talented International, 11*, 84–88.

Doll, E. & Lyon, M. A. (1998). Risk and resilience: Implications for the delivery of educational and mental health services in schools. *School Psychology Review, 27*, 348–363.

Elder, G. H., Caspi, A., & van Nguyen, T. (1986). Resourceful and vulnerable children: Family influence in hard times. In R. K. Silbereisen & K. Eyferth (Eds.), *Development as action in context* (pp. 167–186). Berlin: Springer-Verlag.

Emerick, L. J. (1992). Academic underachievement among the gifted: Students' perceptions of factors that reverse the pattern. *Gifted Child Quarterly, 36*, 140–146.

Ford, D. (1994). Nurturing resilience in gifted Black youth. *Roeper Review, 17*, 80–85.

Ford, D. Y., & Harris, J. J., III (1990). On discovering the hidden treasures of gifted and talented Black children. *Roeper Review, 13*, 27–32.

Forman, S. G., & Kalafat, J. (1998). Substance abuse and suicide: Promoting resilience against self-destructive behavior in youth. *School Psychology Review, 27*, 398–406.

Garland, A. F., & Zigler, E. (1999). Emotional and behavioral problems among highly intellectually gifted youth. *Roeper Review, 22*, 41–44.

Garmezy, N. (1985). Stress-resistant children: The search for protective factors. In J. E. Stevenson (Ed.), *Recent research in developmental psychopathology: Journal of Child Psychology and Psychiatry book* (Supp. 4, pp. 213–233). Oxford, England: Pergamon.

Garmezy, N., & Rutter, M. (1983). *Stress, coping, and development in children*. New York: McGraw-Hill.

Garmezy, N., & Tellegen, A. (1984). Studies of stress-resistant children: Methods, variables, and preliminary findings. In F. Morrison, C. Ford, & D. Keating (Eds.), *Advances in applied developmental psychology* (Vol. 1, pp. 1–52). New York: Academic.

**120**

Glueck, S., & Glueck, E. (1950). *Unraveling juvenile delinquency*. New York: The Commonwealth Fund.

Gordon, E. W., & Song, L. D. (1994). Variations in the experience of resilience. In M. C. Wang & E. W. Gordon (Eds.), *Educational resilience in inner-city America: Challenges and prospects* (pp. 27–43). Hillsdale, NJ: Erlbaum.

Haggerty, R. J., Sherrod, L. R., Garmezy, N., & Rutter, M. (Eds.). (1994). *Stress, risk, and resilience in children and adolescents: Process, mechanisms, and interventions*. Cambridge, England: Cambridge University Press.

Hébert, T. P., & Beardsley, T. M. (2001). Jermaine: A critical case study of a gifted Black child living in rural poverty. *Gifted Child Quarterly, 45*, 85–103

Herman, J. L. (1992). *Trauma and recovery*. New York: Basic Books.

Kline, B. E., & Short, E. B. (1991a). Changes in emotional resilience: Gifted adolescent females. *Roeper Review, 13,* 118–121.

Kline, B. E., & Short, E. B. (1991b). Changes in emotional resilience: Gifted adolescent boys. *Roeper Review, 13,* 184–187.

Lazarus, R. S., & Folkman, S. (1984). *Stress appraisal and coping*. New York: McGraw-Hill.

Luthar, S. S., & Zigler, E. (1991). Vulnerability and competence: A review of research on resilience in childhood. *American Journal of Orthopsychiatry, 61,* 6–22.

Magnusson, D., & Bergmum, L. R. (1990). A pattern approach to the study of pathways from childhood to adulthood. In L. N. Robins & M. Rutter (Eds.), *Straight and devious pathways from childhood to adulthood* (pp. 101–115). Cambridge, England: Cambridge University Press.

Masten, A. S., & Garmezy, N. (1990). Resilience and development: Contributions from the study of children who overcome adversity. *Development and Psychopathology, 2,* 425–444.

McMillan, J. H., & Reed, D. F. (1994). At risk students and resiliency: Factors contributing to academic success. *Clearing House, 67,* 137–140.

Moon, S. M., Jurich, J. A., & Feldhusen, J. F. (1998). Families of gifted children: Cradles of development. In R. Friedman & K. B. Rogers (Eds.), *Talent in context: Historical and social perspectives* (pp. 81–99). Washington, DC: American Psychological Association

Murphy, L. B., & Moriarty, A. E. (1976). *Vulnerability, coping, and growth*. New Haven, CT: Yale University Press.

Noble, K., Subotnik, R., & Arnold, K. (1999). To thine own self be true: A new model of female talent development. *Gifted Child Quarterly, 43,* 140–149.

Pajares, F. (1996). Self-efficacy beliefs and mathematical problem solving of gifted students. *Contemporary Educational Psychology, 86,* 543–578.

Pianta, R. C., & Walsh, D. J. (1998). Applying the construct of resilience in schools: Cautions from a developmental systems perspective. *School Psychology Review, 27,* 407–417.

Pufal-Struzik, I. (1999). Self-actualization and other personality dimensions as predictors of mental health of intellectually gifted students. *Roeper Review, 22,* 44–47.

Reis, S. M., Hébert, T. P., Diaz, E. I., Maxfield, L. R., & Ratley, M. E. (1995). *Case studies of talented students who achieve and underachieve in an urban high school* (Research Monograph 95114). Storrs: The National Research Center on the Gifted and Talented, The University of Connecticut.

Rhodes, J. E. (1994). Older and wiser: Mentoring relationships in childhood and adolescence. *The Journal of Primary Prevention, 14,* 187–196.

Rutter, M. (1983). Stress, coping, and development: Some issues and some questions. In N. Garmezy & M. Rutter (Eds.), *Primary prevention of psychopathology: Social competence in children* (Vol. 3, pp. 49–74). Hanover, NH: University Press of New England.

Rutter, M. (1987). Psychosocial resilience and protective mechanisms. *American Journal of Orthopsychiatry, 57,* 316–331.

Schuler, P. (2000). Perfectionism and the gifted adolescent. *Journal of Secondary Gifted Education, 11,* 183–196

Seligman, M. (1995). *The optimistic child.* New York: Harper Perennial.

Sytsma, R. (2000). *Gifted and talented programs in America's high schools: A preliminary survey report.* Storrs: The National Research Center on the Gifted and Talented, The University of Connecticut.

Werner, E. E. (1984). Resilient children. *Young Children, 40,* 68–72

Werner, E. E., & Smith, R. S. (1982). *Vulnerable but invincible: A longitudinal study of resilient children and youth.* New York: McGraw-Hill.

# Gifted Children and Youth With Special Needs

# GIFTED FEMALES IN ELEMENTARY AND SECONDARY SCHOOL

## by Sally M. Reis, Ph.D.

*It is obvious that the values of women differ very often from the values which have been made by the other sex. Yet, it is the masculine values that prevail.*
—Virginia Woolf

Why do some talented women achieve ambitious goals and gain prominence or eminence while others who once had at least as much potential fail to achieve the dreams they had as young girls? Why do some bright young girls begin to underachieve in school, and why do some women who excelled in school remain in unchallenging jobs? Research with talented females has revealed a number of external barriers, personality factors, personal priorities, and social and emotional issues that have consistently emerged as contributing reasons why many either cannot or do not realize their potential. Not all gifted females experience the same issues, but almost all face a combination of the following: dilemmas about abilities and talents, personal decisions about family, ambivalence of parents and teachers toward developing high levels of competence, decisions about duty and caring (meeting the needs of others before one's own), as well as other personal, religious, and social issues (Reis, 1998).

Personal and social and emotional issues occur across women's lifespans. Some affect the youngest girls and some are apparent only to women who become involved in serious relationships as adults or have children later in their lives. Older gifted women can resolve many personal issues they encountered earlier; but, in reality, some of these dilemmas cannot be resolved to the benefit of everyone involved. Rather, some dilemmas shift, are resolved, or are exacerbated when life changes occur, such as the maturation of children, the dissolution or reemergence of relationships, or a change of circumstances at home or work. One cannot, then, discuss gifted girls without discussing gifted women because many young gifted girls believe that they can "do it all" or "have it all," while many older gifted females have learned that they cannot. Preventing discouragement and retreat and learning more about why hopes fade is the reason that much of the research about gifted girls and women continues.

Talented females' belief in their ability and feelings of self-confidence tend to be undermined and diminished during childhood and adolescence. In a study of five talented adolescents, not one of them attributed her success in school to extraordinary ability (Callahan, Cunningham, & Plucker, 1994). Despite a degree of "feminine modesty," some gifted students do, however, acknowledge their abilities despite admitting to having fears about the future (Reis, Hébert, Diaz, Maxfield, & Ratley, 1995). The following review of research focuses on the social and emotional issues faced by gifted females during childhood, adolescence and young adulthood, and includes issues related to the external and internal barriers that they experience.

## External Barriers

Almost from birth, gifted and talented females find themselves in a world of limiting stereotypes and barriers to achievement presented by parents, school, and the larger society. Moreover, when the majority of leaders, politicians, artists, musicians, and inventors are male, a young female may not develop strong philosophical beliefs about her own creative potential. A brief discussion of some external barriers follows.

## Parental Influences on Talented Females

Pre-eminent among the influences on talented females are parents' attitudes and beliefs about their children's academic self-perceptions and achievement (Hess, Holloway, Dickson, & Price, 1984; McGillicuddy-De Lisi, 1985; Parsons, Adler, & Kaczala, 1982; Stevenson & Newman, 1986), which often supercede children's self-perceptions about their own performance (Parsons et al., 1982). Phillips (1987) confirmed this finding in her study of high-ability students, and a recent study of parental influence on math self-concept in gifted female adolescents (Dickens, 1990) found consistently significant correlations between parental expectations and student math self-concept. Parental opinions matter greatly to young girls, and memories of negative parental comments haunt gifted and talented women decades after they have left home (Reis, 1995, 1998).

## Issues Relating to Teachers

Teachers are usually able to identify gifted boys, but are often surprised to learn that a girl is considered smart, frequently because gifted girls are very successful at hiding their intelligence and silencing their voices (Kramer, 1985; Sadker & Sadker, 1994). Teachers are less accurate, too, in nominating girls than boys who are likely to do well on the quantitative subtest of the SAT (Kissane, 1986). Teachers, in fact, often like smart girls less than they like other students. Cooley, Chauvin, and Karnes (1984) found that both male and female teachers regarded smart boys as more competent than gifted girls in critical and logical thinking skills and in creative problem solving, while they saw smart girls as more competent in creative writing. Male teachers viewed female students in a more traditional manner than did female teachers, however, perceiving bright girls to be more emotional, more high strung, more gullible,

**127**

less imaginative, less curious, less inventive, less individualistic, and less impulsive than males.

Teachers have also been found to believe and reinforce one of the most prevalent sex stereotypes: that males have more innate ability, while females must work harder. Fennema (1990), commenting on the role of teacher beliefs on mathematics performance, reported that, in one study (Fennema, Peterson, Carpenter, & Lubinski, 1990), "teachers selected ability as the cause of their most capable males' success 58% of the time, and the cause of their best females' success only 33% of the time" (p. 178). Fennema and her colleagues also concluded that, even though teachers did not tend to engage in sex-role stereotyping in general, they did stereotype their best students in the area of mathematics, attributing characteristics such as volunteering answers, enjoyment of mathematics, and independence to males. Recent research reported by Reis (1996) has further indicated that some teachers expect less from females than from males, especially with regard to achievement in mathematics and science. Girls may internalize these lowered expectations very early in life.

## Grades in School

Girls get higher grades than boys in both elementary and secondary school (Achenbach, 1970; American College Testing Program, 1989; Coleman, 1961; Davis, 1964; Kimball, 1989), but this phenomenon is not necessarily positive for gifted girls. Their attainment of higher grades, when contrasted with their lower scores on some standardized tests, may contribute to their beliefs that they are not as "bright" as boys and can only succeed by working harder.

## Internal Barriers (Personality Factors/ Personal Choices and Decisions)

Talented females have to deal with a number of personality factors, personal priorities, and decisions that have emerged as the reasons why many of them either cannot or do not realize their potential in academic areas and their professions.

## Loss of Belief in Abilities and Self-Confidence

To varying degrees, some gifted girls lose their enthusiasm for learning and their courage to speak out and display their abilities, a loss that begins in elementary school and continues through college and graduate school. These girls may increasingly doubt their intellectual competence, perceive themselves as less capable than they actually are, and believe that boys can rely on innate ability, while they must work harder to succeed (Arnold, 1995; Bell, 1989; Cramer, 1989; Hany, 1994; Kramer, 1991; Leroux, 1988; Perleth & Heller, 1994; Reis & Callahan, 1989; Subotnik, 1988). Some of this research has also indicated that girls try to avoid competition in order to preserve relationships, even if that means that they don't take the opportunity to use their skills.

Reviewing the literature, Kline and Short (1991) found that the self-confidence and self-perceived abilities of gifted girls steadily decreased from elementary grades through high school. Buescher, Olszewski, and Higham (1987) found gifted boys and girls to be more alike than peers not identified as gifted except in one critical area: the recognition and acceptance of their own level of ability. Interviews with middle school gifted females revealed that girls avoided displays of outstanding intellectual ability and searched for better ways to conform to the norm of the peer group (Callahan, Cunningham, & Plucker, 1994).

## Social Problems and Isolation

Being identified as bright or talented may create social problems for females (Bell, 1989; Buescher, Olszewski, & Higham, 1987; Eccles, Midgley, & Adler, 1984; Kerr, Colangelo, & Gaeth, 1988; Kramer, 1991; Reis, 1987, 1995; Reis, Callahan, & Goldsmith, 1996). Bell identified several dilemmas facing gifted girls that may contribute to personality-development issues later in adolescence. She found that gifted girls often perceive achievement and affiliation as opposite issues because, to girls, competition means that someone wins and someone loses. The gifted girls that Bell studied encountered great difficulty with comparisons and downplayed their own accomplishments. The girls also feared social isolation as a consequence of their success.

**129**

Fearing their peers' disapproval, bright young women may deliberately understate their abilities in order to avoid being seen as physically unattractive or lacking in social competence. In other words, they may "play dumb." Parents may also send negative messages about how girls should act, how polite they should be, how they should dress, and how often they should speak out and in what situations.

## Concerns About Future Education, Career, and Family

Reis, Callahan, and Goldsmith (1996) queried gifted male and female adolescents about a number of future issues in their lives. When asked what they would be doing after they graduated from college, boys were more likely than girls to name a specific job or career (46% vs. 27%) and to state that women should not work after they had children (65% versus 25%). Some girls still thought they would need to support the family (19%), but fewer boys thought that support was important (11%). Fourteen percent of the boys (and none of the girls) explicitly stated that taking care of the children was a woman's responsibility. Only a very small number of the boys (5%), as compared to the overwhelming majority of the girls, said they expected both partners to work and to share the childcare.

## Multipotentiality

Women who demonstrate multipotentiality usually have an eagerness to learn or an endless thirst for knowledge (Ehrlich, 1982); uniformly high scores across ability and achievement tests (Sanborn, 1979); multiple educational, vocational, and leisure interests at comparable intensities; and complex personality factors. Women with high potential and multiple interests often have multiple academic, career, and leisure possibilities, and these choices constitute multipotentiality. For some, having many choices is beneficial because they result in a variety of options. Others, however, cannot find their niche, make it on their own, or choose a vocational path (Fredrickson, 1979, 1986; Jepsen, 1979; Kerr, 1981; Marshall, 1981; Sanborn, 1979; Schroer & Dorn,

1986) since it is not possible to do all that they would like to do and are capable of doing.

## Perfectionism

Perfectionism can cause talented women to set unreasonable goals and to spend their lives trying to achieve perfection in work, home, body, children, wardrobe, and other areas (see Schuler, this volume). It is worth noting, however, that some aspects of perfectionism affect gifted women more than men. In a recent study on perfectionism in gifted middle school adolescents, Schuler (1997) found concern over mistakes, perceived parental expectations, and perceived parental criticisms to be salient factors for the gifted unhealthy/dysfunctional female perfectionists. They were fixated on avoiding mistakes, which resulted in a high state of anxiety. Unlike the healthy female perfectionists, the unhealthy females were concerned about making errors because of both their own high standards and those of their parents, and they worked to please others—teachers, peers, or parents—rather than themselves. They viewed their parents' perfectionism negatively and perceived parental expectations as demands to be perfect in everything they did.

## Achievement and Underachievement in Gifted Teenage Girls

Why do some gifted young girls succeed while others of similar ability fail to achieve at levels that might be expected given their potential? Reis et al. (1995) compared culturally diverse groups of young female achievers and underachievers in a low socioeconomic high school and found that the talented, young, achieving women were extremely determined to be independent. Several said they wanted a different life from that of their mothers. Many of the female achievers explained that their parents had helped instill their determination to succeed. The high-achieving female students indicated that they rarely dated or became romantically involved; were extremely supportive of other high-achieving students; became involved in multiple activities; and were independent, resilient, and dedicated to a career.

# Conclusion

In most professional fields and occupations, men surpass women in both the professional and creative accomplishments, at least when we consider traditional standards of accomplishment. It may be argued that these facts alone are not an adequate measurement of female underachievement; however, it is important to recognize that many talented women look back at what they perceive as lost opportunities. If female underachievement is best measured by the many talented women in our society who look back at their lives with feelings of regret, it then becomes our responsibility to help future generations of gifted and talented females before they, too, underachieve.

# References

Achenbach, T. M. (1970). Standardization of a research instrument for identifying associative responding in children. *Developmental Psychology, 2,* 283–291.

American College Testing Program. (1989). *State and national trend data for students who take the ACT Assessment.* Iowa City: American College Testing Program.

Arnold, K. D. (1995). *Lives of promise.* San Francisco: Jossey-Bass.

Bell, L. A. (1989). Something's wrong here and it's not me: Challenging the dilemmas that block girls' success. *Journal for the Education of the Gifted, 12,* 118–130.

Buescher, T. M., Olszewski, P., & Higham, S. J. (1987, May). *Influences on strategies adolescents use to cope with their own recognized talents* (Report No. EC 200 755). Paper presented at the biennial meeting of the Society for Research in Child Development, Baltimore.

Callahan, C. M., Cunningham, C. M., & Plucker, J. A. (1994). Foundations for the future: The socio-emotional development of gifted, adolescent women. *Roeper Review, 17,* 99–105.

Coleman, J. (1961). *The adolescent society.* New York: Free Press.

Cooley, D., Chauvin, J., & Karnes, F. (1984). Gifted females: A comparison of attitudes by male and female teachers. *Roeper Review, 6,* 164–167.

Cramer, R. H. (1989). Attitudes of gifted boys and girls toward math: A qualitative study. *Roeper Review, 11,* 128–133.

Davis, J. A. (1964). *Great aspirations: The school plans of America's college seniors.* Chicago: Aldine.

Dickens, M. N. (1990). *Parental influences on the mathematics self-concept of high-achieving adolescent girls.* Unpublished doctoral dissertation, University of Virginia, Charlottesville.

Eccles, J. S., Midgley, C., & Adler, T. F. (1984). Grade-related changes in the school environment: Effects on achievement motivation. In J. Nicholls (Ed.), *Advances in motivation and achievement* (Vol. 3, pp. 283–331). Greenwich, CT: JAI Press.

Ehrlich, V. (1982). *Gifted children: A guide for parents and teachers.* Englewood Cliffs, NJ: Prentice-Hall.

Fennema, E. (1990). Teachers' beliefs and gender differences in mathematics. In E. Fennema & G. Leder (Eds.), *Mathematics and gender* (pp. 1–9). New York: Teachers College Press.

Fennema, E., Peterson, P. L., Carpenter, T. P., & Lubinski, C. A. (1990). Teachers' attributions and beliefs about girls, boys, and mathematics. *Educational Studies in Mathematics, 21,* 55–69.

Fredrickson, R. H. (1979). Preparing gifted and talented students for the world of work. *Journal of Counseling and Development, 64,* 556–557.

Fredrickson, R. H. (1986). The multipotential as vocational decision-makers. In R. H. Fredrickson & J. W. M. Rothney (Eds.), *Recognizing and assisting multipotential youth* (pp. 179–188). Columbus, OH: Merrill.

Hany, E. A. (1994). The development of basic cognitive components of technical creativity: A longitudinal comparison of children and youth with high and average intelligence. In R. F. Subotnik & K. D. Arnold (Eds.), *Beyond Terman: Contemporary longitudinal studies of giftedness and talent* (pp. 115–154). Norwood, NJ: Ablex.

Hess, R. D., Holloway, S. D., Dickson, W. P., & Price, G. G. (1984). Maternal variables as predictors of children's school readiness and later achievement in vocabulary and mathematics in sixth grade. *Child Development, 55,* 1902–1912.

Jepsen, D. A. (1979). Helping gifted adolescents with career exploration. In N. Colangelo & R. T. Zaffrann (Eds.), *New voices in counseling the gifted* (pp. 277–283). Dubuque, IA: Kendall/Hunt.

Kerr, B. A. (1981). Career education strategies for the gifted. *Journal of Career Education, 7,* 318–324.

Kerr, B., Colangelo, N., & Gaeth, J. (1988). Gifted adolescents' attitudes toward their giftedness. *Gifted Child Quarterly, 32,* 245–247.

Kimball, M. M. (1989). A new perspective on women's math achievement. *Psychological Bulletin, 105,* 198–214.

Kissane, B. V. (1986). Selection of mathematically talented students. *Educational Studies in Mathematics, 17,* 221–241.

Kline, B. E., & Short, E. B. (1991). Changes in emotional resilience: Gifted adolescent females. *Roeper Review, 13,* 118–121.

Kramer, L. R. (1985, April). *Social interaction and perceptions of ability: A study of gifted adolescent females.* Paper presented at the annual meeting of the American Educational Research Association. Chicago.

Kramer, L. R. (1991). The social construction of ability perceptions: An ethnographic study of gifted adolescent girls. *Journal of Early Adolescence, 11,* 340–362.

**133**

Gifted Females

Leroux, J. A. (1988). Voices from the classroom: Academic and social self-concepts of gifted adolescents. *Journal for the Education of the Gifted, 11*, 3–18.

Marshall, B. C. (1981). A career decision making pattern of gifted and talented adolescents: Implications for career education. *Journal of Career Education, 7*, 305–310.

McGillicuddy-De Lisi, A. V. (1985). The relationship between parental beliefs and children's cognitive level. In R. Sigel (Ed.), *Parental belief systems* (pp. 7–24). Hillsdale, NJ: Erlbaum.

Parsons, J. E., Adler, T. F., & Kaczala, C. (1982). Socialization of achievement attitudes and beliefs: Parental influences. *Child Development, 53*, 310–321.

Perleth, C., & Heller, K. A. (1994). The Munich longitudinal study of giftedness. In R. F. Subotnik & K. D. Arnold (Eds.), *Beyond Terman: Contemporary longitudinal studies of giftedness and talent* (pp. 77–114). Norwood, NJ: Ablex.

Phillips, D. A. (1987). Socialization of perceived academic competence among highly competent children. *Child Development, 58*, 1308–1320.

Reis, S. M. (1987). We can't change what we don't recognize: Understanding the special needs of gifted females. *Gifted Child Quarterly, 31*, 83–89.

Reis, S. M. (1995). Talent ignored, talent diverted: The cultural context underlying giftedness in females. *Gifted Child Quarterly, 39*, 162–170.

Reis, S. M. (1996). Older women's reflections on eminence: Obstacles and opportunities. In K. D. Arnold, K. D. Noble, & R. F. Subotnik (Eds.), *Remarkable women: Perspectives on female talent development* (pp. 149–168). Cresskill, NJ: Hampton Press.

Reis, S. M. (1998). *Work left undone: Compromises and challenges of talented females.* Mansfield Center, CT: Creative Learning Press.

Reis, S. M., & Callahan, C. M. (1989). Gifted females: They've come a long way— or have they? *Journal for the Education of the Gifted, 12*, 99–117.

Reis, S. M., Callahan, C. M., & Goldsmith, D. (1996). Attitudes of adolescent gifted girls and boys toward education, achievement, and the future. In K. D. Arnold, K. D. Noble, & R. F. Subotnik (Eds.), *Remarkable women: Perspectives on female talent development* (pp. 209–224). Cresskill, NJ: Hampton Press.

Reis, S. M., Hébert, T. P., Diaz, E. I., Maxfield, L. R., & Ratley, M. E. (1995). *Case studies of talented students who achieve and underachieve in an urban high school.* Manuscript in preparation.

Sadker, M., & Sadker, D. (1994). *Failing at fairness: How America's schools cheat girls.* New York: Charles Scribner's Sons.

Sanborn, M. P. (1979). Career development: Problems of gifted and talented students. In N. Colangelo & R. T. Zaffrann (Eds.), *New voices in counseling the gifted* (pp. 284–300). Dubuque, IA: Kendall/Hunt.

Schroer, A. C. P., & Dorn, F. J. (1986). Enhancing the career and personal development of gifted college students. *Journal of Counseling and Development, 64*, 567–571.

Schuler, P. A. (1997). *Characteristics and perceptions of perfectionism in gifted adolescents in a rural school environment.* Unpublished doctoral dissertation, University of Connecticut, Storrs.

Stevenson, H. W., & Newman, R. S. (1986). Long-term prediction of achievement in mathematics and reading. *Child Development, 57,* 646–659.

Subotnik, R. (1988). The motivation to experiment: A study of gifted adolescents' attitudes toward scientific research. *Journal for the Education of the Gifted, 11,* 19–35.

**135**

# 14 GIFTED MALES

by **Thomas P. Hébert, Ph.D.**

t is a difficult time to be a boy in this country. Such is the message being reported in today's popular press (Kantrowitz & Kalb, 1998; Sommers, 2000a), and, along with the media, bookstores across the country now offer a collection of recently published books calling attention to the plight of the young American male. In addition, psychologists and gender experts are involved in debates over whether or not problems faced by girls are more difficult than those facing boys (Gurian, 1998; Kindlon & Thompson, 1999; Sommers, 2000b). Educators are claiming that the destructive effects of society's failure to recognize boys' emotional needs are becoming evident in classrooms (Pollack, 1998).

Although the controversy regarding the "boys' crisis" remains heated, little attention is being drawn to issues facing gifted young men. While numerous researchers in gifted education have examined issues facing gifted females, research addressing the social and emotional development of gifted males is limited. The small body (Hébert, 2000a, 2000b; Wilcove, 1998) of research on gifted males indicates a number of social and emotional issues central to their development, including: identity and belief in self, appreciating psychological androgyny, emotional sensitivity, and empathy. Several of these same issues have also been examined through a cultural lens. The following discussion will review these research findings and highlight areas for future research.

## Belief in Self

The most important developmental task of adolescence is the formation of a consistent self-identity (Erikson, 1968). Grotevant (1987) stressed the idea of identity development as being a normal process in adolescence when young people take on problem-solving behaviors and search for information about themselves or their environment in order to make important life choices. In Hébert's (2000a) study of gifted, high-achieving males in an urban high school, a strong belief in self was identified as the most important factor influencing the success of the young men. These young men had developed a strong belief in self that provided them with the energy, the drive, and the tools they needed to face life's challenges. They had definite aspirations that were aligned closely with their personal qualities, strengths, and talents. They saw their aspirations as obtainable since they realized they had an internal motivation that kept them driven to succeed. Just as an inner will had allowed them to succeed in their urban school experiences, a motivational force would keep them focused and allow them to reach their goals in life. Several qualities merged in these young men to form this belief in self: sensitivity, multicultural appreciation, aspirations, and an inner will.

An important part of that strong belief in self was a heightened sensitivity, a quality that allowed these young men to appreciate, for example, the individual differences in people around them, the beauty of a poem, or a relationship with a younger handicapped child learning to swim. They had developed empathy, emotional self-awareness, and emotional expressivity, qualities that allowed them to balance their emotional lives as they developed their self-identities. They viewed their ability to express themselves emotionally as a quality that would help them become more successful in life. Their emotions were seen as functional tools that assisted them in making sense of their life experiences and allowed them to feel secure as sensitive males in an urban setting.

Hébert's (2000a) findings are consistent with what theorists have proposed regarding heightened sensitivity within gifted individuals. Emotionally intense males can be sensitive to people around them, the feelings of others, criticism from others, and the injustices of the world in which they live (Piechowski, 1997). In Hébert's study, the young men's sensitivity was appreciated, therefore they were able to express it. However, if a sensitive, intelligent young man grows up experiencing criticism and ridicule in a culture that does not value sensitivity within males, he may suppress his sensitivity and consequently withdraw emotionally from others around him. The cost of this withdrawal may lead to a number of more serious problems (Piechowski). Therefore, it is important that a gifted male who is highly sensitive find others like him who will appreciate this characteristic and support him emotionally. According to Levant (1992), young men who benefit from validation of their sensitivity are capable of developing empathy, emotional self-awareness, and the ability to express their emotions. Developing these skills help men in becoming more successful in relationships, families, and professional settings.

## Psychological Androgyny

Along with emotional sensitivity, psychological androgyny has also been identified as a characteristic of gifted individuals. Psychological androgyny is defined as "a person's ability to be at the same time aggressive and nurturant, sensitive and rigid, dominant and submissive, regardless of gender" (Csikszentmihalyi,

**139**

1996, p. 71). Csikszentmihalyi noted that a psychologically androgynous person "doubles his or her responses and can interact with the world in terms of a much richer and varied spectrum of opportunities" (p. 71). Barron (1957), Roe (1959), and Torrance (1967, 1995) have all cited evidence to support this phenomenon within highly intelligent, creative individuals. Miedzian (1991) and Shapiro (1993) noted that psychologically androgynous men have broader notions of appropriate or inappropriate male behavior, and in no way does this manner of thinking affect their masculine identity.

In a study of gifted university males pursuing elementary education careers, Hébert (2000b) found that, as part of their identity, the gifted young men displayed empathic qualities and comfort with their psychological androgyny. They recognized characteristics traditionally thought to be feminine within their personalities and they valued those traits. Their identity appeared to involve a sincere caring quality. They knew they were empathic, and they appreciated that quality within themselves because they knew it allowed them to be better men and professionals. Their empathy incorporated an appreciation for the developmental struggles faced by young children in elementary classrooms.

Hébert's findings were consistent with Wilcove's (1998) in another study exploring the gender schemata of gifted males. Wilcove's participants all spoke of the importance of their being able to express themselves emotionally. They valued their emotionality, but did not view it as a gender-specific trait, and they acknowledged that, in their desire to express their emotions, they were atypical of most males.

## Culturally Diverse Males

Gifted males from culturally diverse backgrounds may face additional challenges in their social and emotional development as gifted young men. Unfortunately, research concerning Asian American students in general is limited, and there is a paucity of research concerning gifted Asian American males. Most of the literature addresses the identification of gifted Asian American students but does not offer suggestions for teaching or counseling them (Plucker, 1996).

As for gifted Hispanic males, the research is also limited. Research by Cordeiro (1990) and Cordeiro and Carspecken (1993) investigated 20 highly successful Hispanic high school students from low socioeconomic backgrounds in a large southwestern urban center. Cordeiro found that, in order for Hispanic achievers to succeed, they had to construct an identity at school that allowed them to separate themselves from both the school culture and the minority Latino culture of their neighborhoods. Furthermore, the students in Cordeiro's study carried the responsibility for academic success alone, without full understanding or support from their families. Friendships with other achieving Latino students, particularly in middle school, were crucial to their success, and institutional segregation was very important in solidifying the distinctive nature of the achieving Latino youth culture.

Cordeiro and Carspecken (1993) explained that entrance into the achieving Latino group involved the development of a "success-facilitating interpretive scheme" (p. 289). This enabled students to construct Hispanic identities distinct from what they regarded as "typically Hispanic" and "play the achiever's game" (p. 289), which included involvement in part-time jobs and extensive extracurricular activities. Diaz (1998) explored the self and environmental perceptions of talented high school students of Puerto Rican descent who were underachieving and found that the absence of early appropriate academic experiences thwarted the students' possibilities for developing their abilities and talents later in life.

Ford's (1992, 1993, 1995) extensive research on gifted African American youth calls attention to the fact that gifted Black males face additional challenges that impede their achievement and success. Irvine (1991) found, that across the educational spectrum, African American males were more likely to be labeled deviant, be described negatively, receive negative nonverbal cues, be misjudged by teachers, and receive less positive interaction and feedback. Ford (1996) also found that Black males were more pessimistic than Black females regarding the discrimination they experienced in their daily lives. Ford (1992, 1993, 1995) has noted that gifted

Black students may experience more psychological and social and emotional problems than nonidentified Black students because they may feel less accepted by peers, teachers, and parents by assimilating a value system regarding education held by the dominant culture.

## Implications

The research reviewed highlights important considerations for designing interventions for gifted males. Within the body of literature, some evidence of successful strategies has been identified for supporting the emotional development of gifted males. Supportive male mentors have been found to play a significant role in nurturing the emotional health of intelligent young men across cultural groups (Ford, 1996; Hébert, 1995; Hébert & Olenchak, 2000). In addition, Hébert (2000a) found that providing sensitive intelligent young men with outlets for their emotionality, such as community service activities that focus on addressing societal problems, was beneficial.

As researchers and educators begin to examine the needs of males in this country, it is important that we invest our efforts in addressing the specific needs of gifted males. As indicated by the limited research available on this population, more studies are necessary to gain a better understanding of the social and emotional needs facing gifted males and to develop appropriate interventions.

## References

Barron, F. (1957). Originality in relation to personality and intellect. *Journal of Personality, 25,* 730–742.

Cordeiro, P. A. (1990). *Growing away from the barrio: An ethnography of high-achieving at-risk Hispanic youths at two urban high schools.* Unpublished doctoral dissertation, University of Houston.

Cordeiro, P. A., & Carspecken, P. F. (1993). How a minority of the minority succeed: A case study of twenty Hispanic achievers. *Qualitative Studies in Education, 6,* 277–290.

Csikszentmihalyi, M. (1996). *Creativity: Flow and the psychology of discovery and invention.* New York: HarperCollins.

Diaz, E. I. (1998). Perceived factors influencing the academic underachievement of talented students of Puerto Rican descent. *Gifted Child Quarterly, 42*, 105–122.

Erikson, E. H. (1968). *Identity: Youth and crisis.* New York: Norton.

Ford, D. Y. (1992). Determinants of underachievement among gifted, above-average, and average Black students. *Roeper Review, 14*, 130–136.

Ford, D. Y. (1993). An investigation into the paradox of underachievement among gifted Black students. *Roeper Review, 16*, 78–84.

Ford, D. Y. (1995). *Correlates of underachievement among gifted and nongifted Black students.* Storrs: National Research Center on the Gifted and Talented, The University of Connecticut.

Ford, D. Y. (1996). *Reversing underachievement among gifted Black students.* New York: Teachers College Press.

Grotevant, H. D. (1987). Toward a process model of identity formation. *Journal of Adolescent Research, 2*, 203–222.

Gurian, M. (1998). *A fine young man.* New York: Putnam.

Hébert, T. P. (1995). Coach Brogan: South Central High School's answer to academic achievement. *Journal of Secondary Gifted Education, 7*, 310–323.

Hébert, T. P. (2000a). Defining belief in self: Intelligent young men in an urban high school. *Gifted Child Quarterly, 44*, 91–114.

Hébert, T. P. (2000b). Gifted males pursuing careers in elementary education. *Journal for the Education of the Gifted, 24*, 7–45.

Hébert, T. P., & Olenchak, F. R. (2000). Mentors for gifted underachieving males: Developing potential and realizing promise. *Gifted Child Quarterly, 44*, 196–207.

Irvine, J. J. (1991). *Black students and school failure: Policies, practices, and prescriptions.* New York: Praeger.

Kantrowitz, B., & Kalb, C. (1998, May 11). Boys will be boys. *Newsweek*, pp. 55–60.

Kindlon, D., & Thompson, M. (1999). *Raising Cain: Protecting the emotional life of boys.* New York: Ballantine.

Levant, R. (1992). Toward the reconstruction of masculinity. *Journal of Family Psychology, 5*, 379–402.

Miedzian, M. (1991). *Boys will be boys: Breaking the link between masculinity and violence.* New York: Doubleday.

Piechowski, M. M. (1997). Emotional giftedness: The measure of intrapersonal intelligence. In N. Colangelo & G. A. Davis (Eds.), *Handbook of gifted education* (2nd. ed., pp. 366–381). Boston: Allyn and Bacon.

Plucker, J. A. (1996). Gifted Asian American students: Identification, curricular and counseling concerns. *Journal for the Education of the Gifted, 19*, 315–343.

Pollack, W. S. (1998). *Real boys: Rescuing our sons from the myths of boyhood.* New York: Random House.

Roe, A. (1959). Personal problems and science. In C. W. Taylor (Ed.), *The third (1959) University of Utah research conference on the identification of creative scientific talent* (pp. 202–212). Salt Lake City: University of Utah Press.

Shapiro, J. L. (1993). *The measure of a man.* New York: Delacorte.

**143**

Sommers, C. H. (2000a, May). The war against boys. *Atlantic Monthly, 285*(5), 59–74.

Sommers, C. H. (2000b). *The war against boys: How misguided feminism is harming our young men.* New York: Simon & Schuster.

Torrance, E. P. (1967). Mental health and creative functioning. *Gifted Child Quarterly, 11,* 71–78.

Torrance, E. P. (1995). *Why fly? A philosophy of creativity.* Norwood, NJ: Ablex.

Wilcove, J. L. (1998). Perceptions of masculinity, femininity, and androgyny among a select cohort of gifted adolescent males. *Journal for the Education of the Gifted, 21,* 288–309.

# 15

# GIFTED STUDENTS WHO ARE GAY, LESBIAN, OR BISEXUAL

## by Sanford J. Cohn, Ph.D.

Homophobia forms the backdrop for the school lives of many gifted students, regardless of whether they are gay or straight (Anderson, 2001; Lipkin, 1999). Young people who appear to be outside the parameters of local gender-role stereotypes may bear the brunt of taunts by their schoolmates that are intended to remind them of their differences. Verbally gifted boys with artistic interests may be told that they are not masculine enough, and athletically, mathematically, or mechanically talented girls may be told that they are not feminine enough.

In youths who face the reality of being both gifted *and* gay (that is, gay, lesbian, bisexual, or even just questioning), feelings of being marginalized, both externally and internally, are intensified. Instead of being in the top 3% of their age group in intellectual potential, they fall within the 3–10% (depending upon one's source for an esti-

145

mate of gays, lesbians, and bisexuals [GLB] in the population at large) of that top 3%, dropping from a statistical probability of 3 in a 100 to 1–3 in 1,000. Accordingly, in a large urban high school of 3,000 or so students, one might expect to find only 3 to 9 students who are both gifted and gay. Spread across four grade levels, the likelihood of such individuals finding one another or even feeling safe seeking others like themselves is miniscule.

Feelings of alienation and isolation in this group of adolescents may be exacerbated by overwhelming anxiety as they become aware of a strong and outspoken political block of individuals in present-day society who argue, at best, that being gay is a sickness. But, the sense of vulnerability among these youths may be most affected by those mainstream adults in their lives who bear silent witness to acts of hate and intolerance around them. The youths may learn to hide who they really are, and populations in hiding are difficult to study. There have been only a handful of studies, discussed in the next section, that have examined the possible relationships between sexual orientation and cognitive abilities. Most of these studies examine whether or not there is an increased frequency of high verbal ability among boys and young men who identify themselves as gay and, to a lesser extent, high spatial or mathematical ability among girls and young women who identify themselves as lesbian.

Only *three* articles have appeared to date that explore the school experiences of gifted students who are also gay, lesbian, or bisexual. Two of these articles report findings from studies, and the third offers insights based on clinical experience. Methodological hurdles exist for researchers who attempt to study these youths, in addition to politics surrounding gay, lesbian, and bisexual individuals in our society. These include: educators and laypersons who do not acknowledge the historical and present-day contributions to our culture by gifted and talented individuals who were and are homosexual; individuals who do not show sensitivity to the issues and needs of gifted GLB youths; researchers who fear institutional or governmental reprisals for studying gifted GLB youths; and a lack of funding sources. In the relative absence of explicit studies of youths who are both gifted and GLB, inferences must be drawn about the experiences of these "doubly different" youths from the emerging literature concerning the psychology and development of GLB youths in general.

## Sexual Orientation and Cognitive Abilities

Being gifted in ways that run counter to typical sex-role behaviors exposes individuals to a variety of risks. While stereotypes exist in the minds of a vast majority of people in our society, the question remains as to the reality of an association between certain gifts and sexual orientation. Sex-typical behaviors have been well documented in nearly every field in social and behavioral sciences (Halpern, 1992). Examples range from sex-typical psychiatric diagnoses to selection of college majors. Some cognitive behaviors demonstrate no sex differences, others show relatively small differences, and still others reveal substantial and persistent sex differences. One of the largest sex differences favoring males is shown on tasks involving spatial-visual reasoning, particularly those tasks that involve transforming images in visual working memory and mental rotation (Halpern & Wright, 1996). In the context of mathematical reasoning, males have been disproportionately represented in the highest ranges of the mathematics section of the Scholastic Aptitude Test (SAT–M; Benbow, 1988). Some differences that favor females have been found in verbal fluency tasks; synonym generation tasks; reading; and performance on college tests in English composition, literature, and foreign languages (Stanley, 1993).

Differences in cognition among persons of differing sexual orientation yield more complex patterns of results than those demonstrated in studies of sex differences. The most consistent pattern of differences between heterosexual and homosexual males has emerged in studies of spatial-visual abilities. Heterosexual males repeatedly outperformed homosexual males on these tasks, and homosexual males outperformed females of unspecified sexual orientation (Gladue, Beatty, Larson, & Staton, 1990; Sanders & Ross-Field, 1986; Tuttle & Pillard, 1991; Willmott & Brierly, 1984). McCormick and Witelson (1991) found that heterosexual males demonstrated better visual-spatial ability than verbal ability, just the opposite pattern as that shown by heterosexual females. They also found that homosexual males tended to do equally well on tasks of both verbal and visual-spatial abilities.

Findings about verbal abilities have varied widely from study to study, depending in large part on the measures used. Homosexual

**147**

males were shown to perform better than heterosexual males and females (Tuttle and Pillard, 1991; Willmott and Brierly, 1984), somewhere between heterosexual males and females (McCormic and Witelson, 1991), or no different from heterosexual males (Gladue et al., 1990). The inconsistency of these results is understandable: As verbal ability is a heterogeneous construct, so measures of different subtasks would not be expected to yield similar results (Halpern, 1992); different measures of verbal ability assess different cognitive processes that are only slightly correlated with one another (Halpern); each of the studies contained very small numbers of subjects; and the subjects were not representative of the population at large.

In spite of the constraints, there remains an emergent pattern of differences in certain specific cognitive abilities among individuals of different sexual orientation, particularly between heterosexual and homosexual males. We remain without evidence, however, to address the question of whether or not females who are mathematically or visual-spatially talented or males with extreme verbal ability tend to have a disproportionately higher occurrence of homosexual orientation than the general population. Nor do we understand the impact of being homosexual on the development of talent or the influence of being gifted on the emergence of sexual identity. These questions can only be addressed directly in studies that target sexual orientation among highly talented individuals.

## Experiences of Gifted GLB Youths

Only three articles have been published that address the experiences of adolescents who are both gifted and GLB (Friedrichs, 1997; Peterson and Rischar, 2000; Tolan, 1997).

In his survey study of 53 GLB youths who were members of support groups from eight different metropolitan areas, Friedrichs (1997) found over one-third of them to have been in special programs for gifted students in their schools. Even though the sample of respondents was small, the large proportion of gifted youths in this GLB group indicates that educators of the gifted need to become more aware of the circumstances faced by those gifted GLB youths who might be in their charge.

Peterson and Rischar (2000) conducted a qualitative study of 18 GLB college students focusing on their high school experiences and identified three themes. Being twice different did appear to create additional emotional burdens related to depression and feelings of social isolation. Coming to terms with being different from the majority of their agemates in both ability and sexual orientation often resulted in attempts to deny one of these significant aspects of their identity or, more frequently, in social isolation and loss of self-esteem. The school climate experienced by some of these teenagers seemed unsafe because of psychological and physical harassment. In some cases, individuals sought to handle these uncertainties by academic or athletic overachievement, perfectionism, or overinvolvement in extracurricular activities; or, on the other hand, by self-destructive behaviors such as dropping out of school, running away, substance abuse, or suicide. None of the participants reported turning to adults when they were experiencing such internal turmoil. Peterson and Rischar argued that it is essential for parents and teachers to become more alert to such issues; create a school climate in which students with all kinds of differences are safe and accepted; and make themselves available to listen, support, and help solve problems.

Tolan (1997) described psychological challenges that might be faced by highly gifted adolescents and young adults, but these were not data-based. The author noted that premature self-labeling and premature developmental foreclosure of sexual identity might occur among highly gifted adolescents because they become aware of the complex issues surrounding sexuality and sexual stereotypes earlier than their agemates.

## Barriers to Research on Gifted GLB Youths

The studies reported in this research summary have methodological problems, especially the consistently small number of subjects. All of the research on sexual orientation and cognitive abilities focused on individuals who identified *themselves* as gay, lesbian, or bisexual. Two studies reported data collection on sexual orientation to supplement self-reports. In them, tests were administered to dis-

**149**

cern cognitive abilities. The studies on the school experiences of gifted GLB youths relied on the youths themselves to establish both their sexual orientation and their participation in special programs for gifted students. While important themes can emerge from the qualitative study of college students reflecting on their high school experiences, the findings cannot be generalized to other gifted GLB youths. Other barriers affect research on this population.

*Barrier #1: The absence of explicit operational definitions for constructs under study.* Researchers who wish to study gifted GLB youths must define the constructs *gifted* and *GLB* in operational and clear terms. Sexual orientation is a complex psychological construct that requires more than simply asking a person if he or she is gay, lesbian, or bisexual (Walling, 1997).

*Barrier #2: Difficulties in finding subjects willing to take part in studies.* The second and far more difficult problem facing researchers rests in finding subjects willing to participate in studies of this nature. It is impossible to determine the demographic characteristics of GLB youth in America to establish a representative sample (Walling, 1997). Not only are many of the questions asked in pertinent surveys highly personal, but, in many states, homosexual behavior is illegal, and the promise of confidentiality is often not sufficient to allow someone to expose him- or herself to the risks inherent in being known publicly as GLB. Data from some studies have been subpoenaed by the courts, and to choose to not comply with court orders places the researcher in jeopardy. Only the guarantee of anonymity will suffice.

Protection of underage participants in research requires consent from their parents, an added difficulty when many GLB youths do not want their parents to know their sexual orientation. Exposing adolescents to questions of sexual orientation and identity might also be construed as provocative, evoking curiosity and precocious exploration into complex topics of sexuality. That is, by asking them to examine their sexual orientation and identity, investigators may be raising issues that the adolescent is not developmentally ready to address. Consequently, researchers will likely continue to turn to adult subjects and ask them to reflect on their experiences as adolescents.

All of these issues raise important questions about how representative a study sample is of the population of gifted GLB youth at

**150**

large. Such questions severely limit the degree to which study findings can be generalized.

*Barrier #3: Absence of comparison groups.* We know little, if anything, about differences between gifted gay teens and average gay teens. No one has compared the experiences, development, or risk of gifted gay students with gifted students who are not gay. Research designs must incorporate these comparison groups for us to be able to discern the effects of being twice different. Given these constraints, researchers will likely continue to employ qualitative research methods to further study gifted GLB youths. A reasonable course of action might be simply to collect case studies of gifted youths who are also GLB. As these case studies accumulate, emergent themes of experience can be brought to light for further study.

## We Can Learn From Research on GLB Youths in General

The risks faced by GLB youths underscore the seriousness of the problem. In one review article, Gibson (1989) reported that gay and lesbian youth represent about 30% of all teen suicides. Although Gibson's work was criticized for the quantity and quality of the research, numerous studies have confirmed the fact that there are a significant number of GLB-related youth suicides each year (Lipkin, 1999). In a 1987 random survey of psychiatrists, two-thirds of those polled thought the suicide attempts of homosexual adolescents were more serious and lethal than those of heterosexual youth (Lipkin, p. 153).

We also know that one third of homosexual youth report committing at least one self-injurious act. Almost half of GLB youth attempt suicide, and 25% of homeless youth in America are GLB (Gibson, 1989). In general, GLB youth are at higher risk for substance abuse, depression, prostitution, AIDS, running away, truancy, underachievement, and dropping out of school than their same-age peers (O'Connor, 1992; Russell, 1989).

What can we do? Lipkin (1999, pp. 260–262) has offered us a checklist for teachers that is also applicable to counselors, parents, or anyone working with youths. Lipkin stated that a starting point

151

is to inform ourselves about GLB people and homophobia by reading, attending meetings and cultural events of gay and lesbian organizations, and conversing with openly GLB people. We can create safe, equitable classrooms and schools by changing our assumption that everyone is heterosexual unless we are told otherwise, challenging homophobic language and name calling, openly expressing our willingness to support GLB students, and working to establish policies that protect GLB students from harassment and provide counseling services for GLB youth and their families. We are not likely to have hard data anytime soon about the issues faced by gifted GLB teens, but we cannot let their well-being and educational needs slip away for that reason.

# References

Anderson, J. (Ed.). (2001, Spring). Number crunching, *RESPECT, 5*, 18.

Benbow, C. (1988). Sex differences in mathematical reasoning ability in intellectually talented preadolescents: Their nature, effects, and possible causes. *Behavioral and Brain Sciences, 11*, 169–232.

Friedrichs, T. (1997). Understanding the educational needs of gifted gay and bisexual males. *Counseling and Guidance, 6*(3), 3, 8.

Gibson, P. (1989). Gay male and lesbian suicide. In M. R. Reinleib (Ed.), *Report of the secretary's task force on youth suicide* (pp. 3-100–3-137). Washington, DC: U.S. Government Printing Office. (DHHS Pub. No. 89-1622)

Gladue, B., Beatty, W., Larson, J., & Staton, R. (1990). Sexual orientation and spatial ability in men and women. *Psychobiology, 18*(1), 101–108.

Halpern, D. (1992). *Sex differences in cognitive abilities* (2nd ed.). Hillsdale, NJ: Erlbaum.

Halpern, D., & Wright, T. (1996). A process-oriented model of sex differences in cognitive sex differences. *Learning and Individual Differences, 8*, 3–24.

Lipkin, A. (1999). *Understanding homosexuality, changing schools*. Boulder, CO: Westview Press.

McCormick, C., & Witelson, S. (1991). A cognitive profile of homosexual men compared with heterosexual men and women. *Psychoneuroendocrinology, 15*, 459–473.

O'Connor, M. F. (1992). Psychotherapy with gay and lesbian adolescents. In S. H. Dworkin & F. J. Gutierrez (Eds.) *Counseling gay men and lesbians: Journey to the end of the rainbow*. Alexandria, VA: American Association of Counseling and Development.

Peterson, J., & Rischar, H. (2000). Gifted and gay: A study of the adolescent experience. *Gifted Child Quarterly, 44*, 231–246.

Russell, S. T., & Joyner, K. (2001). Adolescent sexual orientation and suicide risk: Evidence from a national study. *American Journal of Public Health, 91,* 1276–1281.

Russell, T. G. (1989). AIDS education, homosexuality, and the counselor's role. *The School Counselor, 36,* 333–337.

Sanders, G., & Ross-Field, L. (1986). Sexual orientation and visuospatial ability. *Brain and Cognition, 5,* 280–290.

Stanley, J. (1993). Boys and girls who reason well mathematically. In G. R. Bock & K. Ackrill (Eds.), *The origins and development of high ability* (pp. 119–138). Chichester, England: Wiley.

Tolan, S. (1997). Sex and the highly gifted adolescent. *Counseling and Guidance, 6*(3), 2, 5, 8.

Tuttle, G., & Pillard, R. (1991). Sexual orientation and cognitive abilities. *Archives of Sexual Behavior, 20,* 307–318.

Walling, D. (1997). Gay and lesbian issues. In D. R. Walling (Ed.), *Hot buttons: Unraveling 10 controversial issues in education* (pp. 147–166). Bloomington, IN: Phi Delta Kappa.

Willmott, M., & Brierly, H. (1984). Cognitive characteristics and homosexuality. *Archives of Sexual Behavior, 13,* 311–319.

**153**

# 16

# RACIAL IDENTITY AMONG GIFTED AFRICAN AMERICAN STUDENTS

## by Donna Y. Ford, Ph.D.

espite ongoing concerns about the social and emotional needs of gifted students, few studies have examined issues for those gifted students who are linguistically, ethnically, and culturally diverse. In this chapter, the psychological difficulties confronting gifted Black[1] students are examined first; then, the most widely investigated theory of racial identity development (Cross, 1971, 1995) is discussed. The chapter concludes with suggestions for academic and counseling interventions appropriate for gifted Black students.

---

1. The terms *Black* and *African American* are used interchangeably, as are the terms *minority*, *diverse*, and *students of color*. The primary focus of this section is on Black students, but other groups face similar issues.

# Psychological Issues Facing Black Students

Since the work of social psychologist Kenneth Clark in the 1950s, hundreds of studies have examined aspects of racial identity with Black adults and children. Many of the studies have used the Cross model (1995), which will be described later. Most studies and theories of racial identity assume that Blacks are more likely than White students to encounter barriers to healthy racial identity development (e.g., Helms, 1989; Parham, 1989; Parham & Helms, 1985; Smith, 1989, Spencer & Markstrom-Adams, 1990). Racial identity concerns the extent to which people of color recognize and value their ethnic background and heritage.

Smith (1989) argued that race creates bonding and feelings of peoplehood, meaning that individuals often define themselves in terms of membership in a particular racial or ethnic group. She has contended that a healthy regard for one's racial status is psychologically important for people of color. Indeed, people of color have been shortchanged in most theories of self-concept because these theories give little attention to racial identity (Ford, 1996). Healthy self-identification includes accurate and consistent use of an ethnic label based on the perception of belonging to an ethnic group (Rotheram & Phinney, 1987).

Race affects one's social, emotional, and psychological health. For Black youth, racial identity has a significant impact on achievement and attitudes toward school, as reported in studies by Ford (1995), Ford, Harris, and Schuerger (1993), and Smith (1989). For example, research by Fordham (1988, 1991, 1996) and Fordham and Ogbu (1986) revealed that, in the earlier stages of racial identity development, African American youth may deliberately underachieve and choose not to participate in gifted programs to avoid peer pressures and accusations of "acting White," or may camouflage their abilities to be accepted socially by their peers. Furthermore, the existence of a negative stereotype about a group to which one belongs may impair performance in a situation (such as school) in which one's behavior might either confirm or disconfirm the stereotype. Black students are becoming increasingly aware of the negative stereotypes that persist regarding the intelligence of Black students. When they are told a test will measure their intelligence (or that of their racial group), many of them become unmotivated—they give up, or second-guess themselves, or both—often feeling inferior to Whites. These negative reactions to tests and their interpretations hinder Black students' performance on tests and their racial pride. For example, in a study by Steele (1997), Black students who were told that they were taking a test of intelligence showed decreased levels of success compared with Black students who were told that the test was racially unbiased. The same differential did not hold for White students, who did not experience the same "stereotype threat."

## A Theory of Black Racial Identity

The most thoroughly investigated theory of racial identity was introduced by Cross in 1971, and has since been used in more than 600 studies of racial identity. In his most recent revision, Cross (1995) describes five stages through which African Americans progress and regress in the process of "becoming Black."

During Stage 1 (Pre-encounter), Blacks hold one of at least three attitudes: *low-salience* attitude, in which blackness seems to play an insignificant role in daily lives (they see themselves as "human beings who just happen to be Black" [p. 89]); *social-stigma attitudes*, in which low-salience attitudes combine with feeling that racial orientation is something to be ashamed of and negotiated; and *anti-Black attitudes*, in which persons feel thoroughly alienated from and antagonistic toward other Blacks and do not see the Black community as a potential support base. All three pre-encounter types favor European cultural perspectives.

In Stage 2 (Encounter), individuals experience an "identity metamorphosis" (p. 104) in which one or a series of events induces cognitive dissonance, pushing them toward increased awareness of their status as racial beings. Negative feelings are associated with their pre-encounter attitudes, but now individuals feel anxious and confused about the level of "Blackness" to which they should aspire, and they spend a good deal of time gathering information about their ethnic and cultural heritage.

During Stage 3 (Immersion-Emersion), representing what Cross (1995) referred to as the "vortex of psychological

**157**

Nigrescence" (p. 106), individuals are anxious about becoming the "right kind of Black person" (p. 106). Importantly, these individuals tend to perceive all that is White to be evil, oppressive, and inhumane, and all that is Black to be superior. In the early, *immersion* phase, African Americans engross themselves in Black culture; concern themselves with Black issues of justice and equity; show dedication, selflessness, and commitment to other Blacks; and, while feeling conflicting feelings of rage and guilt, they also experience a developing sense of pride and progress toward accepting themselves as racial beings. In this stage, Blacks may experience creative, inspirational busts of energy that express the richness of their racial heritage. Progressing through this stage to the *emersion* phase, there is eventually a marked decline in racist and hyper-emotional attitudes. Through experiences such as encounters with healthy role models who display sophisticated and calm personas, Blacks learn to substitute idealistic and romanticized notions of Blackness with a deeper and more serious understanding of Black issues.

During Stage 4 (Internalization), there is integration of a new identity that is more authentic and natural. The sense of Blackness can now include biculturalism and multiculturalism, and Blacks may also become committed to addressing the problems and needs of other ethnic groups. An internalized identity offers protection from problems associated with living in a society where race matters, provides a sense of belonging and social affiliation, and provides a base for interacting with people, cultures, and situations beyond the world of Blackness.

Internalization leads to Stage 5 (Internalization-Commitment), during which African Americans find ways to translate their personal sense of Blackness and high racial salience into a commitment to minority affairs and to improving the circumstances of people of color. This stage is the essence of multiculturalism and pluralism. It is the action stage whereby concerted efforts are taken to bring about social justice for African Americans and other people of color.

According to Cross (1995), whether an individual regresses, becomes stuck, or progresses through the stages of racial identity depends heavily on personality characteristics, support systems, resources, and experiences, but not on age. African Americans in predominantly White settings may experience more negative racial encounters than those in predominantly Black settings (Smith, 1989) and may do so at an earlier age. Furthermore, because of their insightfulness, intuitiveness, sensitivity, and keen sense of justice, gifted Black students may be especially aware of and sensitive to racial injustices.

One's stage of racial identity may be related to achievement in a curvilinear fashion, with those in the earliest and last stages having the highest achievement orientation. Even so, pre-encounter individuals, because of their low-salience or anti-Black attitudes, are likely to be rejected by the Black community. Conversely, those in later stages, because of their strong and positive racial identification and pluralistic perspectives, are more likely to be accepted. Individuals in the middle stages of racial identity may be so consumed with finding their identity that academic achievement is much less important to them than is self-understanding.

## Implications for Gifted Black Students

Blacks (and other diverse students) encounter more barriers to racial identity development than do White students. Moreover, gifted Black students may experience more psychological and emotional problems than Black students not identified as gifted (Ford, 1995; Fordham & Ogbu, 1988). On this note, Lindstrom and San Vant (1986) argued that gifted diverse children find themselves in a dilemma in which they must choose between academic success and social acceptance. They quoted one gifted Black student who said, "I had to fight to be gifted and then I had to fight because I am gifted" (p. 584). Thus, some gifted or high-achieving minority students may perceive academic achievement as a pyrrhic victory (Fordham, 1988). They win in one respect—academically—but lose socially, with subsequent feelings of loneliness, isolation, and rejection. When caught in this tug-of-war, some Black students attempt to sabotage their achievement (e.g., procrastinating, failing to do assignments, exerting little effort). Efforts are reprioritized, with energy devoted to seeking and securing social acceptance and belonging as the need for affiliation outweighs the need for achievement.

## Discussion and Recommendations

Although many studies have explored the racial identities of diverse students (Banks & Banks, 1995; Ponterotto & Pederson, 1993), only a handful of studies have examined the racial identities of gifted Black students. Interventions are needed to promote positive racial identities among Black and other diverse students.

Gifted students experiencing racial identity difficulties or conflicts can profit from multicultural counseling. They need opportunities to share their concerns with other diverse gifted students. Sessions may focus on such topics as coping with peer pressures and understanding how self-perception influences motivation, choices, achievement, and social relationships (Ford, 1995, 1996). Essentially, counselors should spend a considerable amount of time helping students to get a better understanding of themselves as cultural and racial beings. This can be the first step toward promoting racial self-understanding and pride.

Students often feel they are alone in their pain, confusion, and experiences. Thus, they may not share their concerns with adults and school personnel. Counselors and teachers can use small-group and cooperative learning experiences to facilitate sharing and communication among mixed diverse and White groups of students. These strategies provide diverse students with opportunities to establish friendships with White peers and to decrease feelings of isolation and alienation. Diverse students should also be encouraged to participate in extracurricular activities that promote social interaction and leadership. In essence, social and group experiences will give diverse students an opportunity to talk about their lives and concerns as ethnic beings: To whom can minority students turn for emotional, psychological, and academic support? How do they feel about being identified and placed in a gifted program?

Counseling strategies and initiatives can help minority students with poor racial identities (e.g., pre-encounter and encounter) to understand and appreciate their dual identities of being both gifted and diverse. These students may generalize negative perceptions of Whites in general to White counselors and teachers (Exum & Colangelo, 1981) and reject their help. Counselors will need to be patient and persistent in earning the trust of such students. On this note, a mentor or role model may be helpful in pushing pre-encounter and encounter students into higher and more positive stages of racial identities. A mentor or role model can also help diverse students in the higher racial identity stages maintain their positive self-perception.

School personnel, specifically teachers, curriculum developers, and administrators, must also (re)evaluate the extent to which their curriculum and instruction affirm students' racial identities, while increasing all students' knowledge and acceptance of the nation's multicultural heritage. Mutual understanding and respect between White students and diverse students *and* between White school personnel and diverse students are the ideals of multicultural education (Banks & Banks, 1995; Ford, 1996; Ford & Harris, 1999, 2000; Ford, Howard, Harris, & Tyson, 2000; Lee, 1997; Ponterotto, Casa, Suzuki, & Alexander, 1995; Ponterotto & Pedersen, 1993; Sue & Sue, 1990). The central question for school personnel is: How can we make sure that all students are prepared to live and learn in a culturally diverse society?

Ultimately, to work effectively with diverse students, counselors and teachers require multicultural training. Such training is available through more than 700 ethnic studies and multicultural programs at colleges and universities (Banks & Banks, 1995). Counselors require an understanding of self-perceptions that goes beyond self-esteem and self-concept when working with diverse students. Several professional counseling associations (e.g., American Counseling Association, Association for Multicultural Counseling and Development, American Psychological Association) have guidelines and position statements regarding multicultural competencies internships in urban communities can be found; and publications for teachers on promoting diversity, such as *ReThinking Schools,* can be helpful. At a minimum, such training should focus on:

- understanding cultural beliefs, values, norms, and traditions that impact teaching and learning; in order to recognize and affirm the unique cultural styles of diverse groups relative to communicating and behaving (Boykin, 1994);
- understanding the different learning styles of diverse groups and adapting teaching styles accordingly (Shade, Kelly, & Oberg, 1997);

- understanding the history of diverse groups so that this information can become an integral part of the curriculum through the selection of high-quality, multicultural materials and resources (Ford & Harris, 1999; Ford et al., 2000); and
- building positive, strong relationships with diverse families (Ford, 1996).

When working with gifted diverse students, educators must be mindful of two points. First, such students are gifted and share the concerns and needs of other gifted students. Second, such students are diverse and share the concerns and needs of other diverse students. In essence, diverse gifted students may be in a double bind, and educators must be mindful of these issues and needs.

## References

Banks, J. A., & Banks, C. A. M. (Eds.). (1995). *Handbook of research on multicultural education.* New York: Simon & Schuster.

Boykin, A. W. (1994). Afrocultural expression and its implications for schooling. In E. R. Hollins, J. E. King, & W. C. Haymann (Eds.). *Teaching diverse populations: Formulating a knowledge base* (pp. 225–273). New York: University of New York Press.

Cross, W. E., Jr. (1971, July). Toward a psychology of Black liberation: The Negro-to-Black conversion experience. *Black World*, 13–27.

Cross, W. E., Jr. (1995). The psychology of Nigrescence: Revising the Cross model. In J. G. Ponterotto, J. M. Casas, L. A. Suzuki, & C. M. Alexander (Eds.), *Handbook of multicultural counseling* (pp. 93–122). Thousand Oaks, CA: Sage.

Exum, H. A., & Colangelo, N. (1981). Culturally diverse gifted: The need for ethnic identity development. *Roeper Review, 3*, 15–17.

Ford, D. Y. (1995). *A study of achievement and underachievement among gifted, potentially gifted, and average African-American students.* Storrs, CT: National Research on the Gifted and Talented, The University of Connecticut.

Ford, D. Y. (1996). *Reversing underachievement among gifted Black students: Promising practices and programs.* New York: Teachers College Press.

Ford, D. Y., & Harris, J. J., III (1999). *Multicultural gifted education.* New York: Teachers College Press.

Ford, D. Y., & Harris, J. J., III (2000). A framework for infusing multicultural curriculum into gifted education. *Roeper Review, 23*, 4–10.

Ford, D. Y., Harris, J. J., III, & Schuerger, J. M. (1993). Racial identity development among gifted Black students: Counseling issues and concerns. *Journal of Counseling and Development, 71*, 409–417.

Ford, D. Y., Howard, T. C., Harris, J. J., III, & Tyson, C. A. (2000). Creating culturally responsive classrooms for gifted minority students. *Journal for the Education of the Gifted, 23*, 397–427.

Fordham, S. (1988). Racelessness as a factor in Black students' school success: Pragmatic strategy or pyrrhic victory? *Harvard Educational Review, 58*(1), 54–84.

Fordham, S. (1991). Peer-proofing academic competition among Black adolescents: "Acting White" Black American style. In C. E. Sleeter (Ed.), *Empowerment through multicultural education* (pp. 69–93). Albany: State University of New York Press.

Fordham, S. (1996). *Blacked out: Dilemmas of race, identity, and success at Capital High*. Chicago: The University of Chicago Press.

Fordham, S., & Ogbu, J. U. (1986). Black students' school success: Coping with the burden of "acting White." *The Urban Review, 18*, 176–207.

Helms, J. E. (1989). Considering some methodological issues in racial identity counseling research. *The Counseling Psychologist, 17*, 227–252.

Lee, C. (Ed.). (1997). *Multicultural issues in counseling: New approaches to diversity* (2nd ed.). Alexandria, VA: American Counseling Association.

Lindstrom, R. R., & San Vant, S. (1986). Special issues in working with gifted minority adolescents. *Journal of Counseling and Development, 64*, 583–586.

Parham, T. A. (1989). Cycles of psychological Nigrescence. *The Counseling Psychologist, 17*, 187–226.

Parham, T. A., & Helms, J. E. (1985). Relation of racial identity attitudes to self-actualization and affective states of Black students. *Journal of Counseling Psychology, 32*, 431–440.

Ponterotto, J. G., Casas, J. M., Suzuki, L. A., & Alexander, C. M. (Eds.). (1995). *Handbook of multicultural counseling*. Newbury Park, CA: Sage.

Ponterotto, J. G., & Pedersen, P. B. (1993). *Preventing prejudice: A guide for counselors and educators*. Newbury Park, CA: Sage.

Rotheram, M. J., & Phinney, J. S. (1987). Introduction: Definitions and perspectives in the custody of children's ethnic socialization. In J. S. Phinney & M. J. Rotheram (Eds.), *Children's ethnic socialization* (pp. 7–10). Newbury Park, CA: Sage.

Shade, B. J., Kelly, C., & Oberg, M. (1997). *Creating culturally responsive classrooms*. Washington, DC: American Psychological Association.

Smith, E. M. J. (1989). Black racial identity development. *The Counseling Psychologist, 17*, 277–288.

Spencer, M. B., & Markstrom-Adams, C. (1990). Identity processes among racial and ethnic children in America. *Child Development, 61*, 290–310.

Steele, C. M. (1997). A threat in the air: How stereotypes shape intellectual identity and performance. *American Psychologist, 52*, 613–619.

Sue, W., & Sue, D. (1990). *Counseling the culturally different: Theory and practice* (2nd ed.). New York: Wiley.

# 17 CREATIVELY GIFTED CHILDREN

by **Maureen Neihart, Psy.D.** and
**F. Richard Olenchak, Ph.D.**

Although there has been more than a century of interest in and research on the adjustment of gifted children, the majority of studies have examined academically or intellectually gifted children who participate in some kind of special educational programming. There has been much less effort to explore social and emotional issues among creatively gifted youth. A large body of literature describes the personality traits, motivation, social environment, and cognitive style of creatively gifted adults (Davis, 1992; MacKinnon, 1961, 1962, 1965; Ochse, 1990; Panter, Panter, Virshup, & Virshup, 1995; Roe, 1952; Rothenberg, 1990; Subotnik, in press; Walberg & Stariha, 1992; Walberg & Zeiser, 1997), while only a handful of studies examine similarly gifted adolescents (Bloom, 1985; Csikszentmihalyi, Rathunde, & Whalen, 1993; Fishkin, Cramond, & Olszewski-Kubilius, 1999; Getzels, 1963; Winner, 1996;

Winner & Martino, 1993). A consistent finding from both the adult and adolescent studies is that several affective characteristics, personality traits, and environmental factors facilitate the development of high levels of creativity and creative-productive giftedness and that all should be viewed as part of an interactive system (Csikszentmihalyi, 1998; Feldman, Csikszentmihalyi, & Gardner, 1994; Sternberg, 1999; Sternberg & Lubart, 1993). This chapter highlights the major findings about affective components associated with high levels of creative achievement, the environmental factors that are more likely to result in the actualization of creative giftedness, and the implications for nurturing creative talent.

## Personality Traits and Affective Characteristics

Much of the work on personality and affective factors associated with high creative achievement concludes that there is a consistent psychological profile of creative achievers, though there is considerable variety from one person to the next (Barron, 1969; Bloom, 1985; Csikszentmihalyi, 1996; Csikszentmihalyi, Rathunde, & Whalen, 1993; Fishkin, Cramond, & Olszewski-Kubilius, 1999; Getzels, 1963; Luhman & Fundis, 1987; MacKinnon, 1978; Ochse, 1990; Roe, 1952; Udvari & Schneider, 2000; Simonton, 1988; Torrance, 1962, 1978). This cluster of personality traits distinguishes creative individuals from average people. Creative persons are considered to be open to new experience, persevering, nonconforming, and intellectually and emotionally independent. They may be emotionally labile and impulsive, yet self-confident, and they often have good insight into their abilities. They are less group-oriented, more introverted, and tend to marginalize themselves, seeking more time alone than average people. Additionally, the emotional propensity for originality and imagination in thought and in action (Daniels, 1997; Paget, 1982) as well mature perception (Daniels) has consistently been identified.

Other social and emotional traits that researchers and theorists have associated with creative giftedness include awareness of one's own creativity (Daniels, 1997; Karnes, 1965, 1979) and emotional maturity, including the courage to actualize one's abilities (Landau

& Weissler, 1998; Sternberg & Lubart, 1993; Subotnik, in press). Creative achievers withdraw more often, seeking solitude, and for good reason: Some creative tasks require long stretches of concentration without interruption. Creatively gifted individuals also tend to be much less motivated by external rewards like grades and public recognition, and they tend to be more driven by a love of engagement in creative work.

More recent work has also concluded that youngsters who are exceptionally creative engage in sophisticated, detailed fantasy and are comfortable in openly expressing emotion (Russ, Robins, & Christano, 1999). The same study also found that their emotional expression was relatively stable over time; young people who expressed more emotion in their early years also did so later on in their childhood.

## Environmental Factors

The work of many researchers also suggests that some environments are more conducive to nurturing high levels of creative ability and achievement than others (Amabile, 1989; Barron, 1969; Csikszentmihalyi, 1990; Ericcson, 1996; MacKinnon, 1962, 1978; Olszewski-Kubilius, Kulieke, & Buescher, 1987). For instance, families with moderate levels of stress may promote creativity in children because children learn to tolerate tension, ambiguity, and are less pressured to conform (see Olszewski-Kubilius, this volume). Yet, the creative person also needs support. For example, MacKinnon (1962, 1978) concluded that creative talent requires an enormous need for understanding from others to convey confidence in abilities. This reinforcement and affirmation seems to address the anxieties that may be associated with creative ideation, while neither belittling the intensity, nor dismissing the reality, of the creative ideas.

Runco (1992) elaborated on this concept, finding that creativity requires an environment that nurtures and then actively supports independence of judgment. Runco also found that creative individuals tend to be self-evaluative by nature, but this self-evaluation cannot be sustained without external support systems; and, when support is unavailable, frustration may develop.

Creatively Gifted

Torrance (1962, 1965, 1977, 1978, 1988) determined that the creative personality so strongly requires a variety of social and emotional support mechanisms that denial of them would likely result in both physiological and psychological illnesses. These needs include parental support, understanding of frustration as it develops (Karnes, 1965), and reinforcing experimentation. In other words, the creatively gifted individual is more likely to thrive in environments where risk taking is valued and promoted and where there is less pressure to conform to prescribed conventions (Wildauer, 1984). These needs do not end with adolescence, but continue throughout life (Willings, 1983).

In their studies of artistically or musically gifted adolescents, Bloom (1985) and Subotnik (in press) pointed to the important influence of gifted peers who match or surpass a student's abilities and who share the motivation needed for persistent effort over a prolonged period. Access to a peer group of students with similar passions and abilities prepares creatively gifted adolescents to cope with the realities of the intense competition and stardom that characterizes some creative careers.

## Creative Giftedness and Mood Disorders

Concentrating primarily on writers and visual artists, an additional body of research has focused specifically on the emotional health of artistically gifted adults (Andreasen, 1988; Jamison, 1989, 1993; Panter et al., 1995; Prentky, 1980; Richards, 1981, 1989; Rothenberg, 1990; Rothenberg & Burkhardt, 1984). These studies consistently conclude that there is a significantly higher incidence of mood disorders and suicide among gifted writers and visual artists. Many of these studies provide compelling evidence that high creative achievement in writing or visual arts shares three characteristics with mood disorders: alteration of mood, certain types of thinking processes, and a tolerance for irrationality. Several investigators have attempted to explain the connection.

Jamison (1993) suggested that elevated mood precedes periods of creative productivity, with mood changes opening or inhibiting thought, thus stimulating greater creativity. Depression may have an

**168**

important role in slowing the pace of thought, putting feelings and ideas into perspective, and eliminating irrelevant notions. In other words, it may be the cognitive processes associated with certain moods that link creativity and mood disorders (Prentky, 1980; Rothenberg, 1990; Rothenberg & Burkhardt, 1984). Cognitive traits common to both creativity and hypomania are fluency, rapidity, and flexibility of thought coupled with the ability to combine ideas to form new, original thinking relationships (Jamison). Rothenberg concluded that the cognitive ability to combine paradoxes or superimpose discrete objects characterizes both psychotics and persons predisposed to high levels of creativity. However, his research also describes a narrow but distinct boundary between psychotic processes and creative thought.

Although no similar studies have been conducted with artistically gifted adolescents, Csikszentmihalyi's (1996) ethnographic research on the creative individual lends indirect support to the hypothesis that creatively gifted adolescents may be more psychologically vulnerable than academically or intellectually gifted students. First, the pursuit of high creative achievement among adolescents is likely to result in reduced popularity and perhaps increased marginalization or alienation from peers. "Unfortunately, one cannot be expected to be exceptional and normal at the same time" (p. 177). Creatively gifted persons may appear particularly odd to peers when they have interests and passions that differ from the mainstream and a proclivity for unique thinking and self-expression. Second, development of creative talent often necessitates more time spent alone than is typical for average teens, and the amount of time allocated to mental play appears to inhibit sexual awareness and independence.

## Nurturing Creative Ability: Implications for Social and Emotional Supports

If one of the goals of education is to realize potential, then the research highlighted here suggests that social and affective factors should be explicitly targeted and incorporated into any efforts to nurture creative ability and promote healthy development of cre-

169

atively gifted students. There is disagreement about whether trait- and need-specific interventions (Bloom, 1985; Daniels, 1997; Hennessey, 1997; MacKinnon, 1978; Subotnik, in press) or global supports (Alamprese & Erlanger, 1989; Karnes, 1979; Runco, 1992; Wildauer, 1984) for creativity are more effective in nurturing creative talent. In a comprehensive review of the literature, Paulsen (1984) concluded that the development of creative giftedness requires that schools view children with creative potential in their totality, not singling out and serving their needs one-by-one, but serving them through integrated physical, social, emotional, and mental programming. However, Russ, Robins, and Christano (1999) found that specific interventions like time in school for imaginative or fantasy play and for role playing ultimately produced creatively gifted students who sustained their ability for ingeniously attacking problems over time. In similar fashion, Starko (1989) found that students who took risks in writing by manipulating and otherwise toying with their ideas were better than average at problem finding.

Interventions include providing a psychologically nonthreatening environment that values independence of thought and action, shifting the focus of learning to each student's personal interest and motivations and setting reasonable limits for experimentation and risk taking. Daniels' (1997) research has also advocated allowing for physical movement and acknowledging and showcasing humor. Subotnik (in press) has found that young people capable of elite talent development benefit from learning how to achieve the psychological balance needed to tolerate frequent disappointments and how to maintain composure in frustrating situations. She also found that students interested in pursuing high levels of creative achievement should receive practical information about how to conduct themselves in auditions, how to dress, and how to present an interesting portfolio or program. Their work should be evaluated regularly by appropriate audiences.

## Conclusion

**170**

Although creatively gifted persons share some of the same social and emotional attributes as those who are intellectually gifted, there are a number of affective characteristics and accompanying needs that creatively gifted people embody that are not necessarily attributable to intellectually gifted people. The literature confirms that creative thinking and creative behavior require not only creative abilities and a threshold of intelligence, but also an array of temperaments, perceptions, attitudes, and motivations (Barron, 1969, 1988; Davis, 1992; MacKinnon, 1961, 1978; Torrance, 1962, 1988). The literature also suggests that creatively gifted students in the visual arts and writing may be more vulnerable psychologically than gifted students whose talents and interests lie in other domains.

The particular traits and resultant needs of creatively gifted students necessitate specific attention by schools to enable individual students to discern and develop their creative giftedness and, at the same time, protect them from the potential risks that may accompany the pursuit of high creative achievement. The realization of high creative potential requires a variety of social and emotional support mechanisms including, but not limited to, understanding from others, positive attention to one's abilities, and freedom to be self-evaluative. The environment should tolerate the creatively gifted child's desire for more solitude and be cautious about interpreting withdrawal as pathological. Adults should value and nurture self-evaluation and independence of thought and action and also help to arrange access to gifted peers with similar ability and drive.

If we hope to realize creative potential in visual arts and writing, then we may need to pay attention to the role of mood and the way in which moods can enhance or interfere with creative productivity. It may be useful to model and teach attitudes and practices that build ego strength and manage mood states (Neihart, 1998) and to be explicit with creative young people about why it is valuable to have these psychological skills.

There is much that we still do not know about the social and emotional development of creatively gifted children and adolescents. Research is needed to determine whether the results of adult studies are similar to those conducted with youth and to determine whether the apparent association between mood disorders and high achievement in writing and visual arts is observable in adolescence. Studies are needed that compare the effectiveness of different environments and interventions in realizing creative potential.

# References

Alamprese, J. A., & Erlanger, W. J. (1989). *No gift wasted: Effective strategies for educating highly able, disadvantaged students in mathematics and science.* Washington, DC: U.S. Department of Education, Educational Information Center. (ERIC Document No. ED312802)

Amabile, T. (1989). *Growing up creative: Nurturing a lifetime of creativity.* New York: Crown.

Andreasen, N. (1988). Bipolar disorder and creativity: Implications and clinical management. *Comprehensive Psychiatry, 29,* 207–217.

Barron, F. (1969). *Creative person and creative process.* New York: Holt.

Barron, F. (1988). Putting creativity to work. In R. J. Sternberg (Ed.), *The nature of creativity* (pp. 76–98). New York: Cambridge University Press.

Bloom, B. (Ed.). (1985). *Developing talent in young people.* New York: Ballantine Books.

Csikszentmihalyi, M. (1990). *Flow: The psychology of optimal experience.* New York: Harper and Row.

Csikszentmihalyi, M. (1996). *Creativity: Flow and the psychology of discovery and invention.* New York: HarperCollins.

Csikszentmihalyi, M. (1998). Creativity and genius: A systems perspective. In A. Steptoe (Ed.), *Genius and the mind: Studies of creativity and temperament* (pp. 85–104). New York: Oxford University Press.

Csikszentmihalyi, M., Rathunde, K., & Whalen, S. (1993). *Talented teenagers: The roots of success and failure.* New York: Cambridge University Press.

Daniels, S. (1997). Creativity in the classroom: Characteristics, climate, and curriculum. In N. Colangelo & G. A. Davis (Eds.), *Handbook of gifted education* (2nd ed., pp. 292–307). Boston: Allyn and Bacon.

Davis, G. A. (1992). *Creativity is forever.* Dubuque, IA: Kendall/Hunt.

Ericcson, K. A. (1996). *The road to excellence: The acquisition of expert performances in the arts and sciences, sports, and games.* Mahwah, NJ: Erlbaum.

Feldman, D. H., Csikszentmihalyi, M., & Gardner, H. (1994). *Changing the world: A framework for the study of creativity.* Westport, CT: Praeger.

Fishkin, A. S., Cramond, B., & Olszewski-Kubilius, P. (Eds.). (1999). *Investigating creativity in youth: Research and methods.* Cresskill, NJ: Hampton Press.

Getzels, J. (1963). The highly intelligent and the highly creative adolescent: A summary of some research findings. In C. W. Taylor & F. Barron (Eds.), *Scientific creativity: Its recognition and development* (pp. 161–172). New York: Wiley.

Hennessey, B. A. (1997). Teaching for creative development: A social-psychological approach. In N. Colangelo & G. A. Davis (Eds.), *Handbook of gifted education* (2nd ed, pp. 282–291). Boston: Allyn and Bacon.

Jamison, K. (1989). Mood disorders and patterns of creativity in British writers and artists. *Psychiatry, 52,* 152–134.

Jamison, K. R. (1993). *Touched with fire: Manic depressive illness and the artistic temperament.* New York: Free Press.

Karnes, M. B. (1965). *Culturally disadvantaged children of higher potential, intellectual functioning, and educational implications.* Washington, DC: U.S. Department of Education, Educational Information Center. (ERIC Document No. ED018505)

Karnes, M. B. (1979*). Creative art for learning.* Reston, VA: Council for Exceptional Children.

Landau, E., & Weissler, K. (1998). The relationship between emotional maturity, intelligence, and creativity in gifted children. *Gifted Education International, 13,* 100–105.

Luhman, A. L., & Fundis, R. J. (1987). *College studies for the gifted: An academic approach for the gifted, talented, and creative student.* Washington, DC: U.S. Department of Education, Educational Information Center. (ERIC Document No. ED304242)

MacKinnon, D. W. (1961). Creativity in architects. In D. W. MacKinnon (Ed.), *The creative person* (pp. 291–320). Berkeley: Institute of Personality Assessment and Research, University of California.

MacKinnon, D. W. (1962). The nature and nurture of creative talent. *American Psychologist, 17,* 484–495.

MacKinnon, D. W. (1965). Personality and the realization of creative potential. *American Psychologist, 20,* 273–281.

MacKinnon, D. W. (1978). *In search of human effectiveness.* Buffalo, NY: Creative Education Foundation.

Neihart, M. (1998). Creativity, the arts, and madness. *Roeper Review, 21,* 47–50.

Ochse, R. (1990). *Before the gates of excellence: The determinants of creative genius.* New York: Cambridge University Press.

Olszewski-Kubilius, P., Kulieke, M. J., & Buescher, T. (1987). The influence of the family environment on the development of talent: A literature review. *Journal for the Education of the Gifted, 11,* 6–28.

Paget, K. D. (1982). The creative abilities of children with social and emotional problems. *Journal of Abnormal Child Psychology, 10,* 107–112.

Panter, B., Panter, M., Virshup, E., & Virshup, B. (1995). *Creativity and madness: Psychological studies of art and artists.* Burbank, CA: American Institute of Medical Education.

Paulsen, W. J. (1984). *Creativity and giftedness: A comparative perspective.* Washington, DC: U.S. Department of Education, Educational Information Center. (ERIC Document No. ED292276)

Prentky, R. A. (1980). *Creativity and psychopathology: A neurocognitive perspective.* New York: Praeger.

Richards, R. (1981). Relationships between creativity and psychopathology: An evaluation and interpretations of the evidence. *Genetic Psychology Monographs, 103,* 261–326.

Richards, R. (1989). Compelling evidence for increased rates of affective disorder among eminent creative persons. *Comprehensive Psychiatry, 30,* 272–273.

Roe, A. (1952). A psychologist examines 64 eminent scientists. *Scientific American, 187*(5), 21–25.

Rothenberg, A. (1990). *Creativity and madness: New findings and old stereotypes.* Baltimore: Johns Hopkins University Press.

Rothenberg, A., & Burkhardt, P. E. (1984). Difference in response time of creative persons and patients with depressive and schizophrenic disorders. *Psychological Reports, 54,* 711–717.

Runco, M. A. (1992). The evaluative, valuative, and divergent thinking of children. *Journal of Creative Behavior, 25,* 311–319.

Russ, S., Robins, A., & Christano, B. (1999). Imaginative youngsters become creative problem solvers. *Creativity Research Journal, 12,* 129–139.

Simonton, D. K. (1988). *Scientific genius: A psychology of science.* Cambridge, England: Cambridge University Press.

Starko, A. J. (1989). Problem finding in creative writing: An exploratory study. *Journal for the Education of the Gifted, 12,* 172–186.

Sternberg, R. J. (1999). *Handbook of creativity.* Cambridge, England: Cambridge University Press.

Sternberg, R. J., & Lubart, T. (1993). Creative giftedness: A multivariate investment approach. *Gifted Child Quarterly, 37,* 7–15.

Subotnik, R. (in press). Transforming elite level musicians into professional artists: A view of the talent development process at the Juilliard School. In L. Shavinina & M. Ferrari (Eds.), *Beyond knowledge: Extracognitive facets in developing high ability.* Mahwah, NJ: Erlbaum.

Torrance, E. P. (1962). *Guiding creative talent.* Englewood Cliffs, NJ: Prentice–Hall.

Torrance, E. P. (1965). *Rewarding creative behavior.* Englewood Cliffs, NJ: Prentice-Hall.

Torrance, E. P. (1977). *Creativity in the classroom.* Washington, DC: National Education Association.

Torrance, E. P. (1978). Healing qualities of creative behavior. *Creative Child and Adult Quarterly, 3,* 146–158.

Torrance, E. P. (1988). The nature of creativity as manifest in its testing. In R. W. Sternberg (Ed.), *The nature of creativity* (pp. 43–75). New York: Cambridge University Press.

Udvari, S. J., & Schneider, H. (2000). Competition and adjustment of gifted children: A matter of motivation. *Roeper Review, 22,* 212–216.

Walberg, H. J., & Stariha, W. E. (1992). Productive human capital: Learning, creativity, and eminence. *Creativity Research Journal, 5,* 323–340.

Walberg, H. J., & Zeiser, S. (1997). Productivity, accomplishment, and eminence. In N. Colangelo & G. A. Davis (Eds.), *Handbook of gifted education* (2nd ed., pp. 328–334). Boston: Allyn and Bacon.

Wildauer, C. A. (1984). *Identification and nurturance of the intellectually gifted young child within the regular classroom: Case histories.* Washington, DC: U.S. Department of Education, Educational Information Center. (ERIC Document No. ED254041)

Willings, D. (1983). *The gifted child grows up*. Washington, DC: U.S. Department of Education, Educational Information Center. (ERIC Document No. ED252038)

Winner, E. (1996). *Gifted children: Myths and realities*. New York: Basic Books.

Winner, E., & Martino, G. (1993). Giftedness in the visual arts and music. In K. A. Heller, F. J. Mönks, & A. H. Passow (Eds.), *International handbook of research and development of giftedness and talent* (pp. 253–281). New York: Pergamon Press.

**175**

# 18 GIFTED STUDENTS WITH LEARNING DISABILITIES

by **F. Richard Olenchak, Ph.D.**
and **Sally M. Reis, Ph.D.**

The balancing act required for students with both high potential and learning disabilities to find suitable opportunities that nurture their abilities and concurrently accommodate their impediments may cause frustrations that contribute to potential social or emotional difficulties. Many gifted students have disabilities, with some estimates ranging from between 120,000 to 180,000 in American schools (Davis & Rimm, 1985). Prater and Minner (1986) suggested that the majority of these students have learning disabilities. Minner (1990) found that classroom teachers, including teachers of gifted students, "may hold some rather stereotypical notions about learning disabled and/or gifted students which, in turn, may cause them not even to consider such children in a program for gifted youngsters" (p. 38). Whitmore and Maker (1985) summarized this population as misjudged, misunderstood, and neglected and found that teachers, counselors, and others are inclined to overlook signs of intellectual giftedness and to focus attention on such deficits as poor spelling, reading, and writing. They further believe that gifted students with learning disabilities are often told that college study is inappropriate for them and that professional careers will be unattainable.

Most of the publications about gifted students with learning disabilities (gifted/LD) are descriptive. For example, Baum and Owen (1988) found that gifted/LD students had unique characteristics related to persistence and individual interests and possessed lower academic self-efficacy than their gifted peers without learning disabilities. Baum and Owen further found that 36% of the students in their study who had been identified by school personnel as possessing a learning disability simultaneously demonstrated behaviors associated with giftedness.

## The Interaction of Giftedness and Learning Disabilities

Psychological and educational research has expanded in recent years with the study of various special populations and new theories of intelligence and assessment (Gardner, 1983; Sternberg, 1981). These expanded views of giftedness propose that traditional testing procedures may not accurately assess the potential of some students; giftedness, according to these newer views, is not synonymous with test scores. These expanded views of giftedness may provide a useful theoretical framework for identifying gifted students with learning disabilities.

High-ability students with learning difficulties have been studied for many years. In 1937, Orton found wide ranges of intelligence among nonreaders with specific reading and writing disabilities known as dyslexia, indicating that many high-ability students had learning problems. Some of the lower achieving high-IQ students in Terman and Oden's (1947) study may also have had learning disabilities. Many of these students exhibited feelings of inferiority, an inability to persevere in the accomplishment of goals, and a general lack of self-confidence, all characteristics that are common among high-ability students with learning disabilities (Baum, Owen, & Dixon, 1991; Daniels, 1983; Olenchak, 1995; Whitmore & Maker, 1985).

**178**

Current research has indicated that the interaction of high ability and learning disabilities is confusing for children and young adults and can create affective difficulties for students as they struggle to understand why they can do some things very well while struggling so much with others (Olenchak, 1995). In a recent study of academically successful gifted college students with learning disabilities, all of the participants recalled negative and, in many cases, painful memories of situations that had occurred during their elementary and secondary school years (Reis, Neu, & McGuire, 1997). The negative school experiences that these students encountered included: repeated punishment for not completing work on time, retention (repetition) of a grade attributed to the participant's learning disability; placement in a self-contained special education class in which the majority of students were developmentally delayed or had been identified as mentally retarded; and negative, inappropriate treatment by peers and teachers. The participants in this study were often criticized, punished, or repeatedly told to work harder. Most of their teachers understood they were smart, as many of the participants had superior oral skills, but had below-average writing or reading skills. Participants, however, recounted numerous instances in which their teachers, confused because of the superior abilities they displayed in some areas, repeatedly called these students "lazy" and told them to "shape up" and "work harder."

An examination of the lives of highly accomplished individuals who lived in the past may provide insight into the experiences of some talented persons with learning disabilities. Eminent individuals often experienced difficulties with the educational system. For example, when Goertzel and Goertzel (1962) studied the lives of famous individuals, they found that many avoided school, had different learning styles from those used for instruction, and utilized unique compensation styles to overcome learning problems.

## Identification of Gifted Students With Learning Disabilities

Identification of students with talents and disabilities is problematic and challenges educators. As early as 1957, Gowan noted discrepancies between ability, potential, or both as measured on IQ instruments and by academic performance, and these early findings may have influenced discrepancy formulas often used to identify learning disabilities. For example, a discrepancy may exist between ability and achievement, or high scores in a performance area might be coupled with low scores in a verbal area. Mauser (1981) found that 2.3% of 5,000 identified students with learning disabilities had IQ scores over 120. A comparison of the scores of three groups of students (gifted students, gifted students with learning disabilities, and other students with learning disabilities) on the WISC-R (Schiff, Kaufman, & Kaufman, 1981) revealed discrepancies between verbal and performance scores of gifted/LD students. The conclusions drawn from the discrepancies on WISC-R subtests have caused debate about the use of discrepancies formulae (Brown & Yakimowski, 1987; Silverman, 1989). The current consensus seems to indicate that gifted students with learning disabilities may have discrepancies in their IQ profiles, but that the isolation of specific subtests (e.g., Coding, Arithmetic, and Digit Span) as a sole means to identify gifted/LD students is inappropriate (Baum, Owen, & Dixon, 1991; Hansford, Whitmore, Kraynak, & Wingenbach, 1987; Silverman).

The controversy about how to identify this population continues (Sternberg & Grigorenko, 1999), and, for identification purposes, most school personnel rely on discrepancy formulae between intelligence and ability test scores, analyses of intelligence test results for differences across subtests ("scatter"), and multidimensional approaches that incorporate structured interviews, observations, and other qualitative data (Lyon, Gray, Kavanagh, & Krasnegor, 1993). Identification of this population still continues to be challenging. In one recent study, many gifted students with learning disabilities were identified later in their school career, either in middle school or high school, even though most were referred by teachers or parents for testing or various types of assistance because of difficulties encountered in reading or writing in primary or elementary school (Reis, Neu, & McGuire, 1997). Learning problems were evident in this population in the early grades, although most students who were referred were not identified as having a learning disability until later in school.

The identification of this group is complicated by the fact that abilities of gifted students often mask their disabilities, and, in turn, their disabilities may disguise their giftedness. As a result, students who are gifted and also have learning disabilities are at risk of under-identification (Baum, Owen, & Dixon, 1991; Olenchak, 1994; Reis, Neu, & McGuire, 1995) or exclusion from both programs for students with learning disabilities and programs for the gifted and talented. This is also true of gifted students with other exceptionalities such as AD/HD (Moon, this volume) and Asperger's syndrome (Neihart, 2000).

## Social and Emotional Characteristics of Gifted/LD Students

Gifted students with learning disabilities may demonstrate some of the following affective characteristics: strong, personal need for excellence in performance and in outcomes that approaches or embodies unhealthy perfectionism (Rosner & Seymour, 1983); intensity of emotions (Daniels 1983; Olenchak, 1994; Silverman, 1993; Vespi & Yewchuck, 1992) that may resemble the oversensitivity described by Dabrowski and Piechowski (1977); and unrealistic expectations of self (Baum & Owen, 1988; Daniels, 1983; Silverman, 1989). Other affective characteristics of gifted/LD students may include a tendency toward intense frustration with difficult tasks (Baum, Owen, & Dixon, 1991; Olenchak) that often produces a general lack of motivation (Olenchak; Silverman), as well as disruptive or withdrawn behavior (Baum & Owen); feelings of learned helplessness (Whitmore, 1981; Whitmore & Maker, 1985); and low self-esteem (Baum & Owen; Baum, Owen, & Dixon).

A recent comprehensive discussion of these characteristics of gifted/LD students (Reis, Neu, & McGuire, 1995) found that more characteristics were negative than positive. In addition, in this research study almost half of the postsecondary gifted/LD students studied had sought counseling for their social and emotional problems, ranging from mild depression to contemplation of suicide. The variable academic achievements of this population hindered

181

early identification of their learning disability and prevented several students from inclusion in a gifted education program despite high IQ scores. Students reported negative school experiences and difficulties typically associated with learning disabilities, such as social problems, difficulty with teachers, and frustration with certain academic areas. Participants indicated that educators rarely, if ever, addressed the strengths or gifts of this group and instead focused on their deficits. Some participants in this study indicated that school personnel considered having a learning disability to be synonymous with having below-average ability. This was supported by numerous accounts of negative school experiences related by students and verified by parents.

Using case studies, Olenchak (in press) found that current attempts at "differentiation," defined as adjusting curriculum and instruction around the needs of gifted and talented students with respect to programming and teaching provided to other students, had particularly negative ramifications for gifted/LD students. Generally, gifted/LD students expressed feelings of greater disparity from peers than before differentiation was implemented, and specifically they displayed behaviors associated with anxiety and possible depression after differentiation was implemented. However, once differentiation strategies were adjusted to meet the unique needs of gifted/LD students, those studied demonstrated substantial improvements in both social and emotional status and academic performance. Hence, even efforts appropriate for accommodating gifted students must be carefully examined for their effects on gifted/LD students who do not necessarily fit accommodation techniques that are gauged globally around the gifted label alone. Similar issues have been found in gifted students with AD/HD. For example, they may struggle in self-contained classrooms for gifted students unless they receive special accommodations for their disability (Zentall, Moon, Hall, & Grskovic, 2001).

Reis, McGuire, and Neu (2000) studied the compensation strategies used by gifted/LD students who were able to regulate their social and emotional difficulties and succeed in college. Several of these students were also identified with AD/HD. The following compensation strategies were used: deliberate study strategies, cognitive/learning strategies, compensatory supports, environmental

**182**

accommodations, opportunities for counseling, self-advocacy, and the development of an individual plan incorporating a focus on metacognition and executive functions.

Unfortunately, most studies of the social and emotional characteristics of gifted students with learning disabilities have not examined the possible effects of co-occurring AD/HD, making it difficult to determine how the affective characteristics of gifted/LD students might be affected by the presences or absence of AD/HD. Given what is known about gifted students with AD/HD (Moon, this volume; Moon, Zentall, Grskovic, Hall, & Stormont-Spurgin, 2001), it seems reasonable to hypothesize that gifted students with both exceptionalities will have even greater affective difficulties than gifted students with learning disabilities alone.

## Implications for Educating Gifted/LD Students

Gifted/LD students require unique educational programs and services for both their academic and affective development (Nielsen, Higgins, & Hammond, 1995; Nielsen, Higgins, Wilkinson, & Webb, 1994). By studying eminent adults with learning disabilities, Gerber and Ginsberg (1990) concluded that certain behaviors contributing to success can be cultivated and shaped, and their conclusions about successful adults with learning disabilities can be reasonably applied to the education of gifted/LD students. Educators are more likely to succeed with gifted/LD students when they nurture self-control and empowerment, increase a desire to succeed, and establish an orientation toward establishing and attaining reasonable goals. Further, when schools reframe the learning disability as a personal attribute for which compensatory strategies can be learned and exercised, increase individual persistence, emphasize student abilities, and de-emphasize the disabilities, gifted/LD students have more opportunities to be successful. Differentiation on an individual level that personalizes instruction and curricula is critical for emphasizing talent development and de-emphasizing remediation (Olenchak, in press). The presence of AD/HD in addition to a learning disability would make many of the interventions recommended here more difficult for students to implement, slowing progress and requiring additional understanding and patience from educators. This is yet another reason it is important to assess whether AD/HD is present in addition to a learning disability.

Baum, Owen, and Dixon (1991) found that, when schools implement comprehensive programs that identify and develop individual gifts and talents, gifted/LD pupils begin to behave socially, emotionally, and academically more like gifted students without disabilities than like nongifted students with learning disabilities. These findings, later corroborated by Bender and Wall (1994) and Olenchak (1994), indicate that, as educators diminish the attention to and importance of the disability and concentrate instead on the gifts, gifted/LD students become creatively productive. Reis, Neu, and McGuire (1997) also found evidence of the need to focus on gifts and talents in successful university students with learning disabilities. This attention to talent development produced a determination in parents to fight for additional opportunities and also resulted in higher levels of confidence in gifted students with learning disabilities.

Each of these studies reinforces a need for a shift in the educational paradigm, from remediation of weaknesses to the development of gifts and talents (Baum, Owen, & Dixon, 1991; Reis, Neu, & McGuire, 1995). Minner (1990) found that teachers invariably focus on learning disabilities, even to the point of declining to refer or otherwise involve gifted/LD students in gifted educational programs. Sadly, the orientation toward repairing problems versus one aimed at nurturing strengths dominates educational emphases for gifted/LD students even at the collegiate level (Ferri, Gregg, & Heggoy, 1997; Reis, Neu, & McGuire). Even when programs emphasize strengths, efforts must be geared to provide individual attention to each gifted/LD student in order to enhance self-esteem and self-concept in relation to other gifted students (Olenchak, in press).

## Promising Educational Interventions

Current research suggests possible approaches for differentiating education for gifted/LD students while simultaneously considering their social and emotional growth (Brody & Mills, 1997). However, it should be noted that few programs actually exist for this population. Boodoo, Bradley, Frontera, Pitts, and Wright (1989) found, for example, that the majority of responding school systems they surveyed reported having no gifted/LD children in their district and no special programming available. Many creative alternatives can be used for educational interventions for this population, including those suggested in Table 1.

A program of individually tailored enrichment activities, such as those advocated in the Enrichment Triad Model (Renzulli, 1977; Renzulli & Reis, 1985, 1997), that ultimately leads toward personal creative productivity has been shown to enhance self-esteem and to reduce frustration among gifted/LD students (Baum, Owen, & Dixon, 1991; Olenchak, 1995). In addition, Olenchak (1995) found that optimistic attitudes on the part of educators inspired those same feelings among the pupils, facilitating their achievement. Mentorships are also particularly effective with this population, especially in shifting the way in which students perceive the purpose of schooling (i.e., from a remediation orientation to one targeting their individual growth; Olenchak, 1994, 1995). In a college program for gifted/LD students, opportunities for counseling and acquisition of compensation strategies coupled with the choice of a major of strong interest provided the best possible combination for a successful academic career (Reis, Neu, & McGuire, 1997)

Providing instruction in higher order problem solving and information processing enhances the development of academic coping strategies, and may help to improve both students' self-esteem as problem solvers and their academic performance (Hansford, 1987; Reis, McGuire, & Neu, 2000). Furthermore, because gifted/LD students tend to be more resourceful and strategic in approaching problems than nongifted students who have learning disabilities, classroom activities that emphasize these skills may also improve self-esteem (Coleman, 1992).

Inclusion of group and individual counseling and other specific affective strategies or programs can help to address the unique issues faced by gifted/LD students. Counseling strategies used with other academic compensation strategies can help to keep academic

Table 1

# Educational Interventions
# for Gifted/LD Students

1. **Programming:**

- Gifted/talented program in elementary or secondary schools that focus on strengths as opposed to deficits (Baum, Owen, & Dixon, 1991)
- Acceleration in areas of academic strength (Daniels, 1983; Jacobson, 1984; Rosner & Seymour, 1983)
- Individualized Education Plans (IEP) enabling students to have various accommodations should address both the gift and the disability, the strengths and the needs of the students.
- Interest-based independent studies (Renzulli, 1977)
- Special classes (either part-time or full-time) for students who are gifted and learning disabled
- Opportunities for advanced level courses, online and in person, in areas of strength in middle and high school (Reis, Neu, & McGuire, 1995)

2. **Support personnel:**

- Learning-disability specialist assigned to this population in larger schools (instead of having a learning-disability specialist provide service to a heterogeneous population, he or she can focus on high-potential students with learning disabilities in larger schools)
- Mentorships/internships with a successful adult with learning disability (Silverman, 1989; Weill, 1987; Williams, 1988)

3. **Regular classroom strategies:**

- Modifications that allow students to be successful in the regular classroom (books on tape, keyboarding, spell check, etc.; Reis, Neu, & McGuire, 1995)

- Advanced opportunities in technology (computer dictation, books read by computers) that will help to accommodate for learning disabilities (Reis, Neu, & McGuire)

4. **Counseling:**

- Discussion groups for gifted/LD, led by facilitator with expertise in the area such as a guidance counselor, learning-disability specialist or gifted education specialist (Reis, Neu, & McGuire, 1995)
- Proactive counseling provided by guidance counselor with expertise in the area of social and emotional issues for this population (Reis, Neu, & McGuire, 1995)
- Positive peer support programs that enable successful gifted students with learning disabilities to mentor younger students

6. **Out-of-school options:**

- Summer or after-school programs that provide instruction in compensatory strategies (Daniels, 1983; Reis, Neu, & McGuire, 1995; Rosner & Seymour, 1983; Silverman, 1989)
- Summer programs that provide transitional support to the next level of education (e.g., middle to high school)
- After-school programs focusing on strengths and interests (Renzulli, 1977; Renzulli & Reis, 1985, 1997)

---

achievement steady (Reis, Neu, & McGuire, 1997) and provide forums for discussion of appropriate coping techniques for releasing emotions and for dealing with heightened sensitivities (Bredekamp, 1996; Coleman, 1992; Olenchak, 1995). The research of Bender and Wall (1994) and Osman and Blinder (1995) has advocated group social development and counseling programs for students with learning disabilities without giftedness that seem to have direct educational implications for gifted/LD students, as well. Counseling with groups of gifted/LD students could well serve as a

**187**

forum for the development of positive peer relationships among pupils who may have low academic achievement and problems related to social and emotional regulation.

A carefully articulated research agenda for this population would include studies focusing on the use of various interventions on the identification of and programming for gifted/LD students from elementary through postsecondary. Another type of study would involve descriptive information on areas such as depression and other social and emotional issues on a large sample of gifted/LD students in secondary school and college. Both types of studies should examine differences among gifted students with learning disabilities alone, AD/HD alone, and learning disabilities in combination with AD/HD.

## Conclusion

Gifted students with learning disabilities are a unique population who are at special risk for social and emotional issues because of the incompatibility of extraordinary talent with significant learning problems. These issues can result in unresolved social and emotional problems and serve to diminish the full development of talent in gifted students, resulting in the underachievement of many talented young people.

## References

Baum, S., Owen, S. V., & Dixon, J. (1991). *To be gifted and learning disabled: From definitions to practical intervention strategies.* Mansfield Center, CT: Creative Learning Press.

Baum, S., & Owen, S. V. (1988). High-ability/learning-disabled students: How are they different? *Gifted Child Quarterly, 32*, 321–326.

Bender, W. N., & Wall, M. E. (1994). Social-emotional development of students with learning disabilities. *Learning Disabilities Quarterly, 17*, 323–341.

Boodoo, G. M., Bradley, C. L., Frontera, R. L. Pitts, J. R., & Wright, L. B. (1989). A survey of procedures used for identifying gifted learning-disabled children. *Gifted Child Quarterly, 33*, 110–114.

Bredekamp, C. M. (1996). *The gifted/learning-disabled student: A contradiction in the classroom.* Washington, DC: U.S. Department of Education, Educational Information Center. (ERIC Document No. ED374579)

Brody, L. E., & Mills, C. J. (1997). Gifted children with learning disabilities: A review of the issues. *Journal of Learning Disabilities, 30,* 282–296.

Brown, S. W., & Yakimowski, M. E. (1987). Intelligence scores of gifted students on the WISC-R. *Gifted Child Quarterly, 31,* 130–135.

Coleman, M. R. (1992). A comparison of how gifted/LD and average/LD boys cope with school frustration. *Journal for the Education of the Gifted, 15,* 239–265.

Dabrowski, K., & Piechowski, M. M. (1977). *Theory of levels of emotional development.* Oceanside, NY: Dabor.

Daniels, P. R. (1983). *Teaching the gifted/learning disabled child.* Rockville, MD: Aspen.

Davis, G. A., & Rimm, S. B. (1985). *Education of the gifted and talented.* Englewood Cliffs, NJ: Prentice-Hall.

Ferri, B. A., Gregg, N., & Heggoy, S. J. (1997). Profiles of college students demonstrating learning disabilities with and without giftedness. *Journal of Learning Disabilities, 30,* 552–559.

Gardner, H. (1983). *Frames of mind: The theory of multiple intelligences.* New York: Basic Books.

Gerber, P. J., & Ginsberg, R. J. (1990). *Identifying alterable patterns of success in highly successful adults with learning disabilities: Executive summary.* Washington, DC: U.S. Department of Education, Educational Information Center. (ERIC Document No. ED342168)

Goertzel, V., & Goertzel, M. G. (1962). *Cradles of eminence.* Boston: Little, Brown.

Gowan, J. C. (1957). Dynamics of the underachievement of gifted students. *Exceptional Children, 24,* 98–102.

Hansford, S. J. (1987). *Intellectually gifted learning-disabled students: A special study.* Washington, DC: U.S. Department of Education, Educational Information Center. (ERIC Document No. ED287242)

Hansford, S. J., Whitmore, J. R., Kraynak, A. R., & Wingenbach, N. G. (1987). *Intellectually gifted learning-disabled students: A special study.* Reston, VA: Council for Exceptional Children. (ERIC Document Reproduction Service No. ED 287 242)

Jacobson, V. (1984). *The gifted learning disabled.* Clumer, IN: Purdue University. (Eric Document No. ED254981)

Lyon, G. A., Gray, D. B., Kavanagh, J. F., & Krasnegor, N. A. (Eds.). (1993). *Better understanding learning disabilities: New views from research and their implications for education and public policies.* Baltimore: Brookes.

Mauser, A. J. (1981). Programming strategies for pupils with disabilities who are gifted. *Rehabilitation Literature, 42,* 270–275.

Minner, S. (1990). Teacher evaluations of case descriptions of LD/gifted children. *Gifted Child Quarterly, 34,* 37–39.

Moon, S. M., Zentall, S. S., Grskovic, J., Hall, A., & Stormont-Spurgin, M. (2001). Emotional, social, and family characteristics of boys with AD/HD and giftedness: A comparative case study. *Journal for the Education of the Gifted, 24,* 207–247.

Neihart, M. (2000). Gifted children with Asperger's syndrome. *Gifted Child Quarterly, 44*, 222–230.

Nielsen, E., Higgins, D. H., & Hammond, A. (1995). *Twice-exceptional learners: Gifted students with disabilities.* Albuquerque: University of New Mexico.

Nielsen, M. E., Higgins, L. D., Wilkinson, S. C., & Webb, K. W. (1994). Helping twice-exceptional students to succeed in high school. *Journal of Secondary Gifted Education, 5*, 35–39.

Olenchak, F. R. (1994). Talent development: Accommodating the social and emotional needs of secondary gifted/learning-disabled students. *Journal of Secondary Gifted Education, 5*(3), 40–52.

Olenchak, F. R. (1995). Effects of enrichment on gifted/learning-disabled students. *Journal for the Education of the Gifted, 18*, 385–399.

Olenchak, F. R. (in press). Lessons learned from gifted students about differentiation. *Teacher Educator, 36.*

Orton, S. (1937). *Reading and writing and speech problems in children.* New York: W. W. Norton.

Osman, B. B., & Blinder, H. L. (1995). *No one to play with: The social side of learning disabilities.* Novato, CA: Academic Therapy Publications.

Prater, G., & Minner, S. (1986). *Identification of atypical gifted children* (Technical Report. No. 2). Murray, KY: Murray State University, Department of Special Education.

Reis, S. M., McGuire, J. M., & Neu, T. W. (2000). Compensation strategies used by high-ability students with learning disabilities who succeed in college. *Gifted Child Quarterly, 44*, 123–134.

Reis, S. M., Neu, T. W., & McGuire, J. M. (1995). *Talents in two places: Case studies of high ability students with learning disabilities who have achieved* (Research Monograph 95113). Storrs: National Research Center on the Gifted and Talented, The University of Connecticut.

Reis, S. M., Neu, T. W., & McGuire, J. M. (1997). Case studies of high-ability students with learning disabilities who have achieved. *Exceptional Children, 63*, 463–479.

Renzulli, J. S. (1977). *The enrichment triad model: A guide for developing defensible programs for the gifted and talented.* Mansfield Center, CT: Creative Learning Press.

Renzulli, J. S., & Reis, S. M. (1985). *The schoolwide enrichment model: A comprehensive plan for educational excellence.* Mansfield Center, CT: Creative Learning Press.

Renzulli, J. S., & Reis, S. M. (1997). *The schoolwide enrichment model: A how-to guide for educational excellence.* Mansfield Center, CT: Creative Learning Press.

Rosner, S., & Seymour, J. (1983). The gifted child with a learning disability: Clinical evidence. In L. Fox, L. Brody, & D. Tobin (Eds.), *Learning Disabled/Gifted Children: Identification and Programming* (pp. 77–97). Baltimore: University Park Press.

Schiff, M., Kaufman, A. S., & Kaufman, N. L. (1981). Scatter analysis of WISC-R profiles for learning disabled children with superior intelligence. *Journal of Learning Disabilities, 14*, 400–404.

Silverman, L. K. (1989). Invisible gifts, invisible handicaps. *Roeper Review, 12,* 37–42.

Silverman, L. K. (1993). *Counseling the gifted and talented.* Denver: Love.

Sternberg, R. J. (1981). A componential theory of intellectual giftedness. *Gifted Child Quarterly, 25,* 86–93.

Sternberg, R. J., & Grigorenko, E. L. (1999). *Our labeled children.* Reading, MA: Perseus Books.

Swesson, K. (1994). Helping the gifted/LD. *Gifted Child Today, 17*(5), 24–26.

Terman, L. M., & Oden, M. H. (1947). *The gifted child grows up.* Stanford, CA: Stanford University Press.

Vespi, L., & Yewchuck, C. (1992). A phenomenological study of the social/emotional characteristics of gifted learning-disabled children. *Journal for the Education of the Gifted, 16,* 55–72.

Weill, M. P. (1987). Gifted/learning disabled students: Their potential may be buried treasure. *The Clearing House, 60,* 341–343.

Whitmore, J. R. (1980). *Giftedness, conflict, and underachievement.* Boston: Allyn and Bacon.

Whitmore, J. R. (1981). Gifted children with handicapping conditions: A new frontier. *Exceptional Children, 48,* 106–114.

Whitmore, J. R., & Maker, C. J. (1985). *Intellectual giftedness in disabled persons.* Rockville, MD: Aspen.

Zentall, S. S., Moon, S. M., Hall, A., & Grskovic, J. A. (2001). Learning and motivational characteristics of boys with AD/HD and/or giftedness. *Exceptional Children, 67,* 499–519.

# 19
# GIFTED CHILDREN WITH ATTENTION-DEFICIT/ HYPERACTIVITY DISORDER

by **Sidney M. Moon, Ph.D.**

ifted children with attention-deficit/hyperactivity disorder (AD/HD) are at risk for difficulties with social and emotional adjustment (Leroux & Levitt-Perlman, 2000; Moon, Zentall, Grskovic, Hall, & Stormont-Spurgin, 2001). The issues that place them at risk are directly related to their impairments and include misidentification, emotional immaturity, peer rejection, family stress, and school stress. To understand the social and emotional issues of this special population of gifted students, it is important to understand the nature of their disorder. This is not an easy task, both because AD/HD is controversial and because little empirical research has examined the unique issues that arise when AD/HD and giftedness co-occur.

# AD/HD

The terminology used to describe AD/HD has evolved during the past century as researchers have come to understand more about the disorder. Early terminology such as "minimal brain dysfunction" and "hyperkinetic reaction of childhood" has been replaced with "Attention Deficit/Hyperactivity Disorder." In the current edition of the *American Psychiatric Association Diagnostic and Statistical Manual of Mental Disorders,* four subtypes of AD/HD are recognized: Predominately Hyperactive/Impulsive, Predominately Inattentive, Combined, and Not Otherwise Specified (American Psychiatric Association, 1994). Diagnosis requires (a) establishing that six of nine behavioral criteria for hyperactivity/impulsivity and/or inattention are present; (b) documenting that those behaviors are persistent and present in at least two settings; and (c) ruling out other disorders that have similar symptoms.

The etiology of AD/HD has not been clearly established, but most researchers who have studied the disorder believe it can result from both genetic predisposition and environmental factors such as prenatal smoking (Kaufmann, Kalbfleisch, & Castellanos, 2000). It appears to be a neurobiological disorder that impairs executive functioning. Brain dysfunctions associated with AD/HD include abnormalities in the prefrontal-basal ganglia circuit and/or the anatomy of the cerebellum, or both, and deficiencies in the neurotransmitter dopamine (Kaufmann et al.). Cognitive tests of prefrontal brain functioning show developmental delays of two to three years (Kaufmann & Castellanos, 2000). Some AD/HD researchers have concluded that the core cognitive impairments of AD/HD are in impulse-control processes (Barkley, 1997), while others have put more emphasis on attentional processes (Brown, 1999). All agree, however, that these students have deficiencies in executive functioning that influence their behavior at home and at school.

**194**

Estimates of the prevalence of the disorder in the general population range from 0–16%, with an average of 2% across studies (Lahey et al., 1994). Girls with AD/HD in the general population are less likely to be identified and less likely to be referred for treatment if identified (Grskovic, 2000). The prevalence of AD/HD in gifted populations is unknown, in part because of a lack of research on this issue (Kaufmann & Castellanos, 2000) and in part because of the misidentification issues discussed in the next section.

## Misidentification

Since some symptoms of AD/HD overlap with the characteristics of giftedness, scholars in the field of gifted education have theorized that a gifted child might be labeled and treated for AD/HD when he or she does not actually have the disorder (Baum, Olenchak, & Owen, 1998; Cramond, 1995). This type of misidentification would have negative consequences for the social and emotional development of a gifted child because his or her real needs would not be met and because he or she might receive inappropriate treatment, such as unnecessary psychotropic medication. No empirical research has been conducted to document the frequency of this type of misidentification (Kaufmann & Castellanos, 2000; Kaufmann, Kalbfleish, & Castellanos, 2000).

Our primary concern here, however, is a different type of misidentification, that is, failure to identify AD/HD, giftedness, or both in children who actually have both exceptionalities. This type of misidentification can occur for several reasons. As with other dual exceptionalities, giftedness can mask an attention-deficit disorder for a time. There is empirical evidence that giftedness delays the age of AD/HD diagnosis (Castellanos, 2000). The higher the IQ, the later the AD/HD diagnosis tends to occur. Hidden AD/HD has negative effects on the self-concept of the gifted child because trying harder has little effect on such AD/HD as disorganization, daydreaming, incessant talking, inability to sit still, and social immaturity (Leroux & Levitt-Perlman, 2000). Hence, a gifted child whose giftedness is recognized, but whose attention deficit is hidden, can easily develop learned helplessness in the areas affected by his or her disorder. In extreme cases, such a child may appear "average" in ability, so both exceptionalities will be hidden.

**195**

In addition, cognitive-processing inefficiencies and attentional difficulties lead to lowered scores on IQ tests. Children with AD/HD typically score 5–10 points lower on IQ tests than normal children at the same ability level (Castellanos, 2000). A typical pattern is near-normal scores on verbal subtests and scores 10–40 points below normal on performance subtests. When identification procedures for gifted programs rely heavily on intelligence tests, gifted children with AD/HD may be missed.

A third reason for misidentification of this population is their unusual attentional profile (Kaufmann & Castellanos, 2000). The reinforcement gradient for children with AD/HD differs from that of normal children (Kaufmann, Kalbfleish, & Castellanos, 2000). The reinforcement gradient is the rate at which reinforcement strength decreases as the time interval between a behavior and its consequence increases. For children with AD/HD, the gradient is lower than normal when reinforcement is delayed and higher than normal when it is immediate. In practical terms, the first pattern means that a primary characteristic of the disorder is that children with AD/HD have more difficulty than normal children sustaining attention to low-interest, low-stimulation activities with distal reinforcers. Unfortunately, such tasks characterize much of the work assigned in schools (repetitive homework, studying for unit tests, researching topics that are not interesting to the student, etc.). At the same time, however, the second pattern means that children with AD/HD can sustain attention *better* than normal children when interest is high, tasks are challenging, and reinforcement is rapid. Examples include working under deadline pressure, video games, and self-selected creative expression. Under these conditions, children with AD/HD enter a state called "hyperfocus" that bears a strong resemblance to the state of "flow" described by (Csikszentmihalyi, 1990; 1997). In this state, their attentional problems disappear, leading observing adults to believe that their problems sustaining attention on more routine tasks are due to a failure of will, rather than to a cognitive handicap. The discrepancy between these two attentional profiles in a gifted child with AD/HD is frustrating for teachers and may lead them to not nominate such students for gifted programs.

In summary, the characteristics of gifted children with AD/HD can mask one or both of their exceptionalities, leading to their underidentification for gifted programming and misunderstanding of their behaviors by themselves and their caretakers. Misinterpretation of their behaviors, in turn, can create emotional distress. In addition, their disorder can create emotional problems for them, as discussed in the next section.

## Emotional and Motivational Immaturity

Gifted children with AD/HD have difficulty regulating their emotions (Moon et al., 2001). They are more emotionally immature, but more advanced cognitively, than their age peers. As a result, they experience tremendous internal asynchrony between their cognitive and affective abilities. To others, they often appear moody and unpredictable. These difficulties need to be addressed as developmental immaturities in young gifted children with AD/HD. Such children need more help than other children to learn to label, control, and appropriately express their emotions. Counseling may be required to assist them with these skills.

## Peer Rejection

Children with AD/HD are also socially immature, lagging as much as two to three years behind other children in their social development (Kaufmann & Castellanos, 2000). They exhibit annoying and sometimes aggressive behaviors that are disliked by their peers and can lead to social rejection (Moon et al., 2001). Social rejection may be especially likely for gifted students with AD/HD when such students are placed in self-contained classes for gifted students because gifted education classrooms tend to have advanced norms of social and motivational behavior that highlight their developmental immaturities (Moon et al.). This is a difficult issue to resolve, and research has not yet provided much guidance on how to facilitate friendship development in gifted children with AD/HD.

## Family Stress

Living with a child with AD/HD is a family stressor (Barkley, 1995; Everett & Everett, 1999). In addition, since AD/HD has a genetic component, one or more parents of the gifted child with AD/HD often has the disorder (Barkley, 1990). For both of these reasons, the families of gifted children with AD/HD tend to be more stressed, conflicted, and disorganized than is typical of families of gifted children (Moon et al., 2001). Parents of these children need to learn about both giftedness (Walker, 1991; Webb, Meckstroth, & Tolan, 1993) and AD/HD (Barkley, 1995; Cohen, 1998; Weiss, 1996) in order to understand the behaviors of their child and facilitate their development. Parenting these children requires understanding, skill, and patience (Leroux & Levitt-Perlman, 2000). Families of gifted children with AD/HD that have developed dysfunctional interaction patterns can benefit from family therapy (Everett & Everett, 1999; Moon & Hall, 1998). Early intervention is important to prevent AD/HD from progressing to problems with substance abuse, oppositional defiant disorder, conduct disorder (Biederman, Newcorn, & Sprich, 1991; Herrero, Hechtman, & Weiss, 1994; Levin & Kleber, 1995; Lynskey & Fergusson, 1995)

## School Stress

Gifted children with AD/HD have difficulties sustaining attention to routine tasks, shifting attention, transitioning between tasks, monitoring their progress on long-term projects, keeping track of homework, organizing their desks and lockers, and following directions (Kalbfleisch, 2000; Zentall, Moon, Hall, & Grskovic, 2001). School stress is inevitable when a child has difficulty focusing attention and completing schoolwork. Resolving school stress in gifted children with AD/HD is a difficult task. There are usually insufficient numbers of such children to provide programs designed to address both their giftedness and their AD/HD. One of the best general approaches to working with such children, as with other twice-exceptional children, is individualized planning that accommodates both the child's talents and his or her disability (Baum, Owen, & Dixon, 1991; Birely, 1995; Kaufmann, Kalbfleish, & Castellanos, 2000).

In addition, strength-based interventions are needed that capture the attention of the gifted child with AD/HD. Increasing stimulation often works better than reducing distractions for these students. For example, it may be easier for them to work on routine homework when listening to music or watching television. Similarly, in school settings, these children have preferences for high-stimulation learning contexts (Zentall et al., 2001). They like hands-on activities, computer-based instruction, high-interest content, and one-on-one attention from an adult.

To address their weaknesses, teachers can adapt materials on teaching children who are gifted and learning disabled (Baum, Owen, & Dixon, 1991; Birely, 1995) and children with AD/HD (Reif, 1993) to develop effective strategies until more materials that specifically address children who are both gifted and AD/HD become available. For example, it seems reasonable to assume that gifted children with AD/HD, like other children with AD/HD, might benefit from direct instruction in study skills (Reif). Another approach might be to combine creatively modifications suggested for students with AD/HD with modifications recommended for gifted students (Kaufmann, Kalbfleish, & Castellanos, 2000; Kaufmann & Castellanos, 2000).

In conclusion, gifted children with AD/HD have specific behavioral characteristics and developmental delays that place them at risk for social and emotional problems. These children need early and accurate identification followed by long-term, individualized intervention that addresses both the family and school context in order to maximize their development and realize their talent potential.

# References

American Psychiatric Association. (1994). *Diagnostic and statistical manual of mental disorders* (4th ed.). Washington, DC: Author.

Barkley, R. A. (1990). *Attention deficit hyperactivity disorder: A handbook for diagnosis and treatment.* New York: Guilford.

Barkley, R. A. (1995). *Taking charge of AD/HD.* New York: Guilford.

Barkley, R. A. (1997). *ADHD and the nature of self-control*. New York: Guilford.

Baum, S. M., Olenchak, F. R., & Owen, S. V. (1998). Gifted students with attention deficits: Fact and/or fiction? Or, can we see the forest for the trees? *Gifted Child Quarterly, 42,* 96–104.

Baum, S. M., Owen, S. V., & Dixon, J. (1991). *To be gifted and learning disabled: From identification to practical intervention strategies*. Mansfield Center, CT: Creative Learning Press.

Biederman, J., Newcorn, J., & Sprich, S. (1991). Comorbidity of attention-deficit hyperactivity disorder with conduct, depressive, anxiety, and other disorders. *American Journal of Psychiatry, 148,* 564–577.

Birely, M. (1995). *A sourcebook for helping children who are gifted and learning disabled*. Reston, VA: Council for Exceptional Children.

Brown, T. E. (1999, August). *Inattention and executive functions: New understandings of the ADD syndrome*. Paper presented at the annual meeting of the American Psychological Association, Boston.

Castellanos, X. (2000, November). *ADHD or gifted: Is it either/or?* Paper presented at the annual meeting of the National Association for Gifted Children, Atlanta, GA.

Cohen, M. W. (1998). *The attention zone: A parent's guide to attention deficit/hyperactivity disorder*. Philadelphia: Brunner-Routledge.

Cramond, B. (1995). *The coincidence of attention deficit hyperactivity disorder and creativity*. Storrs: National Research Center on the Gifted and Talented, University of Connecticut.

Csikszentmihalyi, M. (1990). *Flow: The psychology of optimal experience*. New York: Harper & Row.

Csikszentmihalyi, M. (1997). *Finding flow: The psychology of engagement in everyday life*. New York: Basic Books.

Everett, C. A., & Everett, S. V. (1999). *Family therapy for ADHD: Treating children, adolescents, and adults*. New York: Guilford.

Grskovic, J. A. (2000). *Girls with AD/HD*. Unpublished doctoral dissertation, Purdue University, West Lafayette, IN.

Herrero, M. E., Hechtman, L., & Weiss, G. (1994). Antisocial disorders in hyperactive subjects from childhood to adulthood: Predictive factors and characterization of subgroups. *American Journal of Orthopsychiatry, 64,* 510–521.

Kalbfleisch, M. L. (2000). *Electroencephalographic differences between males with and without ADHD with average and high aptitude during task transitions*. Unpublished doctoral dissertation, University of Virginia, Charlottesville.

Kaufmann, F. A., & Castellanos, F. X. (2000). Attention-deficit/hyperactivity disorder in gifted students. In K. A. Heller, F. J. Mönks, R. J. Sternberg, & R. F. Subotnik (Eds.), *International handbook of giftedness and talent* (2nd ed., pp. 621–632). Amsterdam: Elsevier.

Kaufmann, F., Kalbfleisch, M. L., & Castellanos, F. X. (2000). *Attention deficit disorders and gifted students: What do we really know?* Storrs, CT: National Research Center on the Gifted and Talented.

Lahey, B. B., Applegate, B., McBurnett, K., Biederman, J., Greenhill, L., Hynd, G. W., Barkely, R. A., Newcorn, J., Jensen, P., & Richters, J. (1994). DSM-IV field trials for attention deficit hyperactivity disorder in children and adolescents. In H. C. Quay & A. E. Hogan (Eds.), *Handbook of disruptive behavior disorders* (pp. 23–48). New York: Plenum.

Leroux, J. A., & Levitt-Perlman, M. (2000). The gifted child with attention deficit disorder: An identification and intervention challenge. *Roeper Review, 22,* 171–176.

Levin, F. R., & Kleber, H. D. (1995). Attention deficit hyperactivity disorder and substance abuse: Relationships and implications for treatment. *Harvard Review of Psychiatry, 2,* 246–258.

Lynskey, M. T., & Fergusson, D. M. (1995). Childhood conduct problems, attention deficit behaviors, and adolescent alcohol, tobacco, and illicit drug use. *Journal of Abnormal Child Psychology, 23,* 281–302.

Moon, S. M., & Hall, A. S. (1998). Family therapy with intellectually and creatively gifted children. *Journal of Marital and Family Therapy, 24*(1), 59–80.

Moon, S. M., Zentall, S., Grskovic, J., Hall, A., & Stormont-Spurgin, M. (2001). Emotional, social, and family characteristics of boys with AD/HD and giftedness: A comparative case study. *Journal for the Education of the Gifted, 24,* 207–247.

Reif, S. F. (1993). *How to reach and teach ADD/ADHD children.* West Nyack, NY: The Center for Applied Research in Education.

Walker, S. Y. (1991). *The survival guide for parents of gifted kids.* Minneapolis: Free Spirit.

Webb, J. T., Meckstroth, E. A., & Tolan, S. S. (1993). *Guiding the gifted child.* Dayton: Ohio Psychology Press.

Weiss, L. (1996). *Give your ADD teen a chance.* Colorado Springs: Pinon Press.

Zentall, S. S., Moon, S. M., Hall, A. M., & Grskovic, J. A. (2001). Learning and motivational characteristics of boys with AD/HD and/or giftedness. *Exceptional Children, 67,* 499–519.

**201**

Attention-Deficit/Hyperactivity Disorder

# Promising Practices and Interventions and Recommendations for Future Action

# 20 PARENTING PRACTICES THAT PROMOTE TALENT DEVELOPMENT, CREATIVITY, AND OPTIMAL ADJUSTMENT

by **Paula Olszewski-Kubilius, Ph.D.**

t is clear from the research literature on talent development and creativity that families play a very important role in the realization of promise and potential (Bloom, 1985). At the most fundamental level, parents provide the resources to support talent development, including their money for lessons, instruments, equipment, and outside-of-school educational opportunities, as well as their time spent on arranging lessons, searching out programs, driving, and monitoring practices. Some talent domains, particularly those typically not dealt with in schools, (e.g., ice skating, gymnastics, music) require a great deal of disposable parental resources of both types.

Parents espouse values conducive to talent development (Olszewski, Kulieke, & Buescher, 1987). These may include the importance of finding and developing one's abilities, achievement at the highest levels possible, independent thought and individual expression, active-recreational pursuits, and cultural and intellectual pursuits (Olszewski et al.). Csikszentmihalyi and Beattie (1979) asserted that families have systems of cognitive coding and patterns of explanations for events or circumstances that affect and determine children's values and attitudes (e.g., "get an education and find a fulfilling career to avoid poverty" versus "get a stable job and save your money").

Parents enact their values (Olszewski et al., 1987). They can demonstrate a love of work and learning. They model independent learning outside of structured or traditional activities and settings. They also model personality dispositions that are essential to talent development such as risk taking and coping with setbacks and failures. They demonstrate that success requires a great deal of hard work and sustained effort over long periods of time.

Another very important role for parents is helping their talented children build social networks that can give them emotional support for their abilities and talent development activities (Subotnik & Olszewski-Kubilius, 1997). Social networks consist of the people within a child's life and their interconnections. Size, memberships, and degree of interconnectedness among members affects the extent to which social networks are psychologically and physically supportive of an individual. The social world of the child begins with the family; but, over time, as higher levels of talent development are achieved, it expands to include teachers, coaches, mentors, and a wider scope of peers. Participation in special activities, such as competitions or after-school and summer programs, can augment and populate social networks with peers who provide specific emotional support for achievement in the talent domain. Friends and companions who are also involved in the talent field can be essential to sustaining commitment during critical times (Subotnik & Olszewski-Kubilius).

**206**

While research generally supports the positive role families can play in developing talent, the literature also suggests that different kinds of family dynamics yield different outcomes for children. Specifically, family dynamics greatly influence children's motivations to achieve or produce, and different patterns of family attitudes, behaviors, and parenting styles may engender different kinds of motivations. Creatively gifted children are found to have families that stress independence, rather than interdependence, between family members; are less child-centered; have somewhat tense family relationships (ones with "wobble"); and have more expressions of negative affect and competition between family members, resulting in motivation toward power and dominance (Albert, 1978, 1983). High scholastic achievers come from families that are cohesive and child-centered and where parent-child identification is strong, resulting in high levels of achievement motivation (Albert).

Research studies of creative eminent adults yield retrospective accounts of family environments characterized by stress, trauma, conflict, and dysfunction. Research on high-IQ individuals—most of whom do not end up being eminent, but are highly productive, competent, well-adjusted individuals—find families that are intact and happy, with normal and moderate levels of stress (Olszewski-Kubilius, 1997). What can we glean from these different profiles of families of gifted individuals? Can we reconcile the pictures of tumultuous families with relatively peaceful, connected families into an understanding of the family's role in talent development? The answer lies in the realization that the effect of the family is complex and multifaceted. Different mixtures of family variables may, in fact, yield different outcomes for children that are more or less supportive of creativity, scholastic achievement, talent development, and general mental health.

Studies suggest that an important family-environment factor is the degree to which the family creates an atmosphere where children are free to develop a unique identity and have their own individual thoughts and express them freely. Individuals who come from such families are more likely to be very creative, as well as highly competent, in their work. Such families foster creativity and intellectual risk taking. The circumstances within homes and families that create environments conducive to the development of independent identities and thought are many and varied. They include anything that results in a reduction in parent-child identification, an "emo-

**207**

tional space" between parent and child, lower levels of parental monitoring of children, and less conventional socialization of children by parents. Circumstances cited in the literature that create this "space" include both negative ones, such as imbalanced parental or difficult family relationships, as well as more benign, typical circumstances such as parents who are less involved with children because they have interests or careers (Ochse, 1993; Olszewski-Kubilius, 1997). These conditions are thought to result in children being more independent, autonomous, and less sex-stereotyped. They also cause children to retreat from interpersonal relationships at home (if very difficult circumstances exist) or contribute to the development of a preference for time alone (if more benign circumstances exist), resulting in more time and opportunity for both practice and skill acquisition in the talent area and a rich internal fantasy life (Ochse, 1993; Simonton, 1992).

On the other hand, in families where members are emotionally close and parents are very involved in their children's lives, strong psychological identifications occur between parents and children, and children internalize parental values and expectations regarding achievement. Through this process, children can also acquire very strong motivations to achieve, both to please significant others and to enact their own acquired values.

A second family-environment factor that appears to play an important role in creating the motivation for high levels of achievement is stress or challenge. *Stress* is a broad concept that is difficult to define. It may be a highly individualized experience—what is very stressful or challenging for one person may be only moderately so for another. Researchers have speculated on the role of stress in engendering powerful motivations to succeed, specifically on how individuals may strive to achieve in order to acquire admiration and affection from others and compensate for unmet or unfulfilled psychological needs, to ameliorate rejection, or to prove that they are worthwhile (Ochse, 1993). "A stressful setting can become the catalyst for potentially talented individuals to meet their deficiency needs for attention, love, and approval through D (deficiency)-creative efforts providing self-expression and rewards" (Rhodes, 1997, p. 260).

Stressful family circumstances may propel a child to seek refuge in safe, controllable intellectual activities or to use a creative activity as an outlet for emotions (Ochse, 1993, Piirto, 1992), and they may force an earlier psychological maturity for the child (Albert, 1978, 1980). Childhood challenges may prepare individuals to cope with the intellectual tensions and marginal existences that are characteristic of highly creative people (Feldman, 1994; Gardner, 1994). Some individuals turn stressful or difficult childhood events into positive challenges that motivate them to "right a wrong" or solve a broader social problem through their adult work and careers (Csikszentmihalyi, 1990).

Although research on eminent individuals seems to suggest that family stress and unhappy childhoods can be major components of the process of producing a creative individual, are they necessary ingredients? Not according to Csikszentmihalyi, Rathunde, and Whalen, (1993), who talked about a balance of support and tension within the family as conducive to high levels of talent development *and* good mental health. They made the point that, because researchers studying families of talented individuals have lacked a conceptual classification for families with a balance of support and tension, they have simply not looked for or studied these kinds of families. These families provide contexts for children that are both integrated (family members are connected and supportive of one another), yet also differentiated (there were high expectations from parents that individual children would develop their talents to the highest degree possible and encouragement of individual thought and expression). Such families produce autotelic personalities in children or individuals who are self-motivated and self-directed. According to Csikszentmihalyi, Rathunde, and Whalen, an overemphasis on one of these can result in individuals who are either highly talented and creative, but not well adjusted (primacy of differentiation), or very well adjusted, but not talented or creative (primacy of integration). It may be that the development of high levels of talent requires the motivation and characteristics born from childhood tragedy, possibly at the expense of good psychological development; other levels of both talent and mental health result from a more balanced blend of tension or challenge and support.

Similarly, Therival (1999a, 1999b) also asserts that stress and tragedy are not essential elements of creative productivity. He offered a model of creativity that includes the following components: genetic endowment (G), parental or other "confidence building" assistances (A), and misfortunes (M). According to Therival, creativity can develop in individuals who experience great misfortunes as long as there are also great assistances present. He distinguished between creators who are dedicated (have high levels of genetic endowment, many assistances in youth, and no major misfortunes) and creators who are "challenged" (have high genetic endowment, some assistances, and some misfortunes). Both produce creative work, but the "challenged" personalities are more overtly driven to prove themselves and to receive recognition (Therival, 1999b). Therival also noted that psychologically abusive childhood challenges that elicit anger are less likely to result in creativity in substantive work.

Most families experience more moderate levels of stress and tensions—more aptly called *challenges*—and it appears that these can be positive influences for children, depending upon how they are interpreted and handled by families. It is also true that family-environment factors interact with others, such as a person's basic constitution, which may make a person more or less vulnerable to stress and more or less resilient and able to cope with challenges (Olszewski-Kubilius, 1997).

Therefore, parenting styles that help a child to find his or her own identity, rather than prescribe it, allow for open expression of ideas and independent thought; reduce parent-child identification, but not necessarily affiliation or affection; and provide support in the presence of challenges, which aids in the development of talent and creativity and good mental health. Parents need to establish and maintain bonds with children, but also allow them autonomy, independence, and psychological and emotional space. They can be very involved in their child's achievement, directly and actively supporting it, but not overly invested in it emotionally or psychologically.

Parents also help children to succeed by allowing them to experience and cope with challenges and difficulties in their lives. Parents should not shield or try to protect children from risks or hard work. Parents also need to allow children to experience the tensions and stress that arise from challenging ideas and high expectations to live up to one's potential. They can support the

**210**

development of coping strategies for stress, such as a rich internal fantasy life, use of time alone to decompress and rejuvenate, expression of emotions via creative work, active use of leisure time, and other ways that help children gain control over their circumstances.

## References

Albert, R. S. (1978). Observation and suggestions regarding giftedness, familiar influence, and the achievement of eminence. *Gifted Child Quarterly 28*, 201–211.

Albert, R. S. (1980). Family positions and the attainment of eminence: A study of special family positions and special family experiences. *Gifted Child Quarterly, 24*, 87–95.

Albert, R. S. (Ed). (1983). *Genius and eminence: The social psychology of creativity and exceptional achievement.* Oxford, England: Pergamon Press.

Bloom, B. (1985). *Developing talent in young people.* New York: Ballantine.

Csikszentmihalyi, M. (1990). *Flow: The psychology of optimal experience .* New York: Harper & Row.

Csikszentmihalyi, M., & Beattie, O. (1979). Life themes: A theoretical and empirical explorations of their origins and effects. *Journal of Humanistic Psychology, 19*, 45–63.

Csikszentmihalyi, M., Rathunde, K., & Whalen, S. (1993). *Talented teenagers: The roots of success and failure.* Cambridge, England: Cambridge University Press.

Feldman, D. H. (1994). Creativity: Dreams, insights, and transformations. In D. H. Felman, M. Csikszentmihalyi, & H. Gardner (Eds.)., *Changing the world: A framework for the study of creativity* (pp. 85–102). Westport, CT: Praeger.

Gardner, H. (1994). The fruits of asynchrony: A psychological examination of creativity. In D. H. Felman, M. Csikszentmihalyi, and H. Gardner (Eds.), *Changing the world: A framework for the study of creativity* (pp. 47–68). Westport, CT: Praeger.

Ochse, R. (1993). *Before the gates of excellence: The determinants of creative genius.* Cambridge, England: Cambridge University Press.

Olszewski-Kubilius, P. (1997, August). *The development of childhood giftedness into adult talent: The role of psychological characteristics and social supports.* Paper presented at the annual convention of the American Psychological Association, Chicago.

Olszewski, P., Kulieke, M. J., & Buescher, T. (1987). The influence of the family environment on the development of talent: A literature review. *Journal for the Education of the Gifted, 11*, 6–28.

Piirto, J. (1992). *Understanding those who create.* Dayton: Ohio Psychology Press.

Rhodes, C. (1997). Growth from deficiency creativity to being creativity. In M. A. Runco and R. Richards (Eds.), *Eminent creativity, everyday creativity, and health* (pp. 247–264). Greenwich, CT: Ablex.

**211**

Simonton, D. K. (1992). The child parents the adult: On getting genius from gift-edness. In N. Colangelo, S. G. Assouline, & D. L. Ambroson (Eds.), *Talent development: Proceedings from the 1991 Henry B. and Jocelyn Wallace National Research Symposium on Talent Development* (pp. 278–297). New York: Trillium.

Subotnik, R. F., & Olszewski-Kubilius, P. (1997). Restructuring special programs to reflect the distinctions between children's and adult's experiences with gift-edness. *Peabody Journal of Education, 72,* 101–116.

Therival, W. A. (1999a). Why are eccentrics not eminently creative? *Creativity Research Journal, 12,* 47–55.

Therival, W. A. (1999b). Why Mozart and not Salieri. *Creativity Research Journal, 12,* 67–76.

# COUNSELING NEEDS AND STRATEGIES

by **Sidney M. Moon, Ph.D.**

ounselors who work with gifted children and adolescents agree that these young people have unique social and emotional issues related to their giftedness (Moon, in press; Moon & Hall, 1998; Neihart, 1999; Silverman, 1993a; Webb, 1993). The most common counseling need of this population is assistance in coping with stressors related to growing up as a gifted child in a society that does not always recognize, understand, or welcome giftedness. For example, a survey of 335 parents, educators, and counselors suggested that the areas in which gifted youth have the greatest need for differentiated counseling that addresses issues they face because of their giftedness are peer relationships, emotional adjustment, social adjustment, and stress management (Moon, Kelly, & Feldhusen, 1997). Underachievement, school/work relationships, and parenting/family relationships are also perceived as having unique dimensions in the gifted population.

**213**

Counselors who specialize in working with gifted and talented youth find that these children experience both internal stressors (e.g., internal dyssynchrony or existential depression) and environmental stressors (e.g., inappropriate school placements or peer cultures that are hostile to achievement; Webb, 1993). Stressors related to giftedness in both children and families can be alleviated by stress-management techniques (Genshaft, Greenbaum, & Borovksky, 1995; Webb, Meckstroth, & Tolan, 1982), counseling provided by counselors with training in the characteristics and needs of gifted individuals (for a specific example of such counseling, see Moon, Nelson, & Piercy, 1993), or both. The need for counseling appears to be greatest during early adolescence, when many gifted students face achievement/affiliation conflicts (Clasen & Clasen, 1995) and at points of transition from one type of school programming to another, especially when the new school program is much more challenging than the old (Coleman & Fults, 1982, 1985; Moon, Swift, & Shallenberger, in press). Families of gifted children also experience unique issues such as feelings of parental inadequacy and confusion about the role they should play when schools are not meeting their child's needs (Hackney, 1981). Stressors related to giftedness in both children and families can be alleviated by stress management techniques (Genshaft, Greenbaum, & Borovksky, 1995; Webb, Meckstroth, & Tolan, 1982) and/or counseling provided by counselors with training in the characteristics and needs of gifted individuals (for a specific example of such counseling see Moon, Nelson, & Piercy, 1993). The need for counseling appears to be greatest during early adolescence when many gifted students face achievement/affiliation conflicts (Clasen & Clasen, 1995) and at points of transition from one type of school programming to another, especially when the new school program is much more challenging than the old (Coleman & Fults, 1985; Coleman & Fults, 1982; Moon, Swift, & Shallenberger, in press).

Several subgroups of gifted students have an especially strong need for counseling related to issues of giftedness. These include highly gifted children placed in general education classrooms (Gross, 1993; Silverman, 1998); twice-exceptional students (Baum, Owen, & Dixon, 1991; Reis, Neu, & McGuire, 1997); under-achievers (Dowdall & Colangelo, 1982; Peterson, 2001; Peterson &

Colangelo, 1996); adolescent and adult females (Hollinger, 1995; Reis, 1998); gays and lesbians, especially during adolescence (Peterson & Rischar, 2000); and cultural or ethnic minorities (Ford, Harris, & Schuerger, 1993).

Several counseling formats have been recommended for working with gifted students, ranging from psycho-educational formats like affective curricula that can be delivered by teachers as one component of a comprehensive gifted program, to more traditional therapeutic interventions such as group counseling, individual counseling, and family counseling (Colangelo & Peterson, 1993; Kerr, 1991; Moon, in press; Silverman, 1993a). Counseling strategies for gifted youth can be preventative or corrective.

## Preventative Counseling Strategies

One of the most common preventative strategies is an affective curriculum implemented by teachers (Betts, 1986; Betts & Neihart, 1986). Some programs for gifted students have substantial affective components that are designed to help participating students understand and discuss issues related to their giftedness in a supportive educational and peer environment (Betts & Kercher, 1999). When a gifted program lacks a developed affective component, teachers should consider developing their own with guidance from appropriate resources on the affective needs of gifted students and assistance from school counselors or psychologists (Delisle, 1992).

Another preventative strategy that can be implemented by parents, teachers, or counselors is reading and discussing self-help books. There are three types of self-help books written for gifted children and their families: (a) survival guides that help gifted youth understand and cope with giftedness (Delisle & Galbraith, 1987; Galbraith, 1983, 1984); (b) collections of quotations from gifted children (Delisle, 1987); and (c) guides to parenting gifted children (Alvino, 1985; Rimm, 1994; Walker, 1991; Webb, 1993). Bibliotherapy (reading books about gifted persons) or cinematherapy (watching movies about gifted individuals) can serve as a different kind of self-help experience. True stories, such as biographies of famous people, and fictional stories, like *Little Man Tate* (1991) and

**215**

*Good Will Hunting* (1997), can help gifted youth understand their giftedness, overcome difficulties, and persist in developing their talents (Hébert, 1991, 2000b, 2000c; Silverman, 1993c). Through vicarious identification with main characters, readers and moviegoers can try on new roles and attitudes, express feelings, and safely explore alternative solutions to conflicts.

Group counseling is an excellent preventative strategy if trained counseling personnel are available to implement the groups (Colangelo & Peterson, 1993). Groups can be helpful to both students and parents. Counseling groups focused on giftedness can be formed at any grade level, but may be especially effective when implemented at the middle school level to help students cope with achievement/affiliation conflicts and provide educational and career guidance. Since gifted children have advanced career maturity (Kelly, 1992), they can benefit from career guidance prior to high school. Career counseling groups need to address gender issues, especially the effects of societal expectations (Hébert, 2000a; Kerr, 1993; Kerr & Cheryl, 1991).

It may also be effective to provide group counseling at points of transition into a challenging program for gifted and talented students. For example, in a school district that has no gifted program in grades K–3 and challenging, self-contained classes for gifted students in grades 4–6, the fall of fourth grade would be an excellent time for preventative group counseling. Such groups can be unstructured, structured by a specific affective curriculum, or semistructured using resources such as the *Talk with Teens* series to help focus the discussions (Peterson, 1993, 1995).

Finally, differentiated guidance services for families of gifted children have been recommended as a strategy for preventing social and emotional problems and facilitating healthy development (Moon, in press). Support groups for parents of gifted students have been a particular focus of SENG (Social and Emotional Needs of the Gifted), which has produced an excellent guide for facilitators of parental support groups (Webb & DeVries, 1993). Parents of gifted children have unique concerns related to their child's giftedness, such as family adaptations and family-school interactions (Keirouz, 1990), that can be addressed by counseling services focused on the needs of gifted students and their families. Typically, such services are offered by coun-

**216**

selors in private practice (Mahoney, 1997; Silverman, 1993b) or specialized university clinics (Colangelo & Assouline, 2000; Gridley, personal communication, May 24, 2001; Wieczerkowski & Prado, 1991). Family guidance services almost always include an assessment of child characteristics, including ability, motivation, and personality, and recommendations for meeting the child's academic, social, and emotional needs at home and school (Moon). A few family guidance models also include systemic assessment of family characteristics (Colangelo & Assouline; Wendorf & Frey, 1985). Unfortunately, the efficacy of such differentiated family guidance services has not yet been documented by empirical research.

## Counseling Interventions

When preventative strategies are unavailable or ineffective, other counseling interventions may be needed to address the social and emotional issues of gifted students. Gifted children who are underachieving in school or struggling to come to terms with dual exceptionalities can benefit from counseling that focuses simultaneously on the individual and his/her environments (Moon & Hall, 1998; Rimm, 1997). In addition, professional mental-health services are warranted when a gifted student has a co-occurring mood disorder, such as depression or anxiety; a behavior disorder, such as AD/HD or anorexia; or experiences physical or sexual abuse. A few professionals with training in both a counseling specialty and gifted studies have provided guidance for counseling professionals who are treating gifted children and their families (Colangelo, 1997; Kerr, 1991; Moon, in press; Moon & Hall, 1998; Silverman, 1993a). However, very few of the strategies these authors suggest have been empirically tested.

For example, we do not know whether family counseling is more effective than individual counseling in resolving social and emotional problems for gifted individuals. We also do not know which approaches to individual or family counseling work best with gifted children and adolescents. Is structural/strategic family therapy more effective than narrative family therapy when working with gifted children and their families? We don't know. Both approaches

**217**

have been recommended for addressing social and emotional issues with gifted children and their families (Moon, Nelson, & Piercy, 1993; Thomas, 1999; Wendorf & Frey, 1985; Zuccone & Amerikaner, 1986), but the two approaches have not been compared. In summary, there is almost no outcome research available on the efficacy of specific counseling modalities, approaches, or strategies with gifted individuals and their families.

In addition, we know very little about how the process of therapy might be different when clients are gifted. One study of clients at a university-based family counseling center for gifted students suggested that parents of gifted children approach therapy with a medical model mindset (i.e., they expect therapists to diagnose and "treat" their child's or family's problems; Bordeaux, 2001). The same study suggested, however, that families of gifted children respond well to client-centered, postmodern approaches to therapy if the therapist is successful in negotiating a collaborative therapeutic contract with such families at the beginning of the therapy process. More process research of this kind is needed to guide therapists in working with gifted and talented individuals and their families.

In addition, most mental-health professionals are not adequately trained to recognize or address the needs of gifted children (Ford & Harris, 1995; Klausmeier, Maker, & Mishra, 1987). Few graduate training programs provide training in counseling gifted individuals and their families, which results in two problems: First, very few mental health professionals know how to adapt their counseling strategies to better meet the needs of individuals with high abilities, and second, untrained counselors may pathologize normal characteristics of gifted individuals, such as adaptive perfectionism and overexcitabilities.

In summary, gifted children and their families experience unique psychosocial stressors related to giftedness. Although gifted youth in general appear to be well adjusted, preventative counseling for stresses related to giftedness is recommended for all gifted youth to ensure healthy social and emotional adjustment. More research is needed to determine how both preventative counseling and individual and family counseling for more severe presenting problems like depression and eating disorders should be differentiated when working with gifted and talented clients.

# References

Alvino, J. (1985). *Parents' guide to raising a gifted child.* New York: Ballantine Books.

Baum, S. M., Owen, S. V., & Dixon, J. (1991). *To be gifted and learning disabled: From identification to practical intervention strategies.* Mansfield Center, CT: Creative Learning Press.

Betts, G. T. (1986). Development of the emotional and social needs of gifted individuals. *Journal of Counseling and Development, 64,* 587–589.

Betts, G. T., & Kercher, J. (1999). *Autonomous learning model: Optimizing ability.* Greely, CO: ALPS.

Betts, G. T., & Neihart, M. F. (1986). Eight affective activities to enhance the emotional and social development of the gifted and talented. *Roeper Review, 8,* 18–23.

Bordeaux, B. (2001). *Therapy with gifted clients: Honest disagreement is often a good sign of progress.* Unpublished manuscript.

Clasen, D. R., & Clasen, R. E. (1995). Underachievement of highly able students and the peer society. *Gifted and Talented International, 10,* 67–76.

Colangelo, N. (1997). Counseling gifted students: Issues and practices. In N. Colangelo & G. A. Davis (Eds.), *Handbook of gifted education* (2nd ed., pp. 353–365). Boston: Allyn and Bacon.

Colangelo, N., & Assouline, S. G. (2000). Counseling gifted students. In K. A. Heller, F. J. Mönks, & R. J. Sternberg (Eds.), *International handbook of giftedness and talent* (pp. 595–607). Amsterdam: Elsevier.

Colangelo, N., & Peterson, J. S. (1993). Group counseling with gifted students. In L. K. Silverman (Ed.), *Counseling the gifted and talented* (pp. 111–129). Denver: Love.

Coleman, M., & Fults, B. A. (1982). Self-concept and the gifted classroom: The role of social comparisons. *Gifted Child Quarterly, 26,* 116–119.

Coleman, J. M., & Fults, B. A. (1985). Special-class placement, level of intelligence, and the self-concepts of gifted children: A social comparison perspective. *Remedial and Special Education, 6*(1), 7–11.

Delisle, J. (1987). *Gifted kids speak out.* Minneapolis: Free Spirit.

Delisle, J. (1992). *Guiding the social and emotional development of gifted youth: A practical guide for educators and counselors.* New York: Longman.

Delisle, J., & Galbraith, J. (1987). *The gifted kids survival guide II: A sequel to the original gifted kids survival guide (for ages 11–18).* Minneapolis: Free Spirit.

Dowdall, C. B., & Colangelo, N. (1982). Underachieving gifted students: Review and implications. *Gifted Child Quarterly, 26,* 179–184.

Ford, D. Y., & Harris, J. J., III (1995). Exploring university counselors' perceptions of distinctions between gifted Black and gifted White students. *Journal of Counseling and Development, 73,* 443–450.

Ford, D. Y., Harris, J. J., III, & Schuerger, J. M. (1993, March/April). Racial identity development among gifted Black students: Counseling issues and concerns. *Journal of Counseling and Development, 71,* 409–417.

**219**

Galbraith, J. (1983). *The gifted kids survival guide (for ages 11–18)*. Minneapolis: Free Spirit.

Galbraith, J. (1984). *The gifted kids survival guide for ages 10 & under*. Minneapolis: Free Spirit.

Genshaft, J. L., Greenbaum, S., & Borovksky, S. (1995). Stress and the gifted. In J. L. Genshaft, M. Birely, & C. L. Hollinger (Eds.), *Serving gifted and talented students: A resource for school personnel* (pp. 257–286). Austin, TX: PRO–ED.

Gross, M. U. M. (1993). *Exceptionally gifted children*. London: Routledge.

Hackney, H. (1981). The gifted child, the family, and the school. *Gifted Child Quarterly, 25*, 51–54.

Hébert, T. P. (1991). Meeting the affective needs of bright boys through bibliotherapy. *Roeper Review, 13*, 207–212.

Hébert, T. P. (2000a). Gifted males pursuing careers in elementary education: Factors that influence a belief in self. *Journal for the Education of the Gifted, 24*, 7–45.

Hébert, T. P. (2000b). Helping high-ability students overcome math anxiety through bibliotherapy. *Journal of Secondary Gifted Education, 8*, 164–178.

Hébert, T. P. (2000c). Nurturing social and emotional development in gifted teenagers through young adult literature. *Roeper Review, 22*, 167–171.

Hollinger, C. L. (1995). Stress as a function of gender: Special needs of gifted girls and women. In J. L. Genshaft, M. Birely, & C. L. Hollinger (Eds.), *Serving gifted and talented students: A resource for school personnel* (pp. 269–300). Austin, TX: PRO–ED.

Keirouz, K. S. (1990). Concerns of parents of gifted children: A research review. *Gifted Child Quarterly, 34*, 56–63.

Kelly, K. R. (1992). A profile of the career development characteristics of young gifted adolescents: Examining gender and multicultural differences. *Roeper Review, 13*, 202–206.

Kerr, B. (1991). *A handbook for counseling the gifted and talented*. Alexandria, VA: American Counseling Association.

Kerr, B., & Cheryl, E. (1991). Career counseling with academically talented students: Effects of a value-based intervention. *Journal of Counseling Psychology, 38*, 309–314.

Kerr, B. (1993). Career assessment for gifted girls and women. *Journal of Career Assessment, 1*, 258–266.

Klausmeier, K., Maker, J. C., & Mishra, S. P. (1987). Identification of gifted learners: A national survey of assessment practices and training needs of school psychologists. *Gifted Child Quarterly, 31*, 135–137.

Mahoney, A. S. (1997). In search of gifted identity: From abstract concept to workable counseling constructs. *Roeper Review, 20*, 222–227.

Moon, S. M. (in press). Counseling families. In N. Colangelo & G. A. Davis (Eds.), *Handbook of gifted education* (3rd ed.). Boston: Allyn and Bacon.

Moon, S. M., & Hall, A. S. (1998). Family therapy with intellectually and creatively gifted children. *Journal of Marital and Family Therapy, 24*, 59–80.

Moon, S. M., Kelly, K. R., & Feldhusen, J. F. (1997). Specialized counseling services for gifted youth and their families: A needs assessment. *Gifted Child Quarterly, 41,* 16–25.

Moon, S. M., Nelson, T. S., & Piercy, F. P. (1993). Family therapy with a highly gifted adolescent. *Journal of Family Psychotherapy, 4,* 1–16.

Moon, S. M., Swift, M., & Shallenberger, A. (in press). Perceptions of a self-contained class for fourth and fifth grade students with high to extreme levels of intellectual giftedness. *Gifted Child Quarterly.*

Neihart, M. (1999). The impact of giftedness on psychological well-being: What does the empirical literature say? *Roeper Review, 22,* 10–17.

Peterson, J. S. (1993). *Talk with teens about self and stress: 50 guided discussions for school and counseling groups.* Minneapolis: Free Spirit.

Peterson, J. S. (1995). *Talk with teens about feelings, family, relationships, and the future: 50 guided discussions for school and counseling groups.* Minneapolis: Free Spirit.

Peterson, J. S. (2001). Successful adults who were adolescent underachievers. *Gifted Child Quarterly, 45,* 236–250.

Peterson, J. S., & Colangelo, N. (1996). Gifted achievers and underachievers: A comparison of patterns found in school files. *Journal of Counseling and Development, 74,* 399–407.

Peterson, J. S., & Rischar, H. (2000). Gifted and gay: A study of the adolescent experience. *Gifted Child Quarterly, 44,* 231–246.

Reis, S. M. (1998). *Work left undone: Choices and compromises of talented females.* Mansfield Center, CT: Creative Learning Press.

Reis, S. M., Neu, T. W., & McGuire, J. M. (1997). Case studies of high-ability students with learning disabilities who have achieved. *Exceptional Children, 63,* 463–479.

Rimm, S. (1997). Underachievement syndrome: A national epidemic. In N. Colangelo & G. A. Davis (Eds.), *Handbook of gifted education* (2nd ed., pp. 416–434). Boston: Allyn and Bacon.

Rimm, S. B. (1994). *Keys to parenting the gifted child.* Hauppauge, NY: Barron's.

Silverman, L. K. (Ed.). (1993a). *Counseling the gifted and talented.* Denver: Love.

Silverman, L. K. (1993b). A developmental model for counseling the gifted. In L. K. Silverman (Ed.), *Counseling the gifted and talented* (pp. 51–78). Denver: Love.

Silverman, L. K. (1993c). Techniques for preventive counseling. In L. K. Silverman (Ed.), *Counseling the gifted and talented* (pp. 81–109). Denver: Love.

Silverman, L. K. (1998). The highly gifted. In J. VanTassel-Baska (Ed.), *Excellence in educating gifted & talented learners* (pp. 115–128). Denver: Love.

Thomas, V. (1999). David and the family Bane: Therapy with a gifted child and his family. *Journal of Family Psychology, 10,* 15–24.

Walker, S. Y. (1991). *The survival guide for parents of gifted kids.* Minneapolis: Free Spirit.

Webb, J. T. (1993). Nurturing social-emotional development of gifted children. In K. A. Heller, F. J. Mönks, & A. H. Passow (Eds.), *International handbook of research and development of giftedness and talent* (pp. 525–538). Oxford: Pergamon Press.

**221**

Webb, J. T., & DeVries, A. R. (1993). *Training manual for facilitators of SENG model guided discussion groups*. Scottsdale, AZ: SENG.

Webb, J. T., Meckstroth, E. A., & Tolan, S. S. (1982). *Guiding the gifted child*. Dayton: Ohio Psychology Press.

Wendorf, D. J., & Frey, J. (1985). Family therapy with the intellectually gifted. *The American Journal of Family Therapy, 13*, 31–38.

Wieczerkowski, W., & Prado, T. M. (1991). Parental fears and expectations from the point of view of a counseling centre for the gifted. *European Journal for High Ability, 2*, 56–72.

Zuccone, C. F., & Amerikaner, M. (1986). Counseling gifted underachievers: A family systems approach. *Journal of Counseling and Development, 64*, 590–592.

**222**

# 22 CAREER COUNSELING FOR GIFTED AND TALENTED STUDENTS

by **Meredith J. Greene, M.Ed.**

ppropriate career counseling recognizes that career development is a process that is interconnected with multiple concurrent life issues, including developmental, social, and psychological transitions (Kelly, 1996; Perrone, 1997; Stewart, 1999; Super, 1980; Watts, 1996). A lifelong approach to career development is explained by Watts, who believes that "careers are now forged, not foretold . . . [and] are based on a long series of iterative decisions made throughout our lives" (p. 46). Career plans can rarely be set in stone anymore, as plans must be constantly revised to adapt to a continually changing world.

Career counseling helps students develop necessary attitudes for career exploration and planning, and it also helps them self-reflect, restructure their beliefs, and deepen their personalities to answer the all-important "Who am I?" question. Unfortunately, much of the high school and college programming for gifted students still focuses primarily on addressing the individual's academic needs (Berger, 1989; Gladieux & Swail, 2000; Kelly & Colangelo, 1990; Peterson, 2000) even though academic ability is only one variable in career development. In a survey report by the National Research Center on the Gifted and Talented, Sytsma (2000) reported that only 13% of the respondents' high schools offered affective/counseling components in addition to academic opportunities for gifted and talented students. In a survey of over 300 parents, school personnel, and related counseling professionals Moon, Kelly, and Feldhusen (1997) found that, while many counseling needs of the gifted were recognized, trained personnel were not readily available to deliver services that addressed these needs. The job of career counseling is often left to already overburdened guidance counselors, most of whom have too little time for career counseling and many of whom have no background in the needs of gifted and talented students (Moon, Kelly, & Feldhusen, 1997; Peterson), or else gifted students are left to figure career plans out for themselves. Choosing a school, a program, and a major are initial stages of career planning, yet are considered by many to be an end goal.

Different stages exist in career awareness and career maturity (Kelly & Colangelo, 1990; Super, 1977), but central to all of these stages are the common issues of decision making, development of identity, and exploration. Gifted students may face additional psychosocial issues that impact their career development and planning, including asynchrony and early cognitive maturation (Frederickson, 1986; Kelly & Colangelo, 1990; Kerr, 1990, 1991), moral sensitivity (Hansen & Hall, 1997; Lovecky, 1997; Passow, 1988), emotional giftedness (Piechowski, 1991), multipotentiality (Clark, 1992; Kelly & Hall, 1994; Perrone, 1997; Silverman, 1993), perfectionism (Schuler, 2000; Silverman), and stress from the high expectations of significant others (Clark; Perrone; Schultheiss, 2000). Stress can be magnified to unmanageable levels if a gifted student arrives at college with no real personal desire to attend, no clear career plan due to inadequate career counseling in high school, and then continues to receive inadequate advising in college (Brooks & Dubois, 1995; Stewart, 1999). Gifted individuals who are cre-
‒ (Csikszentmihalyi, 1996), underachieving (Peterson, 2000), or

female (Kerr, 1985, 1994; Reis, 1998; Rimm, 1999) also face further challenges in career development.

Multipotentiality is often thought to be the main source of career indecision for gifted adolescents, but this indecision may also be due to a lack of decision-making skills (Achter, Benbow, & Lubinski, 1997; Berger, 1989); faulty self-observation or worldview generalizations based on inaccurate perceptions or isolated incidents (Stewart, 1999); pressure to make *the* perfect career choice in order to please significant others, including parents, teachers, and peers (Stewart), and, for girls in particular, a need to reduce the discrepancy between career and family goals (Hollinger, 1991; Kerr, 1994; Wolleat, 1979). Career indecision may manifest itself in many different ways, including trying to avoid the inevitable by delaying decision making about careers or frequent change of college major (Frederickson, 1986) resulting in the creation of the proverbial professional student or the disappointing and disappointed college dropout. It is important for the significant adults in the lives of gifted and talented students to recognize that, while college attendance and the particular college chosen still may determine who has access to the best jobs, higher economic rewards, and the best life chances (Gladieux & Swail, 2000), a bachelor's degree is only one measure of success.

Gifted students have demonstrated earlier career maturity by being more certain of career choices earlier than other students (Kelly & Colangelo, 1990; Kerr, 1990). This early, and sometimes premature, certainty may actually limit the further exploration of career possibilities, especially in college, where more choices are offered (Frederickson, 1986; Kerr, 1991). Often, the academically gifted in particular choose careers that require 10 or more years of postsecondary training (Stewart, 1999), and, if this career decision is made early due to cognitive maturation without synchronous emotional maturation, the adolescent may not be able to consider the long-range planning, persistence, and self-sacrifice needed to achieve the intended career goal. The long-term training for most professional careers also requires a certain amount of financial and emotional dependence, while the gifted population often needs to assert more independence at an earlier age (Silverman, 1993).

**225**

In order to provide appropriate career counseling for all gifted and talented students, additional areas seldom addressed in the existing literature need to be further explored. Areas of future consideration include combating the emphasis on college for gifted students (Berger, 1989; Burruss, 2000; Collozi & Collozi, 2000); the career needs of gifted and talented students who underachieve (Peterson, 2000; Reis & McCoach, 2000); members of special populations, such as the emotionally (Passow, 1988; Piechowski, 1991), creatively (Csikszentmihalyi, 1996), or disadvantaged (Kozol, 1991) gifted and talented, as well as gay, lesbian, bisexual, and transsexual gifted students (Peterson & Rischar, 2000); and the importance of chance in career development (Mitchell, Levin, & Krumboltz, 1999).

The emotionally gifted young adult choosing a career path must be helped to consider traits that may create crisis in an occupational setting. It is important to both recognize and value a vocational calling, the sense of personal mission to pursue a certain line of work that some gifted individuals experience, while also ensuring that the sometimes harsh realities of such a calling are understood during the career-planning stages.

For adolescents trying to deal with their giftedness, the additional turmoil of uncontrollable factors such as race, religion, or socioeconomic status can also affect their decision making. For poor, urban, or rural adolescents, career planning and decision making do not take precedence over immediate goals of daily life. For gifted and talented students belonging to racial, ethnic, or religious minorities, career planning may also be more difficult due to the lack of varied adult role models in their own group and value conflicts that may arise. For gifted and talented homosexuals, bisexuals, and transsexuals who have suffered through painful school experiences (Peterson & Rischar, 2000), career decision making may also involve highly personal factors about their physical and emotional safety in certain occupational settings or careers.

According to research by Renzulli, Baum, and Hébert (1995), underachievement can sometimes be reversed with the aid of positive adult encouragement and a focus on strengths and self-selected interests. If counselors rely solely on available school data, such as subject grades or achievement test scores, many gifted underachievers will not be identified or will not receive appropriate career counseling.

Career counseling must train individuals to generate, recognize, and incorporate chance events into their career development by remaining open-minded and adopting an exploratory attitude. The skills of curiosity, persistence, flexibility, optimism, and risk taking are as important to develop as domain-specific knowledge and skills in gifted and talented students, so that they may actively seize any unexpected career opportunities. Career counseling must embrace the idea of a cyclical, rather than a linear, path of career development, thereby alleviating the discomfort with change and allowing for chance opportunities to be welcomed.

With a university degree and financial security considered primary societal measures of success, it is increasingly difficult for young, creatively talented individuals to take the risks necessary to find opportunities to display their talents and to have them valued. Creatively gifted students often continue to be encouraged to pursue conventional careers.

We might serve the gifted population better if we begin to consider career counseling as a logical extension of talent development, a lifelong process that demands accurate perceptions of ability, potential, and achievement (Kelly, 1996). This goal requires commitment and self-reflection on the part of the individual student and a collaborative effort from the adults charged with the care and education of that student, including parents, guidance counselors, and educators. Traditional career counseling has focused on finding a person-occupation fit based on existing abilities and interests, rather than considering potential and creativity over time. The lifespan approach to career counseling is crucial, as it acknowledges that occupational interests, competencies, and preferences may indeed change, especially in the identity-formation stages of adolescence. Gifted and talented adolescents should not have to try to make it alone, and guidance counselors should not be solely responsible for finding the perfect career fit for every student. In Table 1, suggestions for changes in the nature of career counseling are summarized and categorized under five basic assumptions.

Career counseling for the gifted should be an action-oriented and constructivist process; it should not be considered in isolation, but in relationship to other aspects of life. Once the first assumption is accepted, that gifted and talented students require appropri-

## Table 1

### Assumptions Leading to Changes in Career Counseling for Gifted and Talented Students

1. Gifted and talented students require appropriate and adequate career counseling.

   - Schools should provide differentiated career education for high-ability, honors, and AP students.
   - Career planning must address the nonacademic components of career choices, such as personality type, values, desired lifestyle, and societal trends.

2. The traditional definitions of career and career counseling should be broadened for gifted and talented students.

   - Career is a part of identity, and it can be defined as meaning or direction in life, as a career is not merely a job.
   - Career counseling is an extension of talent development.
   - Career planning is a lifelong process; therefore, career counseling should take a life-span approach that regards potential and creativity over time.
   - Career counseling should be action-oriented, constructivist, and related to other aspects of school and life.

3. Career counseling for gifted and talented students should be multidimensional. Combinations of the following can be effective:

   - small groups with age/grade-level peers;
   - small groups with other gifted and talented students;
   - informal discussion opportunities with members of the same subgroup (i.e., ethnic minority, females, etc.);
   - personal interviews with a career/guidance counselor;
   - personal assessment of abilities, interests, or both; and

- exposure to world of work through career fairs, guest speakers, mentorships, campus visits, and so forth.

4. Career counseling for gifted and talented students should be differentiated.

   - Tests that are normed to the "typical" population are not appropriate. Typical age-appropriate tests do not show the actual peaks and valleys in scores of multipotential gifted students.
   - Tests that require rapid, repetitive tasks do not reflect higher order thinking abilities.
   - Forced-choice, rather than ranked, interests can provide more discrimination for students with many interests.
   - Self-reflection and experiential learning should be stressed.
   - Unconventional careers and career paths should be explored.
   - Ability tests must extend beyond math and verbal, for example, including spatial and mechanical assessment.
   - Future studies should be incorporated to examine possibilities for brand-new careers.

5. Guidance counselors should not be the sole person responsible for career counseling.

   - Students themselves must be taught to take personal responsibility for career planning.
   - Counselors, parents, and, in particular, educators of gifted and talented students should collaborate in their career counseling efforts.
   - Educators, whether of gifted programs, honors or AP classes, or regular classroom teachers should try to relate school subjects and/or concepts to careers.
   - Educators should be up-to-date with career trends in their own fields (e.g., best training facilities, scholarship or summer opportunities, trends in the field, etc.).

**229**

ate and adequate career counseling (see Table 1), then, based on this review of research, four other changes seem necessary in their career counseling.

A new model of career counseling must first begin with broader definitions of career and career counseling, to mean not merely choosing an occupation, but also a meaning or direction in life that can be fulfilling and satisfying for the gifted individual over his or her lifespan. Contrary to findings among the general population, many gifted adults do work at the same career for life and also have a tendency to consider their work as a part of their identity (Perrone, 1997).

The next change deals with individualization of services, as noted in Table 1. Group counseling with other gifted students is of benefit because some career issues are shared, but it is important to recognize that all gifted students are not alike. Each student needs to develop a personal definition of achievement and career success after carefully analyzing life goals, values, and identity (Hollinger, 1991). Individualized career counseling addresses unique personal needs and is best used in combination with group sessions that address common needs of a particular group. Even in groups with seemingly similar participants, a counselor must be aware that individuals will have specific issues or concerns. Some students belong to one or more subgroups, such as females, racial or ethnic minorities, nonheterosexuals, and students of low socioeconomic status. For example, discussion groups to explore a new model of female talent development and achievement in which females often achieve eminence later in life and pursue different arenas of success than males (Arnold, Noble, & Subotnik, 1999; Hollinger & Fleming, 1992; Reis, 1991, 1998) could be an important element of career counseling with adolescent females. Stressing personal over predictive measures helps maintain both the individuality and the commonalities of gifted and talented students.

An individualized approach to career counseling must also consider the type of assessments used. Counseling should be multidimensional (Hollinger, 1991; Stewart, 1999), considering abilities, interests, values, likes, and preferred lifestyles. Interest inventories that merely identify, rather than rank, interests are of little value to a student with potential and interest in many areas; therefore, forced-choice inventories can be more useful for students, especially for those who display multipotentiality. Van Wyck (cited in Maree,

1999) predicted that one-quarter of existing jobs will not be practiced in 10 years. Career counseling and its assessments should also be based on future trends, rather than focusing on occupation and lifestyles that may be obsolete by the time the student is ready to enter the work world.

In addition to being individualized and multidimensional, career counseling for the gifted should also employ different and differentiated methods (Hollinger, 1991; Smit, 2000; Stewart, 1999). A summary of suggestions for these qualitative differences is provided in Table 1. Most aptitude and ability tests used in career counseling for the general population are of limited use with the gifted, since the academically gifted reach the ceiling of most of these tests or, conversely, the rapid, repetitive tasks in a battery of tests do not allow for the high-level thinking that typically would be demonstrated by some gifted students. Traditional career-assessment tests and inventories can be useful, but only if they are in formats that help students better judge their real abilities. Our creatively gifted and talented population is largely ignored because most of the traditional ability tests focus on testing only math and verbal abilities, while many of the creative arts rely on spatial and mechanical abilities.

Traditional career inventories are normed to the general population; thus, the results may serve only to exacerbate the perceptions of differences experienced by many highly gifted or talented students. Along with these types of traditional assessment tools, career counselors should encourage student self-reflection, mentorships, and experiential learning to aid students in evaluating their true abilities and interests in on-going, goal-oriented career planning and decision making.

The final, and perhaps most crucial, change needed in the field of career counseling is to absolve guidance counselors from sole responsibility for the future career accomplishments of the gifted student. The notion that career is a distinct and separate entity from the educational process, and that guidance counselors are the only adults responsible for career education and counseling, is outdated and detrimental to all students. The idea of collaboration for career counseling outlined in Table 1 assumes that classroom teachers, teachers of gifted and talented programs, and parents of gifted children may be in the best positions to help gifted and talented stu-

**231**

dents in career decision making because their more frequent and close contact with the students affords them the luxury of time to really get to know their abilities, interests, and values better than most guidance counselors. One drawback to relying solely on high school guidance counselors is that time is lost. Career counseling, development, and planning should be started before high school. Parental support, early exposure to diverse enriching activities, and nurturing of interests are crucial to students' career paths (Silverman, 1993). Students need time to explore and sort through their many interests and abilities, as well as time to search out and prepare for major scholarships such as the Intel Science Search. Certain careers, such as those in the performing arts, require early advanced training. Research suggests that girls in particular lower their career aspirations by age 14 and that unless they receive appropriate guidance during their middle school years, these lowered aspirations may never be raised (Kerr, 1985, 1994; Reis, 1998).

## Conclusion

Guidance career services for the gifted and talented are often inadequate both during high school and after. Our society loses potential contributions, and many gifted and talented individuals continue to be anxious, confused, or frustrated about their career decisions. Some drift aimlessly along, while others tread water until a flotation device passes by. It is time to equip our diverse gifted population with a series of appropriate and interconnected counseling services, including career counseling that emphasizes personal responsibility for decision making and continual adjustment and adaptation to changes in career and in life.

## References

Achter, J., Benbow, C., & Lubinski, D. (1997). Rethinking multipotentiality among the intellectually gifted: A critical review and recommendations. *Gifted Child Quarterly, 41*, 5–15.
Arnold, K., Noble, K., & Subotnik, R. (1999). To thine own self be true: A new model of female talent development. *Gifted Child Quarterly, 43*, 140–147.

Berger, S. L. (1989). *College planning for gifted students*. Reston, VA: Council for Exceptional Children.

Brooks, J., & Dubois, D. (1995). Individual and environmental predictors of adjustment during the first year of college. *Journal of College Student Development, 36*, 347–360.

Burruss, J. D. (2000, November). *The mystery of college selection: Decision making of gifted students*. Paper presented at annual meeting of the National Association of Gifted Children, Atlanta, GA.

Clark, B. (1992). *Growing up gifted* (4th ed.). New York: Macmillan.

Colozzi, E. A., & Colozzi, L. C. (2000). College students' callings and careers: An integrated values-oriented perspective. In D. A. Luzzo (Ed.), *Career counseling of college students: An empirical guide to strategies that work* (pp. 63–90). Washington, DC: American Psychological Association.

Csikszentmihalyi, M. (1996). *Creativity: Flow and the psychology of discovery and invention*. New York: HarperCollins.

Frederickson, R. H. (1986). Preparing gifted and talented students for the world of work. *Journal of Counseling and Development, 64*, 556–565.

Gladieux, L., & Swail, W. (2000). Beyond access: Improving the odds of college success. *Phi Delta Kappan, 181*, 688–692.

Hansen, J. B., & Hall, E. G. (1997). Gifted women and marriage. *Gifted Child Quarterly, 41*, 169–180.

Hollinger, C. L. (1991). Facilitating career development of gifted young women. *Roeper Review, 13*, 135–139.

Hollinger, C. L., & Fleming, E. S. (1992). A longitudinal examination of life choices of gifted and talented young women. *Gifted Child Quarterly, 36*, 207–212.

Kelly, K. (1996). A talent development model of career counseling. *Gifted Education International, 11*, 131–135.

Kelly, K., & Colangelo, N. (1990). Effects of academic ability and gender on career development. *Journal for the Education of the Gifted, 13*, 168–175.

Kelly, K., & Hall, A. (1994). Effects of academic achievement and gender on occupational aspirations and career interests. In N. Colangelo, S. Assouline & D. Ambroson (Eds.), *Talent development volume II: Proceedings from the 1993 Henry B. and Jocelyn Wallace National Research Symposium on Talent Development* (pp. 447–453). Dayton: Ohio Psychology Press.

Kerr, B. A. (1985). *Smart girls, gifted women*. Columbus: Ohio Psychology Press.

Kerr, B. A. (1990). *Career planning for gifted and talented youth*. Reston, VA: ERIC Clearinghouse on Disabilities and Gifted Children. (ERIC Digest No. E492)

Kerr, B. A. (1991). *A handbook for counseling the gifted and talented*. Alexandria, VA: American Counseling Association.

Kerr, B. A. (1994). *Smart girls: A new psychology of girls, women, and giftedness*. Scottsdale, AZ: Gifted Psychology Press.

Kozol, J. (1991). *Savage inequalities: Children in America's schools*. New York: Crown.

**233**

Lovecky, D. V. (1997). Identity development in gifted children: Moral sensitivity. *Roeper Review, 20*, 90–94.

Maree, J. G. (1999). Validating the results of test scores: A case study in career counseling, illustrating how a gifted child may benefit from job analyses. *Gifted Education International, 13*, 204–215.

Mitchell, K., Levin, A., & Krumboltz, J. (1999). Planned happenstance: Constructing unexpected career opportunities. *Journal of Counseling & Development, 77*, 115–124.

Moon, S. M., Kelly, K. R., & Feldhusen, J. F. (1997). Specialized counseling services for gifted youth and their families: A needs assessment. *Gifted Child Quarterly, 41*, 16–23.

Passow, A. H. (1988). Educating gifted persons who are caring and concerned. *Roeper Review, 11*, 13–15.

Perrone, P. A. (1997). Gifted individuals' career development. In N. Colangelo & G. A. Davis (Eds.), *Handbook of gifted education* (2nd ed., pp. 398–407). Needham Heights, MA: Allyn and Bacon.

Peterson, J. S. (2000). Preparing for college: Beyond the getting–in part. *Gifted Child Today, 23*(2), 36–41.

Peterson, J. S., & Rischar, H. (2000). Gifted and gay: A study of the adolescent experience. *Gifted Child Quarterly, 44*, 231–246.

Piechowski, M. M. (1991). Emotional giftedness: The measure of intrapersonal intelligence. In N. Colangelo & G. A. Davis (Eds.), *Handbook of gifted education* (2nd ed., pp. 366–381). Needham Heights, MA: Allyn and Bacon.

Reis, S. M. (1991). The need for clarification in research designed to examine gender differences in achievement and accomplishment. *Roeper Review, 13*, 193–198.

Reis, S. M. (1998). *Work left undone: Choices & compromises of talented females.* Mansfield Center, CT: Creative Learning Press.

Reis, S. M., & McCoach, D. B. (2000). The underachievement of gifted students: What do we know and where do we go? *Gifted Child Quarterly, 44*, 152–170.

Renzulli, J. S., Baum, S. M., & Hébert, T. P. (1995). Reversing underachievement: Creative productivity as a systematic intervention. *Gifted Child Quarterly, 39*, 224–235.

Rimm, S. (1999). *See Jane win: The Rimm report on how 1,000 girls became successful women.* New York: Crown.

Schuler, P. (2000). Perfectionism and gifted adolescents. *Journal of Secondary Gifted Education, 11*, 183–196.

Schultheiss, D. P. (2000). Emotional-social issues in the provision of career counseling. In D. A. Luzzo (Ed.), *Career counseling of college students: An empirical guide to strategies that work* (pp. 43–62). Washington, DC: American Psychological Association.

Silverman, L. K. (1993). *Counseling the gifted and talented.* Denver: Love.

Smit, J.C. (2000, November). *Career counseling for gifted students.* Paper presented at annual meeting of the National Association of Gifted Children, Atlanta, GA.

Stewart, J. B. (1999). Career counseling for the academically gifted student. *Canadian Journal of Counselling, 33*(1), 3–12.

Super, D. (1980). Life-span, life-space approach to career development. *Journal of Vocational Behavior, 16,* 282–298.

Sytsma, R. (2000). *Gifted and talented programs in America's high schools: A preliminary survey report.* Storrs: National Research Center on the Gifted and Talented, The University of Connecticut.

Watts, A. G. (1996). Toward a policy for lifelong career development: A transatlantic perspective. *The Career Development Quarterly, 45,* 41–53.

Wolleat, P. L. (1979). Guiding the career development of gifted females. In N. Colangelo & R. T. Zaffrann (Eds.), *New voices in counseling the gifted* (pp. 331–380). Dubuque, IA: Kendall Hunt Publishing Company.

**235**

# 23 PROMOTING A POSITIVE ACHIEVEMENT ATTITUDE WITH GIFTED AND TALENTED STUDENTS

by **Del Siegle, Ph.D.** and **D. Betsy McCoach, M.A.**

hy one gifted student achieves while another does not remains an enigma. Although the underachievement of gifted students has been the subject of much inquiry and debate (Dowdall & Colangelo, 1982; Reis & McCoach, 2000; Van Boxtel & Mönks, 1992; Whitmore, 1986), very few controlled studies have demonstrated the effectiveness of specific interventions designed to reverse that underachievement. As we define the national educational agenda of the 21st century, "student achievement is of great interest to . . . national policy makers because it is so closely correlated with the productive skills students eventually bring to the labor market" (Office of Educational Research and Improvement, 2000, p.

50). The underachievement of gifted students represents a loss of valuable human resources for the nation, as well as an unrealized fulfillment for the individual. Determining why some high-ability students demonstrate low levels of achievement is difficult because underachievement occurs for many different reasons (Reis & McCoach; Rimm, 1995; Whitmore).

## Causes of Underachievement

Reis and McCoach (in press) suggested that the underachievement of bright students occurs for one of three basic reasons:

1. An apparent underachievement problem masks more serious physical, cognitive, or emotional issues such as learning disabilities, attention deficits, emotional disturbances, psychological disorders, or other health impairments (Busch & Nuttall, 1995; Dowdall & Colangelo, 1982; Gallagher, 1991; Lupart & Pyryt, 1996; Silverman, 1991). In this case, the treatment of academic underachievement should be secondary to the treatment of the primary disorder.
2. The underachievement is symptomatic of a mismatch between the student and his or her school environment (Emerick, 1992; Siegle, 2000).
3. The underachievement results from a personal characteristic such as low self-motivation, low self-regulation, or low self-efficacy (McCoach & Siegle, 2001; Reis & McCoach, 2000; Siegle, 2000; Whitmore, 1980).

## Personal Characteristics Associated With Underachievement

Here we focus on underachievement resulting from the personal characteristics of the student. However, we acknowledge that academic underachievement can sometimes be indicative of a more serious physical, mental, or emotional issue. For example, Moon and Hall (1998) noted that learning disabilities, attention-deficit/hyperactivity disorder, hearing impairment, nontraditional learning styles, emotional problems, or any combination of these issues can contribute to underachievement. Therefore, we recommend that all underachieving gifted students be screened for a wide variety of physical, mental, or emotional problems before making a student's underachievement the primary focus of attention.

Once educators rule out these more serious problems, they can explore the role that students' perceptions, attitudes, and motivation are playing in their underachievement. For example, McCoach and Siegle (2001) compared 122 gifted achievers with 56 gifted underachievers in 28 different high schools. The results of an analysis suggested that gifted underachievers differed from achievers on four factors: attitudes toward teachers, attitudes toward school, goal valuation, and motivation/self-regulation. In addition, they found that gifted underachievers displayed greater variability than the gifted high achievers on four factors: academic self-perceptions, attitudes toward school, goal valuation, and motivation/self-regulation. The results of a multidimensional scaling analysis suggested two separate profiles of gifted underachievers: One set of underachievers valued school goals and displayed near-average self-reported motivation/self-regulation, but reported negative attitudes toward teachers and school, while another set displayed positive attitudes toward teachers and school, but did not value school goals and reported low motivation/self-regulation.

## Personal Characteristics Associated With Achievement: An Avenue for Intervention

Knowing that the factors listed above differentiate gifted underachievers from gifted achievers and underachievers from each other provides researchers with a possible new line of inquiry: designing interventions to change students' attitudes and perceptions in the hope of reversing their patterns of underachievement. Guidance for the design of such interventions comes from research in the field of educational psychology on four characteristics of achievers: self-efficacy, environmental perceptions, goal orientation, and self-regulation. Generally, achievers are self-efficacious. They have high

**239**

academic self-perceptions and they believe that they have the ability to perform well (Bandura, 1986; Schunk, 1984). Second, they trust their academic environment and expect that they can succeed in it. They expect that this environment is conducive to their performance of academic tasks and they have positive attitudes toward their teachers and school. Third, they find school meaningful (Atkinson, 1964). They enjoy school or believe that what they are doing in school will produce beneficial outcomes for them. Finally, they implement self-regulating strategies where they set realistic expectations and implement appropriate strategies to complete their goals successfully.

We explore each of these personal factors associated with achievement in this chapter with an emphasis on how these characteristics can be developed in underachievers. While much of the research on these factors is based on studies with a general student population, there is evidence that interventions designed to enhance these characteristics can help gifted underachievers at the middle and secondary level (Baum, Renzulli, & Hébert, 1995; Emerick, 1992; McCoach & Siegle, 2001). In each section below, we briefly review research on one of these achievement characteristics and suggest interventions to develop that characteristic in gifted students who are underachieving in school.

## Self-Efficacy

Students develop confidence in many ways, and those who are confident about their skills are more likely to engage in a variety of activities. The perceptions students have about their skills influence the types of activities they select, how much they challenge themselves at those activities, and the persistence they exhibit once they are involved (Ames, 1990; Bandura, 1977, 1986; Schunk, 1981). This is true for activities ranging from participation in sports and music, to school achievement. Although research has shown that gifted students hold higher academic self-perceptions than their nongifted peers (Dai, Moon, & Feldhusen, 1998), much of the research literature on gifted underachievers suggests that they demonstrate low self-efficacy or poor self-concepts (Reis & McCoach, 2000; Supplee, 1990; Whitmore, 1980). Recent work by McCoach and Siegle (2001) indicated that gifted underachievers'

**240**

self-efficacy, while slightly lower than gifted achievers' self-efficacy, is still quite strong. Therefore, at present, it is unclear whether gifted underachievers are likely to exhibit low self-efficacy.

For those who suffer from low self-confidence, Siegle (1995) suggested the following strategies to increase self-efficacy. Students who have been successful in the past are more likely to believe they will be successful in the future. The adage "Success breeds success" generally holds true for self-efficacy. To develop self-efficacy in students, educators and parents can help them recognize their successes and growth in specific areas. Rewards can also increase students' self-efficacy when they are tied to specific accomplishments (Schunk, 1989). When teachers give students opportunities to revise their work, they promote efficacious behavior. Students often view exams and projects as static portraits of their abilities at one point in time, instead of seeing the assignments as part of a learning process. Students need to appreciate that any project, no matter how well executed, can be enhanced with revisions and that a first attempt, even if fraught with errors, can be improved. Utilizing portfolios to preserve student work can be an effective way to document student growth and improvement over time (Schunk, 1998).

Teacher compliments should be specific to the skills students are acquiring. A specific compliment, such as, "You really know how to calculate area," provides more information to a student than a general comment, such as, "Good job." Feedback linking successes with ability is more effective if the feedback is provided early in the students' performance (Schunk 1984, 1989). Although feedback linking success to ability can increase self-efficacy, failures should never be attributed to lack of ability. When failure is attributed to lack of effort or poor choice of learning strategies, students are likely to put forth more effort the next time they engage in a similar task. By contrast, failure that is attributed to lack of ability decreases student motivation (Dweck, 1975; Schunk, 1984; Schunk & Cox, 1986) when students perform poorly, educators can help them practice lack-of-effort or poor-strategy use explanations, while drawing attention to something they did correctly. For example, a comment like, "You know how to use a ruler, but you need to be more careful reading the numbers," provides both positive feedback and strategic guidance.

Teachers should also avoid the appearance of unsolicited help, expressions of sympathy following a substandard performance, or praise after an easy task. Students believe that these responses are indicative of low ability (Graham & Barker, 1990). Also, receiving praise for work completed without effort may cause students to doubt others' beliefs in their abilities. Gifted students who remain unchallenged in school and receive high praise for work that is easily accomplished may begin to doubt others' beliefs in their abilities. Similarly, doing the same task repeatedly does not maintain high self-efficacy (Schunk, 1998). Teachers must continually raise the academic hurdle for students who have shown mastery of specific skills or content. Again, gifted students are often repeatedly forced to show mastery of the same concepts and skills, and this constant repetition may sabotage a bright student's self-efficacy. Teachers who help promote self-efficacious learners consistently provide students with challenging assignments, offer specific praise for students accomplishments, and grant opportunities for students to revise their work.

## Environmental Perception

We hypothesize that students' perceptions of their environment play an important role in their achievement motivation. Students who view their environment as friendly and reinforcing may be more likely to demonstrate achievement-oriented behaviors. Students who expect that they will succeed within their environment may be more likely to put forth effort. Phrases such as, "My teacher doesn't like me," or, "I can't learn this way," may be indicators that students do not view their learning environment as friendly or that they have developed a belief that their efforts do not affect outcomes (Rathvon, 1996).

Our belief in the importance of environmental perceptions is inspired by current states of knowledge in a variety of educational arenas. Underachievers appear to display negative attitudes toward school (Bruns, 1992; Clark, 1988; Diaz, 1998; Ford, 1996, 2001; Frankel, 1965; Mandel & Marcus, 1988; McCall, Evahn, & Kratzer, 1992; Rimm, 1995); achievers, on the other hand, tend to be interested in learning and to have positive attitudes toward

**242**

school (Majoribanks, 1992; Mandel & Marcus, 1988; McCoach & Siegle, 2001; Weiner, 1992).

In order to be successful within a system or organization, a student must possess certain prerequisite skills. First, the student must understand the system; second, he or she must fit into the system; Finally, he or she must master the system. Minority students and students from diverse cultures often feel disenfranchised from the culture of the school (Ford, 1996; Ogbu, 1978; Steele, 2000) because they feel that they either do not understand or do not fit into the school system. When the culture of the student is valued, educators are more likely to witness fundamental and essential changes in that student's achievement, motivation, attitudes, and behavior (Ford).

Gifted underachievers often view school negatively (McCoach & Siegle, 2001). They may feel like they do not fit into the system, and, in some cases, giftedness can actually represent a stigma in the schools (Cross, 1997). Gifted students, like other students, wish to "look good" and to avoid embarrassment in front of their peers. They often report that classroom teachers don't call on them when their hands are raised or embarrass them by calling on them when no one else knows the answer. From a teacher's perspective, the gifted child may appear to be the most likely choice when no one else raises a hand; however, gifted students feel embarrassed when they are unable to answer correctly, and they may be teased if they constantly answer the most difficult questions correctly. A second area of concern is how teachers relate to gifted students in their classes. Rather than appreciating the special gifts and talents these students exhibit, some teachers are threatened by the presence of gifted students in their classroom. Therefore, in some situations, underachievement may represent a coping strategy whereby students strive to adapt to an anti-intellectual school environment (Cross).

## Goals

Children's goals and achievement values affect their self-regulation and motivation (Ablard & Lipschultz, 1998; Wigfield, 1994) because goals influence how children approach, engage in, and respond to achievement tasks (Hidi & Harackiewicz, 2000). When students value the goals of the school, they will be more likely to engage in academics, expend more effort on their schoolwork, and become achievers (Wigfield). Peterson (2000) followed achieving and underachieving gifted high school students into college and found that achievers' sureness and earlier determination of career direction suggested that direction may be a factor in successful achievement. Emerick (1992) reported that underachieving high school gifted students were able to reverse the underachievement pattern by developing goals that were both personally motivating and directly related to academic success. Students' motivation to complete tasks stems from the attainment value, utility value, and intrinsic value associated with the task (Wigfield).

Attainment value is the importance students attach to the task as it relates to their conception of their identity and ideals. For example, students who identify themselves as athletes set goals related to their sport. These students are more motivated to attain the goals because they are associated with the students' perceptions of who they are. Providing students with role models who value academic achievement may be one way to increase attainment value. Rimm (1995) suggested that same-sex models who resemble the student in some way are most effective. Educators must personalize the school experience by helping students to integrate academic goals into their ideals. Gordon (2000) cautioned educators to help students own their educational experience by making it meaningful for them.

Utility value is how the task relates to future goals. While students may not enjoy an activity, they may value a later reward or outcome it produces (Wigfield, 1994). The activity must be integral to their vision of their future. Because goals can play a key role in attaining later outcomes, educators and parents should help students see beyond the immediate activity to the long-term benefits it produces. Teachers need to be able to answer the common query, "Why do we have to study this stuff?"

Intrinsic value often results from the enjoyment an activity produces for the participant (Wigfield, 1994). When students enjoy scholastic tasks, they are intrinsically motivated to do well. Both interests and personal relevance produce intrinsic value for a student. Students bring a variety of experiences and interests to the classroom, and learning becomes personally meaningful when their prior knowledge and diverse experiences are connected with the present learning experiences. Educators can aid this by creating an enriching environment and providing opportunities for students to explore their interests. In a recent study, researchers used self-selected enrichment projects based on students' interests as a systematic intervention for underachieving gifted students. This approach specifically targeted student strengths and interests and helped reverse academic underachievement in over half of the sample (Baum, Renzulli, & Hébert, 1995). Emerick (1992) also found that gifted underachievers responded well to interventions that focused on individual strengths and interests.

## Self-Regulation

Self-regulation (Zimmerman, 1989; Zimmerman & Martinez-Pons, 1986) describes students' organization skills and attitude in executing tasks. For self-regulation to occur, a student must have both choice and control. Often, gifted students are not given the control over their own learning that would enable them to demonstrate their capability for self-regulatory processes.

Assuming that students have the skills to do well and are motivated, they must set realistic expectations and implement appropriate management strategies. Gifted students' use of self-regulatory strategies varies considerably (Ablard & Lipschultz, 1998; Zimmerman & Martinez-Pons, 1986). Many gifted students are self-regulated learners; however, some gifted students exhibit low levels of self-regulatory strategy use. Research suggests that some gifted students are able to achieve at high levels without the use of self-regulatory strategies, although students who fail to develop appropriate strategies may be at risk for later underachievement (Ablard & Lipschultz). Because gifted students traditionally progress through the early years of school without being challenged, they sometimes fail to develop the self-management skills that other students master. In the early grades, good memory and fast processing skills can compensate for note taking and other study skills. Often, educators attempt to teach students study skills before students need those skills to be successful. This process usually frustrates both the teachers and the students. Self-regulatory skills are

**245**

more likely to be internalized when they are needed to solve the problem at hand. An obvious solution to the problem is to provide gifted students with an academically challenging curriculum early and throughout their school careers.

Teachers can help students to develop self-regulatory skills by incorporating explicit strategies to teach and model those skills into their classrooms. Zimmerman, Bonner, and Kovatch (1996) have designed an instructional model for developing self-regulated learners that involves training in goal setting, strategy use, and self-monitoring. In their learning academy model, students evaluate their current levels of mastery, analyze the learning task, set their own learning goals, choose the appropriate strategy to master material, and monitor their own performance. When using this model with gifted students, teachers should pay careful attention to the first step, evaluating current levels of mastery. Teachers who allow students to assess their own mastery and set their own goals may be surprised at how well some gifted students' self-assess their prior knowledge and content mastery. When teachers incorporate formal and informal preassessments into the classroom, gifted students benefit in several ways. First, students have the opportunity to demonstrate mastery of content and skills before they are taught and work at a more appropriate level, creating a need for the student to use more self-regulatory strategies in order to be successful. Second, students learn to assess what they know and do not know, which helps to develop their self-monitoring skills. Finally, the students become more actively engaged in the learning process as they begin to see the connection between classroom activities and skill development.

In summary, using programs to develop gifted students' self-regulatory skills will be more successful when the students can show mastery of prior learning and practice developing self-regulatory skills in the context of new learning.

## Conclusion

No single intervention will work with all gifted underachievers. Just as gifted underachievers differ from gifted achievers, gifted underachievers differ from each other. Discovering how the personal factors discussed in this paper interact with each other and the extent to which they influence the achievement of gifted students will provide fertile areas for future research. Research and pedagogy within the fields of educational psychology and gifted education can enhance our efforts to create positive achievement environments for gifted children.

## References

Ablard, K. E., & Lipschultz, R. E. (1998). Self-regulated learning in high-achieving students: Relations to advanced reasoning, achievement goals, and gender. *Journal of Educational Psychology, 90*, 94–101.

Ames, C. A. (1990). Motivation: What teachers need to know. *Teachers College Record, 91*, 409–421.

Atkinson, J. W. (1964). *An introduction to motivation*. Princeton, NJ: Van Nostrand.

Bandura, A. (1977). Self-efficacy: Toward a unifying theory of behavioral change. *Psychological Review, 84*, 191–215.

Bandura, A. (1986). *Social foundations of thought and action: A social cognitive theory*. Englewood Cliffs, NJ: Prentice–Hall.

Baum, S. M., Renzulli, J. S., & Hébert, T. P. (1995). Reversing underachievement: Creative productivity as a systematic intervention. *Gifted Child Quarterly, 39*, 224–235.

Bruns, J. H. (1992). *They can but they don't*. New York: Viking Penguin.

Busch, B., & Nuttall, R. L. (1995). Students who seem to be unmotivated may have attention deficits. *Diagnostique, 21*, 43–59.

Clark, B. (1988). *Growing up gifted* (3rd ed.) Columbus, OH: Merrill.

Cross, T. L. (1997). Psychological and social aspects of educating gifted students. *Peabody Journal of Education, 72*, 180–200.

Dai, D. Y., Moon, S. M., & Feldhusen, J. F. (1998). Achievement motivation and gifted students: A social cognitive perspective. *Educational Psychologist, 33*, 45–63.

Diaz, E. I. (1998). Perceived factors influencing the academic underachievement of talented students of Puerto Rican descent. *Gifted Child Quarterly, 42*, 105–122.

Dowdall, C. B., & Colangelo, N. (1982). Underachieving gifted students: Review and implications. *Gifted Child Quarterly, 26*, 179–184.

Dweck, C. S. (1975). The role of expectations and attributions in the alleviation of learned helplessness. *Journal of Personality and Social Psychology, 31*, 674–685.

Emerick, L. J. (1992). Academic underachievement among the gifted: Students' perceptions of factors that reverse the pattern. *Gifted Child Quarterly, 36*, 140–146.

Ford, D. Y. (1996). *Reversing underachievement among gifted Black students*. New York: Teacher's College Press.

Ford, D. Y. (2001, March). *Achievement and underachievement among gifted, potentially gifted, and Black students.* Presentation at "Instant Access: Critical Findings from the NRC/GT" conference, Orlando, FL.

Frankel, E. (1965). A comparative study of achieving and underachieving boys of high intellectual ability. In M. Kornrich (Ed.), *Underachievement* (pp. 87–101). Springfield, IL: Thomas.

Gallagher, J. J. (1991). Personal patterns of underachievement. *Journal for the Education of the Gifted, 14,* 221–233.

Gordon, E. (2000, September). *Educational access and opportunity.* Paper presented at the U.S. Department of Education and The National Academies' Millennium Conference, Achieving High Educational Standards for All, Washington, DC.

Graham, S., & Barker, G. P. (1990). The down side of help: An attribution-developmental analysis of helping behavior as a low-ability cue. *Journal of Educational Psychology, 82,* 7–14.

Hidi, S., & Harackiewicz, J. M. (2000). Motivating the academically unmotivated: A critical issue for the 21st century. *Review of Educational Research, 70,* 151–179.

Lupart, J. L., & Pyryt, M. C. (1996). "Hidden gifted" students: Underachiever prevalence and profile. *Journal for the Education of the Gifted, 20,* 36–53.

Majoribanks, K. (1992). The predictive validity of an attitude toward school scale in relation to children's academic achievement. *Educational and Psychological Measurement, 52,* 945–949.

Mandel H. P., & Marcus, S. I. (1988). *The psychology of underachievement.* New York: Wiley.

McCall R. B., Evahn, C., & Kratzer, L. (1992). *High school underachievers: What do they achieve as adults?* Newbury Park, CA: Sage.

McCoach, D. B., & Siegle, D. (2001, April). *Factors that differentiate gifted achievers from gifted underachievers.* Paper presented at the annual conference of the American Educational Research Association, Seattle.

Moon, S. M., & Hall, A. S. (1998). Family therapy with intellectually and creatively gifted children. *Journal of Marital and Family Therapy, 24,* 59–80.

Ogbu, J. U. (1978). *Minority education and caste.* New York: Academic Press.

Office of Educational Research and Improvement. (2000). *Elementary and secondary education: An international perspective.* Washington, DC: U.S. Government Printing Office.

Peterson, J. S. (2000). A follow-up study of one group of achievers and underachievers four years after high school graduation. *Roeper Review, 22,* 217–224.

Rathvon, N. (1996). *The unmotivated child: Helping your underachiever become a successful student.* New York: Simon and Schuster.

Reis, S. M., & McCoach, D. B. (2000). Gifted underachievers: What do we know and where do we go? *Gifted Child Quarterly, 44,* 152–170.

Reis, S. M., & McCoach, D. B. (in press). Underachievement in gifted and talented students with special needs. *Exceptionality.*

Rimm, S. (1995). *Why bright kids get poor grades and what you can do about it.* New York: Crown.

Schunk, D. H. (1981). Modeling and attributional effects on children's achievement: A self–efficacy analysis. *Journal of Educational Psychology, 73*, 93–105.

Schunk, D. H. (1984). Self-efficacy perspective on achievement behavior. *Educational Psychologist, 19*, 48–58.

Schunk, D. H. (1989). Self-efficacy and cognitive achievement: Implications for students with learning problems. *Journal of Learning Disabilities, 22*, 14–22.

Schunk, D. H. (1998, November). *Motivation and self-regulation among gifted learners.* Paper presented at annual meeting of the National Association for Gifted Children, Louisville, KY.

Schunk, D. H., & Cox, P. D. (1986). Strategy training and attributional feedback with learning disabled students. *Journal of Educational Psychology, 78*, 201–209.

Siegle, D. (1995). *Effects of teacher training in student self-efficacy on student mathematics self-efficacy and student mathematics achievement.* Unpublished doctoral dissertation, University of Connecticut, Storrs.

Siegle, D. (2000, December). Parenting achievement-oriented children. *Parenting for High Potential,* 6–7, 29–30.

Silverman, L. K. (1991). Family counseling. In N. Colangelo & G. A. Davis (Eds.), *Handbook of gifted education* (pp. 307–320). Boston: Allyn and Bacon.

Steele, C. (2000, September). *Promoting educational success: Social and cultural considerations.* Paper presented at the U.S. Department of Education and The National Academies' Millennium Conference, Achieving High Educational Standards for All, Washington, DC.

Supplee, P. L. (1990). *Reaching the gifted underachiever: Program strategy and design.* New York: Teachers College Press.

Van Boxtel, H. W., & Mönks, F. J. (1992). General, social, and academic self-concepts of gifted adolescents. *Journal of Youth and Adolescence, 21*, 169–186.

Weiner, I. B. (1992). *Psychological disturbance in adolescence* (2nd ed.). New York: Wiley.

Whitmore, J. R. (1980). *Giftedness, conflict, and underachievement.* Boston: Allyn and Bacon.

Whitmore, J. R. (1986). Understanding a lack of motivation to excel. *Gifted Child Quarterly, 30*, 66–69.

Wigfield, A. (1994). The role of children's achievement values in the self-regulation of their learning outcomes. In D. H. Schunk & B. J. Zimmerman (Eds.), *Self regulation of learning and performance: Issues and educational applications* (pp. 101–124). Mahwah, NJ: Erlbaum.

Zimmerman, B. J. (1989). A social cognitive view of self-regulated academic learning. *Journal of Educational Psychology, 81*, 329–339.

Zimmerman, B. J., Bonner, S., & Kovatch, R. (1996). *Developing self-regulated learners.* Washington, DC: American Psychological Association.

Zimmerman, B. J., & Martinez-Pons, M. (1986). Development of a structured interview for accessing student use of self-regulated learning strategies. *American Educational Research Journal, 23*, 614–628.

**249**

# 24

# MODELS AND STRATEGIES FOR COUNSELING, GUIDANCE, AND SOCIAL AND EMOTIONAL SUPPORT OF GIFTED AND TALENTED STUDENTS

by **Sally M. Reis, Ph.D.** and **Sidney M. Moon, Ph.D.**

hile numerous strategies and some models have been suggested for addressing the social and emotional needs of students with gifts and talents, few have been comprehensively implemented by school personnel or even by private counselors who practice with this population. Therefore, determining effectiveness is impossible. As early as 1926, during the same period that Terman (1925) published findings about the low incidence of emotional problems experienced by gifted children in his longitudinal study, Hollingworth discussed the guidance needs of gifted students in the areas of personality, education, social development, and career decisions. The beginnings of the practical application of these needs and specific work in developing strategies for guidance and counseling for gifted and talented students can be traced to the 1950s with Rothney and Gowan at the Research and Guidance Laboratory at the University of Wisconsin and at San Fernando State College (Colangelo & Zaffrann, 1979). Since then, numerous strategies have been suggested for enhancing the social and emotional development of gifted students (see for example Birely & Genshaft, 1991; Colangelo and Zaffrann; Coleman & Cross, 2001, Cross, 2001; Delisle, 1992; Demos, 1965; Drews, 1964; Fine & Pitts, 1980; Frasier & McCannon, 1981; Gowan & Demos, 1964; Hébert, 1991, 1995; Hébert & Kent, 2000; Hébert & Neumeister, 2001; Hickson, 1992; Milne & Reis, 2000; Milgram, 1991; Moon & Hall, 1998; Olenchak, 1991; Perrone, 1986, 1997; Piechowski, 1997; Reis, 1998; Rimm, 1995, 1997; Rimm & Lowe, 1988; Rimm & Olenchak, 1991; Robinson, 1996; Roeper, 1982; Sanborn, 1979; Silverman, 1993; Torrance, 1979; VanTassel-Baska, 1983; Zaffrann & Colangelo, 1979; Zilli, 1971). Some of these strategies are discussed throughout this book; others are referenced within individual chapters. A summary of some of the most commonly suggested strategies is presented in Table 1.

These strategies can be implemented in a variety of ways. For example, gifted programs and sponsor group discussions and panels in which gifted and talented adults discuss some of the issues they faced in developing their own talents, or school counselors can lead small groups of gifted adolescents in discussing social and emotional issues they face because of their giftedness (Colangelo, 1997). Some strategies are suggested for specific populations, but can also be used for other groups. For example, Reis (1998) suggested using multiple resources, such as historical research, biographies, autobiographies, and novels, to facilitate discussion among younger gifted girls of the barriers they may encounter when seeking to develop their full potential as adults. Cross (1997, 2001) suggested numerous strategies that parents and educators can use to address the social and emotional needs of talented youth. These include recognizing and respecting the relationship between academic and social and

**252**

emotional needs, being cautious about applying adults' desires to students based on their perception of student's strength areas, teaching pro-social skill development and stress management, and the enjoyment of nonacademic activities. He advocates that adults model behaviors they want children to exhibit and expose gifted students to knowledgeable counseling. He also supports providing opportunities for down time and relaxation.

Finally, several models for gifted enrichment programs integrate affective components into the services they suggest for talented youth. For example, dimension one of the Autonomous Learner Model (Betts, 1985) includes activities to help students understand their giftedness, analyze their strengths and weaknesses, and build group dynamics. Similarly, enrichment models focusing on creative productivity encourage the use of affective strategies such as guided imagery (Goff & Torrance, 1991) and adult mentoring to create an affective support system during the completion of independent and small-group investigations (Renzulli, 1977; Renzulli & Reis, 1985, 1997).

In summary, many experts in the field of gifted education have suggested specific strategies for facilitating the social and emotional development of gifted children. However, only a few have developed comprehensive models of developmental or intervention processes. The models that have been developed fall into two categories: models of social and emotional development and models of interventions to promote social and emotional development.

## Models of Social and Emotional Adjustment Processes

Sowa, McIntire, May, and Bland (1994) identified common themes related to the social and emotional adjustment of gifted children. Drawing on the work of Lazarus (1961), they distinguished two views of psychological adjustment: adjustment as achievement and adjustment as process. They indicated that previous research with gifted children had focused only on the first perspective, adjustment as achievement. Therefore, they focused on adjustment as process using Lazarus's cognitive appraisal paradigm (Lazarus, 1966, 1993) as a theoretical framework. In this paradigm there are two

Table 1

## Suggested Strategies for Counseling and Meeting the Social and Emotional Needs of Gifted Children

**Family**

- family counseling and therapy in either school or private practice
- parent education programs, such as college and university application workshops and career guidance workshops for students and parents
- parent workshops on accepting differences and nurturing creativity

**Professional**

- training programs for regular education teachers and counselors involved with this population
- training programs for gifted education teachers and program coordinators
- teacher education programs

**Students**

- individual counseling and therapy in either school or private practice
- group counseling and therapy in either school or private practice
- within-school academic programs and grouping options
- strategies related to helping gifted students understand their own abilities and feelings of difference, perfectionism, stress from high expectations, such as discussions and presentations in gifted and talented programs
- proactive strategies to address issues that may affect gifted students, such as teaching decision making or creative problem solving

- panel or individual presentations by gifted adults in areas such as helping gifted students to understand creativity, identifying personal goals, and choosing careers
- coping strategies such as relaxation exercises and guided imagery
- role-playing and simulation
- videotherapy and cinematherapy
- mentorships, positive role models
- journal writing
- bibliotherapy and discussion of appropriate age and content fiction and nonfiction
- college and university workshops for students
- career guidance workshops for students

---

ways of coping with stress: problem-focused coping and emotion-focused coping. In Sowa et al.'s study, coping processes were triggered in gifted children by life stressors similar to those experienced by nonidentified peers. However, the experiences and statements of the gifted children indicated that they were using cognitive appraisal (Lazarus & Folkman, 1984) in ways typical of adults far in advance of their nonidentified peers. Understanding that gifted students have advanced cognitive appraisal skills may help educators to understand more fully conflicting research results about the incidence of adjustment problems in this population. For example, the sample of gifted children studied actively attempted to change their environments based on their own appraisals (problem-focused coping), a strategy more typical of adults than children. This suggests that we must consider both adults and children's models of adjustment in our attempts to understand the social and emotional adjustment of children with talents and gifts. It also suggests that many intellectually and academically gifted children also are talented in the social and emotional realm.

In later work, Sowa and May (1997) proposed a model that applied Lazarus and Folkman's (1984) paradigm to a model they called the Social and Emotional Adjustment of Gifted Children and Adolescents (SEAM). SEAM was derived from a study of the coping mechanisms employed by 20 gifted children as they experienced

**255**

demands and pressures at home and school. This complex model combines patterns in the ways that children and youth respond to stress, with theoretical and empirical information from the fields of child development and gifted education. The model uses family influences (functional vs. dysfunctional) and intrapersonal processes (coping mechanisms, peer comparison processes, and personal identity) to predict functional and dysfunctional patterns of social and emotional adjustment among gifted and talented children. Sowa and May suggested that gifted adolescents may rely on behaviors reflecting social adjustment at the expense of their own emotional needs or express cognitive appraisals that suggest they are emotionally adjusted even though their behaviors do not reflect social adjustments. They further suggested the need to establish both school and home environments that create opportunities and rewards for both the incorporation of others' opinions in decision making and the development of personal opinion.

Another empirically derived mode of adjustment is the Information Management Model (Coleman & Cross, 1998). This model explains social adjustment processes in gifted adolescents, illustrating the ways that external and internal school interactions affect the development of a gifted student's identity. Based on Bandura's (1986) social cognitive framework, the model assumes that gifted individuals actively construct their world and are influenced by expectations of certain behavior in various settings. Some gifted students do not feel different; some feel different, but do not develop social coping strategies; and some feel different and use social coping strategies that fall on a continuum, called the Continuum of Visibility, from high visibility (standing out), to invisibility (blending in), to disidentifying (acting like nongifted students).

More recently, Coleman and Cross (2001) discussed three theoretical models, providing advantages and disadvantages for use with gifted children: the Universal Development Model (for providing a general school program outline), the Behavioral-Cognitive Model (for use with gifted students' strengths to help them problem solve), and the Domain-Specific Developmental Model (to explain advanced development). They also summarized various social and psychological characteristics and features that can accompany gifts and talents in young people that should be addressed to ensure that their talents are developed and they reach the vitally important goal of emerging as emotionally healthy and contributing adults.

Finally, Olszewski-Kubilius (2000) has created a model to summarize the psychological factors and social support systems that aid the successful transition from childhood giftedness to adult creative productivity. Specifically, she examined the role of childhood environments in promoting adult productivity, presenting a model for understanding that the environmental conditions of creative producers result in key responses that help to develop several personality characteristics or coping strategies, which, in turn, facilitate creative productivity. These include a preference for time alone, an ability to cope with high levels of anxiety or tension, freedom from conventionality, and the use of intellectual activities to fulfill emotional needs. The environmental conditions that facilitate these personality characteristics can result from family stress, such as parental loss or dysfunction, threats to security, feelings of isolation, rejection, and need for refuge, among other issues. She explained, of course, that stress during the childhoods of talented persons does not regularly result in creative productive work as adults, but rather that stress during childhood "appears to be a typical pattern for adult creative producers" (p. 68). Exceptions to the pattern exist, as Reis (1996) found that women who achieve eminence and high levels of creative productivity in later life experienced varied childhood environments, including both those that were very happy and those in which stress had occurred.

## Intervention Models

Recent research conducted by Moon, Kelly, and Feldhusen (1997) indicated that parents, school personnel, and counseling professionals believe that gifted and talented children could benefit from differentiated counseling services designed to help them address such issues as peer relations, emotional adjustment, stress management, and underachievement. The work of pioneers in the area of counseling, affective needs, and social and emotional issues of gifted and talented students (Colangelo & Davis, 1997; Colangelo & Zaffrann, 1979; Gowan, 1955, 1957; Gowan &

Demos, 1964; Hollingworth, 1926; Janos & Robinson, 1985; Kerr, 1991; Webb, Meckstroth, & Tolan, 1982; Whitmore, 1980) has laid the foundation for several models of such differentiated counseling services that were proposed during the past decade. The existing models fall into two broad categories: developmental models that are designed to enhance optimal development and intervention models that are designed to address social and emotional difficulties. Most of the models have been proposed by clinicians who have worked with gifted and talented children and their families. Very few studies have been conducted to assess the effectiveness of these models or to test the relative effectiveness of different counseling modalities (e.g., individual vs. family counseling).

## Developmental Counseling Models

One of the most well-articulated and comprehensive intervention models is Silverman's (1993) Developmental Model for Counseling the Gifted. Her model addresses both intellectual and personality characteristics as foundations for intervention and urged counselors to help gifted individuals employ these characteristics in counseling processes. Silverman's model proposes that goals of counseling include *moral* outcomes such as moral courage, compassion, and altruism; *well being* outcomes such as autonomy and self-efficacy; and *achievement* outcomes such as creativity and contribution to society. Her model suggests that these outcomes can be achieved through many types of intervention, including educational ones such as grouping with same ability peers, as well as individual, group, and family counseling.

Mahoney (1997) created another model for counseling gifted individuals that focuses on identity development. His model was developed to guide counselors in helping gifted individuals explore their identity, strengthen their inner self, and enhance their health and development. It provides a grid to guide the counseling process that asks counselors to analyze each of the systems that impact identity formation (self, family, social, etc.) according to four identify formation constructs: validation, affirmation, affiliation, and affinity.

VanTassel-Baska (1998) recommended three types of counseling that are similar to Silverman's suggestions, including academic planning matched to learners' cognitive needs, life and career planning, and psychosocial counseling focusing of the preservation of affective differences. Van Tassel-Baska and Baska (1993) suggested that parents and teachers must become more involved with this responsibility as school counselors often have too many other scheduling and monitoring responsibilities and are restricted by large case loads.

Similarly, Colangelo (1997), one of the best-known researchers in this area, emphasized the importance of specialized counselors in facilitating healthy adjustment of students with gifts and talents. As with the models discussed above, Colangelo emphasizes the need for counselors to understand and factor in the individual's parent and school situation. He went further, however, in proposing methods for counselors to use in assessing how school and home issues might be improved in the process of counseling this population. Colangelo advocates a developmental approach that encourages counselors to establish school environments that are conducive to the educational growth of gifted students. The suggested developmental approach puts the focus on individual counseling as a way of getting to know gifted students better, focusing on understanding their strengths and weaknesses and decision making regarding how they can become the formulators of their own lives. Group counseling in this developmental approach focuses on sharing perceptions and learning effective interpersonal skills. Family work is based on discussion groups in which parents share information and connect with other families. Using Colangelo's approach, the goal of developmental counseling is to consider giftedness "not as a problem to be solved, but a unique challenge to be nourished" (p. 362). A model developmental counseling program, according to Colangelo, would include an articulated rationale; a program of activities based on the affective and cognitive needs of youngsters; counselors with expertise in giftedness; minimal attention to rehabilitative services and strong attention to individual, family, and teacher consultations; input from teachers, administrators, parents, and students being served; and continued professional development to keep the counselor informed of current research on the counseling needs of gifted students.

One other trend that has been evident in the developmental counseling literature is the proliferation of brief parent guidance models designed specifically for parents of gifted children (for review see Moon, in press). Usually these models are developed by and offered at university centers for gifted education, rather than through schools or private practitioners. Some of these models propose one-on-one counseling of families of gifted children, prescribing a brief counseling approach most appropriate for parents of young gifted children that includes a rigorous psychological assessment followed by some combination of recommendations for school programming, counselor-facilitated advocacy with schools, or parent guidance (e.g., Wieczerkowski & Prado, 1991). Other models emphasize sequenced and structured parent support groups (Webb & DeVries, 1993). Both types of parent guidance models are designed to enable parents to serve as better facilitators of the social and emotional development of gifted children.

## Counseling Models for Specific Dysfunctions

Much less work has been done to develop differentiated counseling models for interventions when gifted individuals, their families, or both experience problems such as underachievement, eating disorders, behavior disorders, divorce, or remarriage. There are several case reports in the literature on different approaches to family therapy with families of gifted children (see Moon, in press). These articles provide useful strategies, but not articulated or differentiated intervention models. However, there does appear to be some consensus that family counseling is the preferred modality for helping gifted children with serious social and emotional adjustment difficulties (see also Moon & Hall, 1998).

At the Belin-Blank Center, the Family FIRO model is used to conceptualize the presentation of problems and to organize treatment when families of gifted children experience family conflict (Colangelo & Assouline, 2000). According to the Family FIRO model, family issues can be categorized into a hierarchy of inclusion, control, and intimacy. When families have issues in more than one of these categories, the hierarchy is followed. For example, if issues of inclusion are present, they are addressed before issues of control or intimacy. This model is implemented with families of gifted children in a family counseling program at the Belin-Blank Center that serves as a practicum for advanced doctoral students.

**260**

One intervention model developed specifically for use with families of gifted children is a clinical model developed by a clinician researcher team in 1984 (Frey & Wendorf, 1985; Wendorf & Frey, 1985). Like the parent guidance models, this model began with a two-pronged assessment process. First, the gifted child's academic history was assessed with test scores, records of past achievement, and a clinical interview addressing current school programming and home-school relationships. Then, family dynamics were assessed. At the conclusion of the clinical assessment phase, families were divided into two categories: (a) problem families whose primary problem was between the home and school systems; and (b) clinical families whose primary problem was considered to be family dysfunction. The problem families received parental guidance counseling like that described above. The clinical families received structural-strategic family therapy of varying durations, from brief therapy (3–4 sessions), to extended therapy (20 or more sessions over several years). This intervention model is a good fit with Sowa and May's adjustment model, which predicts that poor adjustment among gifted children is far more likely when there is family dysfunction, and, hence, that it is extremely important to intervene when possible to improve dysfunctional family relationships.

One of the few intervention models developed specifically for a common presenting problem among gifted and talented students is the Trifocal Model, which was developed to help reverse underachievement among gifted children (Rimm, 1995). This model is extremely well elaborated, providing numerous suggestions to both parents and teachers for specific strategies to reverse underachieving patterns. The model includes assessment followed by a five-step intervention process that is implemented collaboratively by parents and teachers. Like the other models discussed in this section, the family is seen as a key to intervention in the Trifocal model. Unlike the family therapy models, the Trifocal model proposes that parents and teachers, rather than family therapists, provide the interventions. In that respect, the Trifocal model is more like some of the developmental models discussed above, especially those advocated by Colangelo (1997).

# Summary

Carefully reviewing the strategies and models to enhance the social and emotional well-being of gifted and talented children and youth may help us to develop a continuum of services that will guide their social and emotional development. This continuum could range from services for gifted individuals who need intensive therapy from trained professionals for serious psychological problems, to services for gifted children who need only minimal developmental interventions from parents and teachers. There are many good ideas in the literature for developmental interventions by parents, teachers, and counselors, but few suggestions for how to help professional counselors best address the needs of their clients who are gifted and talented. What is needed most, however, is solid, empirical research on patterns and interventions that promote the healthy development of gifted students into gifted adults who lead satisfying personal and professional lives. Many models and strategies provide excellent suggestions, but we need research indicating what works best, under what circumstances, for what types of gifted students and their families. Perhaps in the near future, such research can and will occur.

# References

Bandura, A. (1986). *Social foundations of thought and action: A social cognition theory.* Englewood Cliffs, NJ: Prentice Hall.

Betts, G. (1985). *Autonomous learner model for the gifted and talented.* Greeley, CO: Autonomous Learning Publications and Specialists.

Birely, M., & Genshaft, J. (1991). (Eds). *Understanding the gifted adolescent: Educational development and multicultural issues.* New York: Teachers College Press.

Colangelo, N. (1997). Counseling gifted students: Issues and practices. In N. Colangelo & G. A. Davis (Eds.), *Handbook of gifted education* (2nd ed., pp. 353–365). Boston: Allyn and Bacon.

Colangelo, N., & Assouline, S. G. (2000). Counseling gifted students. In K. A. Heller, F. J. Mönks, & R. J. Sternberg (Eds.), *International handbook of giftedness and talent* (pp. 595–607). Amsterdam: Elsevier.

Colangelo, N., & Davis, G. A. (Eds.). (1997). *Handbook of gifted education* (2nd ed.). Boston: Allyn and Bacon.

Colangelo, N., & Zaffrann, R. T. (Eds.). (1979). *New voices in counseling the gifted.* Dubuque, IA: Kendall-Hunt.

Coleman, L. J., & Cross, T. L. (1988). Is being gifted a social handicap? *Journal for the Education of the Gifted, 11*, 41–56.

Coleman, L. J., & Cross, T. L. (2001). *Being gifted in school: An introduction to development, guidance, and teaching*. Waco, TX: Prufrock Press.

Cross, T. L. (1997). Psychological and social aspects of educating gifted students. *The Peabody Journal of Education, 72*, 181–201.

Cross, T. L. (2001). *On the social and emotional lives of gifted children*. Waco, TX: Prufrock Press.

Delisle, J. (1992). *Guiding the social and emotional development of youth*. New York: Longman.

Demos, G. D. (1965). Guidance and counseling with the ablest. In J. C. Gowan & G. D. Demos (Eds.), *Guidance of exceptional children* (pp. 75–78). New York: McKay.

Drews, E. M. (1964). The creative intellectual style in gifted adolescents. In *Being and becoming: A cosmic approach to counseling and curriculum* (Third report of Title VII, Project No. 647–I, National Defense Act of 1958. Grant No. 7-32-0410-140). Washington, DC: Department of Health, Education, and Welfare.

Fine, M. J., & Pitts, R. (1980). Intervention with underachieving gifted children: Rationale and strategies. *Gifted Child Quarterly, 24*, 51–55.

Frasier, M. M., & McCannon, C. (1981). Using bibliotherapy with gifted children. *Gifted Child Quarterly, 25*, 81–85.

Frey, J., & Wendorf, D. J. (1985). Families of gifted children. In L. L'Abate (Ed.), *Handbook of family psychology and therapy* (Vol. 2, pp. 781–809). Homewood, IL: Dorsey Press.

Goff, K., & Torrance, E. P. (1991). Healing qualities of imagery and creativity. *Journal of Creative Behavior, 25*, 296–303.

Gowan, J. C. (1955). The underachieving gifted child: A problem for everyone. *Exceptional Children, 22*, 247–249, 270–271.

Gowan, J. C. (1957). Dynamics of the underachievement of gifted students. *Exceptional Children, 24*, 98–101.

Gowan, J. C., & Demos, G. D. (1964). *The education and guidance of the ablest*. Springfield, IL: Thomas.

Hébert, T. P. (1991). Meeting the affective needs of bright boys through bibliotherapy. *Roeper Review, 13*, 207–212.

Hébert, T. P. (1995). Using biography to counsel gifted young men. *Journal of Secondary Gifted Education, 6*, 208–219.

Hébert, T. P., & Kent, R. (2000). Nurturing social and emotional development in gifted teenagers through young adult literature. *Roeper Review, 22*, 167–171.

Hébert, T. P., & Neumeister, K. L. S. (2001). Guided viewing of film: A strategy for counseling gifted teenagers. *The Journal of Secondary Gifted Education, 14*, 224–235.

Hickson, J. (1992). A framework for guidance and counseling of the gifted in a school setting. *Gifted Education International, 8*, 93–103.

Hollingworth, L. S. (1926). *Gifted children: Their nature and nurture*. New York: Macmillan.

**263**

Janos, P. M., & Robinson, N. (1985). Psychosocial development in intellectually gifted children. In F. Horowitz & M. O'Brien (Eds.), *The gifted and talented: Developmental perspectives* (pp. 149–195). Washington, DC: American Psychological Association.

Kerr, B. A. (1991). *Handbook for counseling the gifted and talented*. Alexandria, VA: American Association for Counseling Development.

Lazarus, R. S. (1961). *Adjustment and personality*. New York: McGraw-Hill.

Lazarus, R. S. (1966). *Psychological stress and the coping process*. New York: McGraw-Hill.

Lazarus, R. S. (1993) From psychological stress to the emotions: A history of changing outlooks. *The Annual Review of Psychology, 44,* 1–21.

Lazarus, R. S., & Folkman, S. (1984). *Stress appraisal and coping*. New York: Springer.

Milne, H. J., & Reis, S. M. (2000). Using video therapy to address the social and emotional needs of gifted children. *Gifted Child Today, 23*(1), 24–29.

Milgram, R. M. (Ed.). (1991). *Counseling gifted and talented children: A guide for teachers, counselors, and parents*. Norwood, NJ: Ablex.

Moon, S. M. (in press). Family counseling. In N. Colangelo & G. A. Davis (Eds.), *Handbook of gifted education* (3rd ed.). Boston: Allyn and Bacon.

Moon, S. M., Kelly, K. R., & Feldhusen, J. F. (1997). Specialized counseling services for gifted youth and their families: A needs assessment. *Gifted Child Quarterly, 41,* 16–25.

Moon, S. M., & Hall, A. S. (1998). Family therapy with intellectually and creatively gifted children. *Journal of Marital and Family Therapy, 24,* 59–80.

Olszewski-Kubilius, P. (2000). The transition from childhood giftedness to adult creative productiveness: Psychological characteristics and social supports. *Roeper Review, 23,* 65–71.

Olenchak, F. R. (1991). Wearing their shoes: A case study of reversing underachievement in a gifted child through role playing. *Understanding Our Gifted, 3*(4), 1–7.

Perrone, P. A. (1986). Guidance needs of gifted children, adolescents, and adults. *Journal of Counseling and Development, 64,* 564–566.

Perrone, P. A. (1997). Gifted individuals' career development. In N. Colangelo & G. A. Davis (Eds.), *Handbook of gifted education* (2nd ed., pp. 398–407). Boston: Allyn and Bacon.

Piechowski, M. M. (1997). Emotional giftedness: The measure of intrapersonal intelligence. In N. Colangelo & G. A. Davis (Eds.), *Handbook of gifted education* (2nd ed., pp. 366–381). Boston: Allyn and Bacon.

Reis, S. M. (1996). Older women's reflections on eminence: Obstacles and opportunities. In K. Arnold, K. Noble, & R. Subotnik (Eds.), *Remarkable women: Perspectives of female talent development* (pp. 149–168). Cresskill, NJ: Hampton Press.

Reis, S. M. (1998). *Work left undone: Compromises and challenges of talented females*. Mansfield Center, CT: Creative Learning Press.

Renzulli, J. S. (1977). *The enrichment triad model*. Mansfield Center, CT: Creative Learning Press.

Renzulli, J. S., & Reis, S. M. (1985). *The schoolwide enrichment model: A comprehensive plan for educational excellence*. Mansfield Center, CT: Creative Learning Press.

Renzulli, J. S., & Reis, S. M. (1997). *The schoolwide enrichment model: A comprehensive plan for educational excellence* (2nd ed.). Mansfield Center: Creative Learning Press.

Rimm, S. (1995). *Why bright kids get poor grades and what you can do about it*. New York: Crown.

Rimm, S. (1997). Underachievement syndrome: A national epidemic. In N. Colangelo and G. A. Davis (Eds.), *Handbook of gifted education*. (2nd ed., pp. 416–435). Boston, MA: Allyn and Bacon.

Rimm, S. B., & Lowe, B. (1988). Family environments of underachieving gifted students. *Gifted Child Quarterly, 32*, 353–358

Rimm, S. B., & Olenchak, F. R. (1991). How FPS helps underachieving gifted students. *Gifted Child Today, 14*(2), 19–22.

Robinson, N. M. (1996). Counseling agendas for gifted young people. *Journal for the Education of the Gifted, 20*, 128–137.

Roeper, A. (1982). How the gifted cope with their emotions. *Roeper Review, 5*, 21–24.

Sanborn, M. P. (1979). Counseling and guidance needs of the gifted and talented students. In A. H. Passow (Ed.), *The gifted and talented: Their education and development* (pp. 424–428). Chicago: University of Chicago Press.

Silverman, L. K. (1993). A developmental model for counseling the gifted. In L. K. Silverman (Ed.), *Counseling the gifted and talented* (pp. 51–78). Denver: Love.

Sowa, C. J., & May, K. M. (1997). Expanding Lazarus and Folkman's paradigm to the social and emotional adjustment of gifted children and adolescents. *Gifted Child Quarterly, 41*, 36–43.

Sowa, C. J., McIntire, J., May, K. M., & Bland, L. (1994). Social and emotional adjustment themes across gifted children. *Roeper Review, 17*, 95–98

Terman, L. M. (1925). *Genetic studies of genius* (Vol. 4). Stanford, CA: Stanford University Press.

Torrance, E. P. (1979). An instructional model for enhancing innovation. *Journal of Creative Behavior, 13*, 23–25.

VanTassel–Baska, J. (1983). School counseling needs and successful strategies to meet them. In J. VanTassel–Baska (Ed.), *A practical guide to counseling the gifted in a school setting* (pp. 40–46). Reston, VA: Council for Exceptional Children.

VanTassel-Baska, J. (1998). Counseling talented learners. In J. VanTassel-Baska (Ed.), *Excellence in educating gifted and talented learners* (3rd ed., pp. 489–510). Denver: Love.

VanTassel-Baska, J., & Baska, L. (1993). The roles of educational personnel in counseling the gifted. In L. K. Silverman (Ed.), *Counseling the gifted and talented* (pp. 181–200). Denver: Love.

Webb, J. T., & DeVries, A. R. (1993). *Training manual for facilitators of SENG model guided discussion groups*. Scottsdale, AZ: SENG.

Webb, J., Meckstroth, E., & Tolan, S. S. (1982). *Guiding the gifted child: A practical source for parents and teachers.* Columbus: Ohio Psychology Press.

Wendorf, D. J., & Frey, J. (1985). Family therapy with the intellectually gifted. *The American Journal of Family Therapy, 13,* 31–38.

Whitmore, J. R. (1980). *Giftedness, conflict, and underachievement.* Boston: Allyn and Bacon.

Wieczerkowski, W., & Prado, T. M. (1991). Parental fears and expectations from the point of view of a counseling center for the gifted. *European Journal for High Ability, 2,* 56–72.

Zaffrann, R. T., & Colangelo, N. (1979). Counseling with gifted and talented students. In N. Colangelo & R. T. Zaffrann (Eds.), *New voices in counseling the gifted* (pp. 142–153). Dubuque, IA: Kendall-Hunt.

Zilli, M. J. (1971). Reasons why the gifted adolescent underachieves and some of the implications of guidance and counseling to this problem. *Gifted Child Quarterly, 15,* 279–292.

# SOCIAL AND EMOTIONAL ISSUES FACING GIFTED AND TALENTED STUDENTS:

What Have We Learned and What Should We Do Now?

by **Nancy M. Robinson, Ph.D., Sally M. Reis, Ph.D., Maureen Neihart, Psy.D.,** and **Sidney M. Moon, Ph.D.**

The previous chapters yield a picture of the social and emotional lives of gifted children and youth that is like a cup both half full and half empty. Although these young people encounter a number of challenges—most, but not all, of them because they live in environments that serve them poorly—the research summarized in this volume points to clear steps to improve matters. Consequently, we conclude with a set of recommendations, the minimum we must do and the best we can do to promote the healthy development of children and youth with high potential, and offer recommendations for research and advocacy.

## Central Conclusions

Admittedly working from a limited research base, the authors of the previous chapters have reached consistent conclusions. These are the major themes derived from the overall thrust of the reviews:

- There is good news. There is no evidence that gifted children or youth—as a group—are inherently any more vulnerable or flawed in adjustment than any other group. We failed to discover evidence of social or emotional vulnerabilities or flaws unique to intellectually gifted learners or those with high creative potential. With the exception of mood disorders in creative writers and artists, indices of serious maladjustment, such as suicide, delinquency, and severe behavior disorders, appear no more (or less) frequently in this group than the general population. Indeed, many gifted young people possess assets that, when supported, may enhance their resilience to highly negative life events and enable them to utilize their talents to achieve productive and satisfying lives.
- When social and emotional problems related to an individual's giftedness do occur in this population, they most frequently reflect the interaction of an ill-fitting environment with an individual's personal characteristics. Gifted students by definition are those whose intellectual advancement is such that they require special educational experiences that are seldom forthcoming in regular classrooms (U.S. Department of Education, 1993). Most of their school days are spent relearning material they have already mastered or could master in a fraction of the time that it takes their chronological peers. Therefore, many never learn strategies to cope with the challenges related to effort and perseverance that other children encounter throughout their childhood and later lives. In addition, the maturity of their personal outlook, which is, in many ways, similar to that of older students, may result in a mismatch, not only with the

**268**

curriculum, but usually also with their classmates. They may encounter a variety of intellectual and social issues in addition to the developmental tasks usually encountered by persons of their age. They may have difficulty finding friends who share their understandings, and far too often they endure not only the burden of loneliness, but also enormous peer pressure to "be like everyone else."

- From this perspective, the news is also good, as much can be accomplished by modifying the contexts in which gifted and talented children grow up. With greater understanding, teachers, parents, counselors, and peers can make many of the changes that will offer the challenges, flexibility, and acceptance that gifted students need to flourish. It is up to caring adults to redesign life experiences so that these young people do not have to resolve challenging issues on their own.

- Far from finding that "gifted children are all alike," the reviewers found marked differences among this highly diverse group. Because no single panacea exists, researchers, educators, parents, and other citizens must join together to implement a range of strategies matched to the needs of individual gifted and talented children and youth. Among the dimensions to consider are:

  - *Degree of advancement.* In IQ terms alone, wide differences exist, even between moderately gifted students and the most gifted, and special programs must take these individual differences into account.
  - *Gender.* Reviewers have found somewhat different issues confronting gifted girls (whose needs have received attention in recent years) and gifted boys (who are seldom studied.)
  - *Age.* Very young gifted children may thrive within their families, but may lose their enthusiasm for learning and even become underachievers when they enter school. Peer pressures and stresses mount for gifted adolescents.
  - *Ethnicity, language, and income.* Gifted students who come from families that differ because of race, ethnicity,

language, socioeconomic status, or a combination of these factors face their own special challenges. Not only may their talents escape recognition, but family and peers may actively discourage or passively fail to support their optimal talent development. Furthermore, they may retreat from some opportunities because they find too few of their own group present.

- *Sexual orientation.* Gays, lesbians, and bisexual gifted persons may face additional burdens of difference that can cause additional pressures and anxiety.
- *Internal discrepancies in ability levels.* It is the rule, rather than the exception, to find gifted students with uneven abilities—higher in verbal than math, or higher in visual-spatial than verbal reasoning, for example, or vice versa. Such discrepancies present their own challenges.
- *Disabilities.* Gifted children are not immune to disabilities in reading, writing, and mathematics; to sensory or motor impairment; to attention deficit disorder; or to serious psychiatric disorders. In this day of increasing specialization, it is often difficult to locate professionals in the field who can address both concerns.

- Contradictions abound about this area. There are, contrary to our major findings, respected authorities in this field who maintain that gifted children are emotionally different from others. Roeper (1996), for example, has asserted that "the self of the gifted child is structured differently" (p. 18). She contended that gifted individuals have a more complex view of the world, that their depth of awareness is different, and that gifted children have an emotional need to develop themselves and to master the world. Dabrowski also maintained that people with the highest potential follow a developmental path that is uniquely different. He believed that they are characterized by an overexcitability and intensity of character and a dissatisfaction with what is (see O'Connor, this volume).

**270**

While such differences may indeed exist, we caution readers to evaluate carefully whether most or all such characteristics are inherently or qualitatively *different,* or whether they reflect primarily the *maturity of viewpoint* that is a part of intellectual and emotional giftedness (Feldhusen, 1989; Jackson & Butterfield, 1986). What appears qualitatively different may be common to other young people of chronological ages equivalent to the mental ages of the individuals being described. We should not expect gifted and talented children to see the world in the same way as do other children of their age. Furthermore, some characteristics (e.g., perfectionism and entelechy) may take on their own flavor because students become accustomed to high levels of achievement, and still other characteristics (e.g., uneven abilities) from the fact that their highest abilities are "so high." Some (e.g., sensitivities and excitabilities), however, may indeed be qualitatively special traits of gifted students. We need considerable research, first to determine whether in fact these characteristics are more common to gifted than nongifted youngsters, and second, to explore to what extent qualitative differences exist and whether or not the dyssynchrony of an "older" mind in a younger body exists.

Nevertheless, it is worthwhile to examine some common characteristics of gifted individuals that may pose challenges to their social and emotional balance and adjustment (see Table 1). Note that many of these characteristics can be assets when the environments in which they live are accepting and appropriately supportive.

Although possible negative consequences resulting from these traits are cited in some research discussed in this book, many of them can also have a positive impact on the individual's social and emotional well-being. For example, Schuler (this volume) found many examples of gifted students who display healthy perfectionism, defined as doing their personal best and consistently wanting to do well. Reis, Neu, and McGuire (1995) found that, although half their sample of high-ability college students with learning disabilities had sought counseling to address social and emotional difficulties, the majority evolved into strong, competent young adults with high levels of resilience and academic success. The same investigators cautioned, however, that their sample includes only those who had survived the secondary school system and who had had very supportive parents.

**271**

Few will disagree that having gifts and talents causes some gifted children and youth to struggle with their identity and with

Table 1

## Social and Emotional Characteristics
## of Gifted Children That May Pose Challenges

- perceptiveness (O'Connor, Neihart & Olenchak)
- high involvement and preoccupation; need to understand (Gross)
- heightened sensitivity (O'Connor, Hébert)
- perfectionism and need for precision (Schuler, Reis, Greene)
- uneven intellectual abilities, even above-average abilities experienced as deficits (Silverman)
- asynchronous development of physical, intellectual, social, emotional aspects (Silverman)
- emotional intensity (O'Connor, Keiley, Hébert)
- feelings and early awareness of being different (Rimm, Reis, Ford)
- anxiety caused by advanced knowledge (Reis & McCoach)
- need for mental stimulation (O'Connor, Neihart & Olenchak, Reis & McCoach, Rogers)
- entelechy—a desire to become all one is capable of becoming (Gross)
- nonconformity and questioning of authority (Neihart & Olenchak)
- excitability and overexcitability (O'Connor)
- tendency toward introversion and internalized locus of control (Silverman, Keiley, Gross)
- multipotentiality—the ability to succeed in any of several domains, requiring difficult choices (Greene, Reis & McCoach)
- tendency toward self-doubt (females) (Reis, Reis & McCoach)

*Note.* Citations are to relevant chapters in this volume.

**272** balancing their own abilities and needs with their academic life, their family life, and their career choices (Moon & Hall, 1998; Olenchak, 1999; Reis, 1998). Social and emotional stress can result when gifted and talented students are teased by peers and subjected to pressure to conform to peer norms. Many talented students learn early on to stop raising their hands in class and to underplay their abilities to avoid labels such as "nerd," "dweeb," or "dork." Consider the experience of an exceptional student who pleaded with her school board to save the program in which she had opportunities to take academically challenging classes with other talented students in both middle and high school:

> In my 12 years in school, I have been placed in many "average" classes—especially up until the junior high school level—in which I have been spit on, ostracized, and verbally abused for doing my homework on a regular basis, for raising my hand in class, and particularly for receiving outstanding grades. (Peters, 1990, p. 10)

The research cited in this book clearly indicates that some students survive these experiences by developing resilience; others begin a spiral of underachievement from which they do not recover; and still others experience continuing negative social and emotional pressures despite academic successes that may or may not last. These outcomes, as we have pointed out, are not the result of inherent vulnerabilities, but often result from a lack of fit with a frequently nonchallenging environment.

## What We Can Learn From Talented Adolescents Who Succeed

Some high-potential teenagers manage to maintain their positive trajectories in developing their talents, and some do not. What can we learn from those who do? In a landmark longitudinal study of 200 talented teenagers, Csikszentmihalyi, Rathunde, and Whalen (1993) found a strong core of personal attributes that distinguished those who did and those who did not maintain their talents from their freshman to their senior year in high school. Among these attributes were intellectual curiosity, active seeking of information, strong desire to achieve, perseverance in attaining goals, preference for leading and controlling, desire to display accomplishments and gain others' attention, and lit-

**273**

tle questioning of their own worth. The productive male teens valued stability and predictability more than did the other group, preferred to avoid physical risks, enjoyed arguments, and had an unusual need for social recognition. The productive female teens were less inclined to identify with "feminine" values (orderliness, neatness, and predictability) than those who abandoned their talents. The successful teens in this study "entered adolescence with personality attributes well suited to the difficult struggle of establishing their mastery over a domain, a desire to achieve, persistence, and a curiosity and openness to experience" (Csikszentmihalyi, Rathunde, & Whalen, p. 82).

Another important finding of this study was the influential role played by families. The successful teenagers were more likely to come from families termed "complex" by the authors. These families were warmly engaged with one another and, at the same time, maintained high expectations for their children. The literature on achievement motivation (McClelland, Atkinson, Clark, & Lowell, 1953; Parsons, Adler, & Kaczala, 1982) has long recognized the importance of supportive families that reward responsibility and expect children to do their best from an early age.

The concepts underlying *resilience theory* (see Neihart, this volume) provides a way to understand why some gifted and talented students who encounter difficult situations manage to remain achievers, while others do not. Studies of risk and resilience point to the powerful effects of certain personal characteristics—above-average intelligence being one of the most powerful—and the availability of social supports (caregivers, mentors, teachers, peers) in mitigating the negative effects of adversity. Preliminary findings from a handful of studies that have specifically examined resilience in gifted youth are consistent with earlier studies of mixed groups, and they demonstrate the advantages of using this research-based framework to address the social and emotional needs of gifted children. Operating within this framework, practitioners and researchers alike might ask about the children with whom they work, "What are the risks (stressors) and the protective mechanisms (social supports, developmental assets, and personal qualities) that contribute to positive and negative outcomes?" All of the means that have been suggested in this volume to support gifted children's positive adjustment can be viewed as either diminishing

**274**

risk factors (e.g., reducing understimulating environments, disabling perfectionism, social isolation) or promoting protective factors (e.g., enhancing supportive relationships with caring adults, talent development, and problem-solving skills, and personal characteristics known to be associated with psychosocial strength and achievement, such as a positive explanatory style, self-efficacy, and androgyny).

## What We Should Do to Address Social and Emotional Issues Faced by Talented Children and Youth

It is time that educators, researchers, and parents put to rest some of the widespread, false myths about high potential youth (e.g., "They are too smart for their own good," "They don't get along with other children") and reach some consensus about those things that can be done to alleviate the situation. Many current explicit and implicit school policies interfere with the full actualization of high ability. Moreover, "Risk is pervasive. If a student is at risk in one area, that student is very likely to be at risk in many other areas" (Frymier et al., 1992, p. 5). Research has clearly delineated the multiple sources of the challenges faced by gifted students, but is yet to develop effective long-range interventions.

Keeping in mind the resilience model described above, it is clear that we can bring about major improvement in the outcomes of the interactions between gifted students and their environment. There are a number of strategies that may work—and others to be developed—that can minimize risks and maximize assets as gifted students interact with all their environments: family, school, peers, and the larger community.

### Preventive Efforts

As we all know, "an ounce of prevention is worth a pound of cure." We already have available a variety of optimizing strategies that can improve the fit of the environment with the student, enhance the knowledge and skills of the adults with whom students

**275**

interact, and encourage the proximal (peer) and distal (community) environments to be more accepting of the gifted students within their midst.

It is important to note that practically none of the section that follows is based on "hard" research data, with the major exception of findings about the effects of various forms of educational adaptations for gifted students. The recommendations for teacher and parent training; for anticipatory and responsive group counseling for students, parents, or both; and for interventions for underachievement and other forms of maladjustment are based on the sparsest of research data. Nevertheless, as we move from our extensive review of the findings about the social and emotional lives of gifted children to making recommendations for action, we feel compelled to offer the following as an agenda of worthy possibilities.

Educational modifications, including teacher training, are probably the single most effective way to prevent social and emotional difficulties in gifted students. They need appropriate levels of academic challenge and time every day to learn with others of similar abilities, interests, and drive. There are no substitutes for this remedy. Although counseling, extracurricular enrichment, mentorships, and so forth are helpful, they should never be considered an adequate alternative to a responsive and flexible educational environment matched to the level and pace of the student's learning, recognition for excellence of work habits and persistence of effort, and some choice of topic in accord with individual interests. These are the rights of every student. Some appropriate opportunities can be provided by well-trained teachers in the regular classroom, and some can be achieved by placing students for all or part of the day in regular classes above their ordinary grade level. Often, special programs, ranging from full-time to part-time, as well as after-school classes, best address these basic needs of gifted students.

Distinctions must be made between efforts that bring about fundamental changes in students' everyday school experience (e.g., compacting and differentiated instructional methods, cluster grouping, self-contained classes, above-grade classes) and those that are add-ons or complementary (e.g., pull-out programs, contests, after-school clubs). While the latter are often of significant value, gifted students need a challenging school day every day. Much of the distress experienced by gifted students who are in ill-fitting school environments could be a thing of the past if we made substantive changes in the schools.

These changes will not occur until we train teachers— both those who do and those who do not specialize in working with gifted children—to recognize and respond to advanced abilities. Furthermore, many students not identified as gifted have advanced abilities in specific domains. Techniques for differentiating teaching and expectations for student performance will empower teachers to forsake a "one-size-fits-all" approach, to the benefit of all students. There is no denying, however, that such approaches require more planning time and energy, as well as imagination, tolerance for a bit of disorder, and a desire to change.

School administrators must lead this effort. They need to value flexibility, cooperation among teachers, and accelerative methods, since these require administrative changes. Unless there is accountability for the continued progress of our most able students and recognition of advanced levels of performance, many teachers will continue to pursue the status quo, and gifted students will be essentially left out of current school reform efforts. At a state level, services are enhanced when a mandate, a legal requirement, exists to meet the needs of identified gifted children and when special certification of teachers of the gifted is required for those who are special teachers or teaching consultants. Even with a mandate, however, economically poor states are likely to eliminate programs for high-ability students (Purcell, 1994).

*Enhancement of parents' understanding and responsiveness to their students' needs.* Parents of gifted children often feel at a loss to know how to best support their development. They want help in understanding the children's needs; in treading the fine line between appropriate expectations and "pushing"; in learning skills of negotiating with teachers and other school personnel; and in widening and deepening their children's learning through family activities, outside tutors, or coaches. The needs are particularly acute for families who do not come from a background of education, for those whose own experiences in school were unfulfilling, and for those who are otherwise at a disadvantage for knowing how to help their

What We Have Learned and What We Must Do

children to be successful in school. In addition to how-to books, parent groups can reach out to these families to offer empowering opportunities. Special efforts are often needed to make such parents feel comfortable even admitting that their child's abilities are advanced and then coming together for discussion. We as professionals have done relatively little in this area, although some parents—typically well-educated and financially comfortable parents—have reached out to each other.

To the extent that young people recognize their actual and potential assets, they can meet the world with optimism and insightfulness, recognize that mismatches are not their fault, and accept their differences from others, rather than try to eradicate them. It is primarily with acceptance, respect, and feedback from caring adults (parents, teachers, counselors) and peers that gifted children will develop this equanimity and the ultimate resilience that accompanies it.

*Changes in the peer culture.* A number of authors in this volume have alluded to the negative effects of anti-intellectualism in the peer group, the deriding of gifted classmates as "nerds," or worse. Teasing of bright students is a form of misbehavior as offensive as hurling epithets at a student of color, a student with a disability, or a member of any other marginalized group (and doubly so when the bright classmate is also such a student).

Bringing about changes in the peer culture is never easy, and it will not occur at all unless respected adults—especially parents and teachers—respond positively to gifted children. Students who do their outstanding academic and artistic work deserve the same kinds of admiration that athletes receive. Prizes for academic accomplishment are but a small part of this effort and may indeed backfire unless the milieu is positive. In those schools that have adopted an integrated curricular preventive approach to social and emotional issues led by teachers or counselors, surely these issues should be a topic of discussion. The best we can expect is probably incremental change, not a revolution, but adults need to remain alert to manifestations of an anti-intellectual peer culture, to deal with the situation as directly as possible, and to support the gifted child who is the target.

**278**

In addition, gifted students need to be made explicitly aware that all of us belong simultaneously to several subcultures, which may be defined by school class, neighborhood, ethnicity, language, or religion. Finding acceptance among intellectual peers at school does not imply that one has rejected one's other subcultures, even when those subcultures fail to appreciate high academic motivation and attainment.

*Efforts to make the broader society accepting of giftedness, especially in those students from nonmainstream families.* We are living in a society that is intensely ambivalent toward its intellectual leaders. Support for research—especially medical research—is generous, and recipients of the Nobel Prize are honored. But, true fortunes and daily headlines are made by athletes and entertainers who may never have even attended college. Rock stars earn far more than leading orchestra conductors. Yet, many beginning teachers are paid so poorly that they cannot afford to house, feed, or educate their families. It will take patience, creativity, and perseverance to reverse this situation. In the meantime, we can show by our own example and advocacy that anti-intellectualism is unacceptable, that it is, in fact, a form of bigotry as pernicious as any other.

At the same time, we can actively welcome talented students to that part of the society that values intellect and creativity, learning and the arts. The adult world enriched by public lectures, book clubs, concerts, drama, painting, sculpture, and dance needs to reach out not only to students with specific talents, but to talented students who may find the kind of acceptance at these events that may be lacking in their home schools.

## Supportive Efforts: Minimizing Stress When It Occurs

Despite preventive efforts, stresses occur in the lives of gifted young people, just as they do in everyone's lives. Supportive services can minimize the effects of such stressors and, indeed, sometimes turn them into assets.

## Models for Counseling and Meeting
## the Affective Needs of Gifted and Talented Students

Both strategies and preliminary models have been suggested for addressing the emotional needs of students with gifts and talents, although few have been used comprehensively by school personnel or even by private counselors who practice with this population. (Reis, this volume). All involve some type of combination of individual and group counseling in home, school, and, if necessary, with professionals working in the health care field. Many excellent suggestions have been made in strategies and models of positive adjustment, counseling, and social and emotional support; however, few are comprehensively implemented, and little empirical evidence exists indicating that any of these strategies actually makes a difference in the lives of gifted and talented children and youth.

*Transitions and shifts in comparison groups.* As discussed by Moon (this volume), many gifted students experience stress when they enter a special class for gifted students, enroll in a more advanced class, enter a summer program, or skip a grade. The transitional shift from being top of one's class to simply one of the group—or even one who might be struggling to keep up—can be difficult. Even very bright students often fail to understand that their comparison group has changed. Some students do not, however, survive the transition and opt out of the very situation that would provide both the academic challenge and the peer group they desire. Anticipatory counseling can ease these types of matters considerably.

*Group counseling.* Similarly, group counseling can be helpful in dealing with many ordinary stressors, such as planning the trajectory of secondary school, choices among colleges, and career choices. Some choices made during secondary school (e.g., whether to take calculus) have long-range ramifications for careers. Stress-management and time-management skills (when schoolwork has been undemanding), inevitable peer issues, and special issues for specific groups (e.g., girls and boys, members of underserved minorities) are all topics that can be handled well in groups.

*Family guidance groups.* As mentioned in the previous section, appropriate readings and parent and family support groups that deal with the same topics as those for their children can reduce parental isolation and increase competence at handling potentially stressful situations. These discussion groups may be especially helpful to economically disadvantaged families who have less experience than others with such matters.

## Interventions When Things Have Gone Wrong

*Underachievement.* It is beyond the scope of this volume to discuss the array of specific interventions for the ills that may befall gifted and talented youth. We will use one area, underachievement, to comment on what should be minimally acceptable standards of support. Student performance that falls noticeably short of potential, especially for young people with high ability, is bewildering and perhaps the most frustrating of all challenges faced by teachers, students, and parents. Despite six decades of research on this topic, the problem of underachievement is still identified as the number one concern among educators of high-ability students (Renzulli, Reid, & Gubbins, 1991).

The causes of underachievement are diverse and emanate from dysfunctional family relationships, motivational difficulties, poor social skills, peer rejection, learning and attentional disabilities that go too long unrecognized, and so on. For most students of high potential, significantly adding to the situation, if not the primary cause, are the daily encounters with material and skills long since mastered, slow pace of progress, low levels of discourse, and content that fails to match interests.

A few strategies have been shown by research to mitigate underachievement. These include curriculum compacting to eliminate reteaching what a student already knows (Reis, Burns, & Renzulli, 1992), self-selected independent or small-group studies (Baum, Renzulli, & Hébert, 1995), and the shift to more challenging and engaging learning environments that provide opportunities for accelerated progress. Because of the diverse sources of underachievement, approaches will need to be individualized and multifaceted (Siegle & McCoach, this volume). For many students,

**281**

counseling should be provided to handle family and personal issues and to enable students to strengthen those personal traits that can serve as assets.

*Counseling and family therapy.* We have mentioned counseling strategies as both preventive and stress-reducing, but the more traditional role of counselors and therapists in treating emotional and behavioral problems when they occur should also be mentioned. Unfortunately, as Moon (this volume) has mentioned, few counselors have been trained to understand the special issues confronting gifted students, and, as a result, they often fail to distinguish between healthy and unhealthy differences. Furthermore, they are all too often ready to blame giftedness as the source of the difficulty because they have, like others, been exposed to the myths regarding the supposedly high rates of serious pathology in this group.

## What Must We Do?

Because there are social and emotional factors associated with high performance, we must address the needs of the whole child. At the very least, three things ought to be done, and three things might characterize our very best efforts:

### The Minimum We Must Do

- Provide appropriate educational choices. No single strategy or setting will fit the needs of every gifted child, but the ordinary classroom, maintaining the usual *status quo,* will fit the needs of none.
- Provide training for teachers, parents, counselors, and others in identifying high ability and understanding its concomitants. Enable them to see that many problems, when they occur, result from the mismatch of the student with an unsuitable environment.
- Recognize the great diversity among those labeled "gifted and talented" and respond to the individual student, not the stereotype. It is particularly important to recognize individual differ-

ences among traditionally underserved populations and to develop sensitivity to the kinds of support they can use.

## The Best We Can Do

- Focus on helping gifted individuals develop resilience. Help them to evaluate their assets and the risk factors with which they deal so they can maximize the former—including developing their own strengths and seeking mentors and advocates when they are lacking—and develop strategies to deal constructively with the latter.
- Develop a continuum of services, including educational, counseling, family, and community programs, from early childhood through college, to enable approaches that meet the needs of specific individuals.
- Continue to advocate for changes in the culture, promoting acceptance and respect for gifted students and the willingness to make the relatively small investments they need for what is potentially an enormous payoff.

## Priorities for Research on the Social and Emotional Needs of High Potential

Throughout this volume, reviewers have decried the lack of systematic research in this field. Designated research funds have been few and far between, and what funding exists (i.e., federal funds under the Jacob Javits Act) has been largely devoted to a single theme, that of developing services for underserved minorities. As a consequence, most studies have enrolled small samples that are easy to identify, and most of our knowledge comes from studies of gifted students who have done well enough to be selected for special programs (and, to an unknown degree, who come from families astute enough to make application for such programs). Research of many kinds is sorely needed. As this report shows, sufficient knowledge is currently available to guide the next generation of research efforts.

Investigators in the "giftedness community" are too often isolated from mainstream research in developmental psychology and

**283**

education, with the result that they are too often seen as parochial and that they fail to profit from the insights developing in those fields. It is important that we not maintain this isolation, but increase the cross-fertilization of interdisciplinary work.

Investigators interested in gifted students should join forces with the currently developing field of "positive psychology" (Seligman & Csikszentmihalyi, 2000; Sheldon & King, 2001) to maximize understanding and encourage the enhancement of human assets, such as those that gifted children possess, to promote the progression of intelligence into wisdom, energy into commitment, and promise into fulfillment.

Any research undertaken should carefully describe the groups of children who are participants. It is not only impossible, but inaccurate to describe gifted children as though they were all the same. As mentioned previously, dimensions of difference include domains and levels of ability, gender, age, ethnicity, and family background; internal discrepancies in development; motivation; and a wide variety of other personal characteristics. Priority should be given to understanding the ways in which demographic and personal variables interact with children's abilities and environments to determine the patterns of their lives.

Many more studies should include a minimum of three groups: a target gifted group, a comparison group of average ability matched to them by chronological age, and an older comparison group of average ability matched by mental age. The addition of a fourth group of gifted students matched with the last group on chronological age would also help to tease out the generalizability of the characteristics being studied. This "MA-CA" research design is familiar to investigators of persons with mental retardation and would help us to distinguish between possible qualitative characteristics and those that are maturity-based.

At the same time, because it has been noted that some personal characteristics (e.g., introversion, perfectionism, and intensities) and some adjustment difficulties (e.g., attention-deficit disorder, eating disorders, and depression) are, or *may be*, more frequent among gifted students, carefully controlled studies that compare well-described groups of gifted children with other children are needed.

Prospective longitudinal studies are needed to identify the antecedents and predictors of positive and negative developmental outcomes for subgroups of gifted children who are growing up under different conditions. Of primary importance are studies comparing the effectiveness of various styles of parenting and various educational programs in promoting the attainment and mental health of gifted participants.

Studies are needed to compare the effectiveness of a variety of supports and interventions for gifted children and their families. Which educational and other strategies promote positive outcomes most effectively? Which new approaches hold promise? More research is needed into the specific kinds of supports that can be of help to specific groups of gifted students who are experiencing difficulties. By evaluating the effectiveness of a variety of approaches to address concerns in well-defined groups of children, the success and efficiency of such efforts should be greatly enhanced.

As noted, most of the existing research has been conducted with academically or intellectually gifted youth who are participating in special programs. We know much less about other types of giftedness in children—for example, those who are artistically or creatively gifted.

We also know little about academically gifted children whose needs are not met in the schools, for example, those for whom there are no existing programs, those who are overlooked for reasons of ethnicity or insufficient mastery of English, those with uneven patterns of abilities, and those whose academic achievement fails to reflect their advanced development. Research is needed to discover reliable ways to identify gifted children who are not effectively served at present.

High priority should also be given to efforts to understand the subtle dynamics of underachievement and loss of potential.

Recent knowledge about the history and nature of mood disorders and suicide among highly creative adults suggests that we should be looking more closely at teenagers who are talented in the visual arts and writing in order to institute preventive efforts to support young people at risk for such conditions.

**285**

Detailed examination is needed of the specific kinds of learning disabilities shown by gifted students in comparison with other learning-disabled students. Intervention efforts will be greatly enhanced by such focused understandings.

Finally, an effective research agenda needs appropriate levels of funding. Good research is almost always expensive. As we have noted, most existing research about social and emotional issues facing high-potential individuals has been carried out with small groups in the absence of carefully selected comparison groups, and it often lacks methodological precision simply because of cost. At present, research funds specifically available for investigations with this population are extraordinarily limited. The incentives and possibilities for carrying out carefully designed, coherent, and ultimately useful research are often fiscal. With funding, this area could be transformed.

## A Final Word

The notion that some people can be "too smart for their own good" permeates contemporary society and creates a social climate in which intellectual and creative efforts by children and adults are undervalued. One consequence of anti-intellectualism has been a damaging tendency on the part of gifted children to deny their talents and to try desperately to become "just like everyone else." In a society in which all citizens should be respected and welcomed for who they are and what they can contribute to others, respect for individuality and appropriate resources must be provided to gifted and talented youth, as well as others. Positive changes will ensue if we create an open climate for the development and support of gifts and talents:

- Understanding will be enhanced that giftedness does not inherently bring with it increased social and emotional vulnerability. Problems do not occur simply because a child demonstrates gifts and talents, and they must be understood in a broader context.
- National efforts to increase the availability of a variety of appropriate instructional and out-of-school provisions must be a high priority since research indicates that many of the emotional or social difficulties gifted students experience disappear when their educational climates are

adapted to their level and pace of learning. Among such educational provisions should be opportunities for academic acceleration and enrichment, together with opportunities for gifted children to find companions of similar maturity, interests, and commitments to develop their gifts and talents. Too many schools across the country actively discourage, or even prohibit, capable students from moving through the curriculum at a pace commensurate with their abilities. Sadly, too, many schools maintain practices that prevent gifted students from working with others of similar ability for all but a couple of hours a week.

- Wider acceptance of the value of high attainment will create an atmosphere that rewards students' best efforts and their courage in the face of life's challenges. These two components are essential to the fulfillment of promise.
- Opportunities should be provided for adults—particularly parents, teachers, counselors, and potential mentors—to enhance their skills at recognizing talent and responding effectively to the social and emotional needs of gifted and talented students in a wide variety of ways. This will lead to the creation of an informed cohort of adults who can support and counsel gifted students as needed and can nip in the bud many potential problems before they fester.

Our society needs to recognize with empathy creative persons who may experience pain and even serious mental health disorders. Continuing support and intervention should be provided to such young people and adults to enable them to weather the difficult times while maintaining their creative trajectories.

## References

Baum, S., Renzulli, J. S., & Hébert, T. P. (1995). *The prism metaphor: A new paradigm for reversing underachievement.* (Collaborative Research Study 95310). Storrs: The National Research Center on the Gifted and Talented, The University of Connecticut.

Csikszentmihalyi, M., Rathunde, K., & Whalen, S. (1993). *Talented teenagers: The roots of success and failure.* New York: Cambridge University Press.

**287**

Feldhusen, J. F. (1989). Why the public schools will continue to neglect the gifted. *Gifted Child Today, 12*(2), 56–59.

Frymier, J., Barber, L., Carriedo, R., Denton, W., Gansneder, B., Johnson-Lewis, S., & Robertson, N. (1992). *Growing up is risky business, and schools are not to blame* (Final report of the Phi Delta Kappa Study of Students At Risk, Vol. 1). Bloomington, IN: Phi Delta Kappa.

Jackson, N. E., & Butterfield, E. C. (1986). A conception of giftedness designed to promote research. In R. J. Sternberg & J. E. Davidson (Eds.), *Conceptions of giftedness* (pp. 151–181). Cambridge, England: Cambridge University Press.

McClelland, D., Atkinson, J., Clark, R., & Lowell, E. (1953). *The achievement motive*. New York: Appleton-Century-Crofts.

Moon, S. M., & Hall, A. S. (1998). Family therapy with intellectually and creatively gifted children. *Journal of Marital and Family Therapy, 24*, 59–80.

Olenchak, F. R. (1999). Affective development of gifted students with nontraditional talents. *Roeper Review, 21*, 293–297.

Parsons, J. E., Adler, T. F., & Kaczala, C. M. (1982). Socialization of achievement attitudes and beliefs: Parental influences. *Child Development, 53*, 310–321.

Peters, P. (1990, July). TAG student defends programs against critic. [Letter to the editor]. *The Register Citizen*, p. 10.

Purcell, J. (1994). *The status of programs for high ability students.* (CRS 94305). Storrs: The National Research Center on the Gifted and Talented, The University of Connecticut.

Reis, S. M. (1998). *Work left undone: Compromises and challenges of talented females.* Mansfield Center, CT: Creative Learning Press.

Reis, S. M., Burns, D. E., & Renzulli, J. S. (1992). *Curriculum compacting: The complete guide to modifying the regular curriculum for high ability students.* Mansfield Center, CT: Creative Learning Press.

Reis, S. M., Neu, T. W., & McGuire, J. M. (1995). *Talent in two places: Case studies of high ability students with learning disabilities who have achieved.* Storrs: The National Research Center on the Gifted and Talented, The University of Connecticut.

Renzulli, J. S., Reid, B. D., & Gubbins, E. J. (1991). *Setting an agenda: Research priorities for the gifted and talented through the year 2000.* Storrs: The National Research Center on the Gifted and Talented, The University of Connecticut.

Roeper, A. (1996). A personal statement of philosophy of George and Annemarie Roeper. *Roeper Review, 19*, 18–19.

Seligman, M. E., & Csikszentmihalyi, M. (2000). Positive psychology: An introduction. *American Psychologist, 55*, 5–14.

Sheldon, K. M., & King, L. (2001). Why positive psychology is necessary. *American Psychologist, 56*, 216–217.

U.S. Department of Education, Office of Educational Research and Improvement. (1993). *National excellence: A case for developing America's talent.* Washington, DC: U.S. Government Printing Office.

**288**

# CONTRIBUTORS

---

**Sanford J. Cohn, Ph.D.,** is a professor in the College of Education at Arizona State University whose research focus is on self-actualization and the development of talent. He has created several graduate programs with specialization in the education of gifted learners. He is also a licensed psychologist, serving highly gifted youths and their families. Dr. Cohn founded the Center for Academic Precocity at ASU in 1979. Since 1991, he has served as the principal investigator for Conexiones, a program that introduces educationally motivated migrant education students to state-of-the-art technology (robotics and video-ethnography) and to the opportunities available on the campus of a major state university.

**Donna Y. Ford, Ph.D.,** is a professor of special education at the Ohio State University, where she teaches courses in gifted education. Dr. Ford's research focuses on recruiting and retaining culturally diverse students in gifted education, reversing underachievement among gifted Black students, and creating multicultural curricula that challenge gifted students. She has published widely in the fields of urban and gifted education, is the author of two books, and consults with school districts nationally.

**Meredith J. Greene, M.Ed.,** is a high school teacher of French and gifted education and a guidance counselor from Nova Scotia, Canada. She is currently pursuing full-time doctoral studies in educational psychology at the Neag Center for Gifted Education and Talent Development at the University of Connecticut. Her research interests include career counseling, gender-role issues in talent development, gifted females, and gifted GLBT students.

**Miraca U. M. Gross, Ph.D.,** is professor of gifted education and director of the Gifted Education Research, Resource, and Information Centre (GERRIC) at the University of New South Wales in Sydney, Australia. She has won several international awards, including the Hollingworth Award, for her research on the social and emotional development of highly gifted children and adolescents.

**Thomas P. Hébert, Ph.D.,** is associate professor of educational psychology in the College of Education at the University of Georgia in Athens. Dr. Hébert teaches graduate courses in gifted education and qualitative research and is a research fellow for the Torrance Center for Creative Studies. He serves as Governor-at-Large for The Association for the Gifted (TAG) Board, and the Council for Exceptional Children. His research interests include counseling issues, underachievement, and problems faced by gifted young men.

**Margaret Keiley, Ed.D.,** is an assistant professor at Purdue University in the marriage and family therapy program of the department of child development and family studies. She is also a practicing family therapist. Dr. Keiley is the principal investigator for several ongoing research projects at Purdue. Her interests include feminist and emotion-focused family therapy; development of affect regulation in families; the role of the regulation of feelings in violence, sexual abuse, addiction, and externalizing/internalizing behaviors; longitudinal data analytic techniques—growth modeling and survival analysis.

**290**

**D. Betsy McCoach, M.A.,** is a doctoral student in the department of educational psychology at the University of

Connecticut, where she is pursuing dual concentrations in gifted education and school psychology. Previously, she was a secondary gifted specialist and a teacher of the gifted in Pennsylvania. Her research interests include the underachievement of academically able students, the identification of students for gifted programs, gifted students with dual exceptionalities, and quantitative research methodology.

**Sidney M. Moon, Ph.D.,** is a professor in the department of educational studies and the director of the Gifted Education Resource Institute at Purdue University. She has been active in the field of gifted education as a parent, counselor, teacher, administrator, and researcher. She has contributed more than 40 books, articles, and chapters to the literature on gifted education. Her research interests include social and emotional issues of gifted students, families of the gifted, differentiated counseling for gifted children and their families, student outcomes of gifted education programs, and the development of personal talent.

**Maureen Neihart, Psy.D.,** is a licensed clinical child psychologist in Laurel, MT. She has worked as a secondary teacher, a school counselor, and a coordinator of gifted programs. She is a former member of the board of directors of the National Association for Gifted Children, and she currently serves on the editorial boards of several education journals. Dr. Neihart's special interests include children at risk and violent youth.

**Kevin J. O'Connor, Ed.M.,** is a doctoral student in educational psychology (gifted education/counseling psychology) at the University of Connecticut. He received his master's degree in counseling from Boston University. Kevin has worked with children of diverse backgrounds and abilities as both a classroom teacher and school counselor. Outside of the school environment, he has provided individual and group counseling to children, specializing in enhancing social competence and self-esteem.

**F. Richard Olenchak, Ph.D.,** is a professor, psychologist, and director of the Urban Talent Research Institute at the University of Houston. Having served in various roles with gifted and talented children for nearly 30 years, he is interested in research and practice about their affective development, as well as intervening issues such as poverty and concurrent disabilities. Often found teaching high-ability children, he feels that practicing what he preaches provides the best foundation of future research.

**Paula Olszewski-Kubilius, Ph.D.,** is the director of the Center for Talent Development at Northwestern University. For over 18 years she has conducted research and published widely on issues of talent development, particularly talent search programs; the effects of accelerated educational programs; and the needs of special populations of gifted children, including minority gifted students, economically disadvantaged gifted students, and gifted females. She has designed and conducted educational programs for learners of all ages and workshops for parents and teachers. She is active in national- and state-level advocacy organizations for gifted children and currently serves on several editorial advisory boards.

**Sally M. Reis, Ph.D.,** is a professor of educational psychology at the University of Connecticut, where she also serves as principal investigator of the National Research Center on the Gifted and Talented. She was a teacher for 15 years, 11 of which were spent working with gifted students. Dr. Reis serves on several editorial boards and is the past president of the National Association for Gifted Children.

**Sylvia Rimm, Ph.D.,** is a child psychologist, director of the Family Achievement Clinic in Cleveland, OH, and a clinical professor at Case Western Reserve University School of Medicine. She is on the board of directors of the National Association for Gifted Children and serves as a reviewer for *Gifted Child Quarterly*. Her interest in giftedness began as a parent advocate and a founding member of the Wisconsin Council for Gifted Children. She is the author or coauthor of numerous articles and books on parenting gifted children and gifted girls. Dr. Rimm writes a syndicated newspaper column and hosts a weekly national call-in program on public radio.

**Nancy M. Robinson, Ph.D.,** is professor emerita of psychiatry and behavioral sciences at the University of Washington and former director of what is now known as the Halbert and Nancy Robinson Center for Young Scholars. Her current research interests include the effects of marked academic acceleration to college, behavioral and family adjustment of gifted children, and verbal and mathematical precocity in very young children. She serves on several editorial boards and is a member of advisory boards for the U.S. State Department Office of Overseas Schools, Johns Hopkins Center for Talented Youth, and the Advanced Academy of Georgia, as well as a member of the board of trustees of the Seattle Country Day School.

**Karen B. Rogers, Ph.D.,** is professor of gifted studies in the curriculum and instruction department at the University of St. Thomas. She has authored approximately 60 articles, 12 book chapters, and a book on a variety of issues concerning the cognitive and affective issues confronting gifted children. She has assessed 150 gifted children and developed educational plans for them and has used the knowledge gained from this to write a book for parents on educational planning.

**Pat Schuler, Ph.D.,** is a national certified counselor and a partner in Creative Insights, a counseling and educational consulting practice, in Rensselaer, NY, that specializes in working with high-ability children. She has master's degrees in gifted education and counseling psychology, as well as a doctorate in educational psychology from the University of Connecticut. Her experiences in education include work as a regular classroom teacher, an examination services specialist for the New York State Department of Education, a coordinator and teacher of elementary through high school schoolwide enrichment programs, and a research associate at the National Research Center on the Gifted and Talented.

**Del Siegle, Ph.D.,** is an assistant professor at the University of Connecticut, where he coordinates the Three Summers Master's Degree program. He serves on the boards of directors for the National Association for Gifted Children, the Council for

Exceptional Children, and The Association for the Gifted. He also serves as coeditor of *The National Research Center on the Gifted and Talented Newsletter.* Prior to earning his Ph.D. in gifted education, he coordinated and taught for eight years in an academically gifted program in Montana, where he was a Montana semifinalist for U.S. West Teacher of the Year. His research interests include motivation, gifted and talented identification bias, and teaching with technology.

**Linda Kreger Silverman, Ph.D.,** is a licensed psychologist and director of the Institute for the Study of Advanced Development and the Gifted Development Center in Denver, CO. She received her Ph.D. in educational psychology and special education from the University of Southern California and served on the faculty of the University of Denver for nine years in counseling psychology and gifted education. She has published several books and nearly 200 articles and chapters. She founded the only journal on adult giftedness and is currently conducting research on profoundly gifted children, the visual-spatial learner, comparative assessment of the gifted on different instruments, the effects of vision therapy, and introversion.

# NAGC Task Force on Social-Emotional Issues for Gifted Students

## Task Force Members and Contributors

George Betts
Carolyn Carr
Sanford Cohn
Victoria Damiani
Donna Y. Ford
Thomas P. Hébert
Mary E. Jacobsen
William Keilty
Barbara Kerr
Maxine Levy
Andrew S. Mahoney
D. Betsy McCoach
Sidney M. Moon

Maureen Neihart, Co-Chair
Helen Nevitt
F. Richard Olenchak
Paula Olszewski-Kubilius
Jean S. Peterson
Michael Piechowski
Sally M. Reis
Sylvia Rimm
Nancy M. Robinson, Co-Chair
Karen Rogers
Patricia Schuler
Carol Shepherd
Linda K. Silverman

## NAGC Association Editor and Lead Reviewer

James J. Gallagher, University of North Carolina

## Reviewers of Selected Chapters and the Executive Summary

Barbara Bickford
Chris Briggs
Carolyn M. Callahan
Elaine Cheesman
Tracy L. Cross
Meredith J. Greene
E. Jean Gubbins
Ellen P. Hench

Richard Herklots
Kevin O'Connor
Jung Pao
Jean Peterson
Anthony A. Pittman
Ric Schreiber
Rachel Sytsma

## NAGC National Office

Jane Clarenbach